TWO ROADS

Dear Reader

It didn't take long after meeting Luke Gamble to realise what a force of nature he was. Only someone with his astonishing energy could manage a busy country practice, oversee a charity sending vets off on projects across the globe, star in two TV series, have a young family, write like a dream and *never* miss a deadline (OK, once).

The Vet takes Luke back to his beginnings as a vet, fresh out of university, with very few country miles under his belt. Joining a mixed practice in Dorset, he is quickly thrust into the real world of veterinary medicine. Across the course of the story, Luke not only learns his trade, but also learns something of his character – and develops a group of close friends (both human and animal . . .) who will stay with him across his career.

Part Dr Doolittle, part young Indiana Jones – and, in its sense of camaraderie and friendship, part Richard Curtis romantic comedy – this is the story of a very 21st century vet who is a natural successor to James Herriot and Gerald Durrell. I love stories about animals that, although warm, aren't afraid to extend into more serious issues. And Luke has both the talent and the experience to tell them.

We hope you enjoy Luke's tales and look forward, as we do, to his next book. Do let us know what you think, we'd love to hear from you. Our details are on the last page.

Lisa Highton
PUBLISHER

The Vet.

My wild and wonderful friends

LUKE GAMBLE

The Vet

My wild and wonderful friends

TWO
ROADS

www.tworoadsbooks.com

First published in Great Britain in 2011 by
Two Roads
An imprint of Hodder & Stoughton
An Hachette UK company

First published in paperback in 2011

I

A CIP catalogue record for this title is available from the British Library.

Hardback ISBN 978 1 444 72175 1
Paperback ISBN 978 1 444 72177 5

Typeset in MT Sabon by Hewer Text UK Ltd, Edinburgh

Printed and bound in the UK by Clays Ltd, St Ives plc

Hodder & Stoughton policy is to use papers that are natural, renewable
and recyclable products and made from wood grown in sustainable
forests. The logging and manufacturing processes are expected to
conform to the environmental regulations of the country of origin.

Two Roads
Hodder & Stoughton Ltd
338 Euston Road
London NW1 3BH

For Cordelia, Noah, Sheba, Leuwen and little Charlie!

AUTHOR'S NOTE

This is my story. Although this is a work of fact, I have deliberately changed the names of the people and places involved, as well as their physical descriptions, and mixed up different incidents from throughout my career. Accordingly, many of the people described are not based on any real person but are imaginary constructs based on different characters I've encountered in my life so far.

I

WHAT GOES AROUND COMES AROUND

'My cat has acute glaucoma!' a shrill voice screeched down the phone.

It was the middle of the night. I sat on the floor just outside my bedroom, holding the mobile to my ear, struggling to recall the conditions that can cause increased pressure of the eyes. The phone only had reception in one isolated spot in the whole house, so I crouched low with my head on one side, praying that the signal would stay strong.

'Acute glaucoma is very rare in cats,' I replied, hoping to gain a little time.

It was only my third night on call but as a freshly gradu-ated vet, encyclopaedic knowledge was supposed to be at my fingertips. Given the number of books I'd crammed into my tiny brain just a few months ago, I should have known a thing or two about a poorly cat.

'How is he behaving?' I asked.

'Not well. I told you he has acute glaucoma!' The voice had got shriller. 'It's very painful and you need to see him.'

I glanced at my watch. In the half-light of the landing, the cracked display was difficult to read.

'Not a problem,' I began. 'I'd be delighted to see him – but it could be tricky getting into town right now . . .'

Somewhere outside, I heard a cheer going up.

'What?' came the terse reply.

'Can you tell me what he is doing to make you think he has acute glaucoma?' I asked.

'My name,' the voice declared, 'is Mrs Beasley – and I have been a client of Mr Spotswode for fifteen years! I worked as an optician for twenty-five years, so I certainly don't need you questioning whether my cat has acute glaucoma or not!' She paused. I could almost see the steam curling from the telephone receiver. 'You will need to remove his eye.'

I had the nagging feeling that whatever I said or did wasn't going to crack it with Mrs Beasley. I screwed up my eyes and took a deep breath.

'Mrs Beasley . . .' I began.

'Are you going to come and help my poor cat or not?'

'I might be some time.'

'And why, exactly, is that?'

'Mrs Beasley,' I said. 'It's almost midnight. And it's New Year's Eve.'

I pictured it: the centre of town packed, the high street shut, me careering through crowds of revellers, screaming, 'Feline glaucoma! Outta my way!'

'That's not good enough,' Mrs Beasley announced. 'Have you been drinking?' There was no hint of shrillness now. The tone was positively menacing.

'Mrs Beasley, I . . .'

'I will see you at the practice at 6 a.m. Do not be late. I will put a cold compress on my poor cat's eye for the next few hours since you refuse to see him.'

The line went dead. At first, I thought it was the dreaded reception and frantically tried to resurrect the caller's number, but finding it withheld, I realised my one bar of reception was as strong as ever and Mrs Beasley had hung up on me. From outside, I could hear passing partygoers begin to count down: five, four, three, two, one. The New Year cries went up.

I had spent years reading epic texts, sitting endless exams, working my socks off to become a fully qualified vet – but none of my training had prepared me for a call like that. People, it seemed, were going to be as much a part of being a veterinarian as dogs and cats and snakes and rats. Balancing the phone on top of a picture hanging on the landing, I padded into my bedroom. Leaving the door open so I could hear it ring, I got into bed and flicked the light off, wishing myself a Happy New Year.

Two minutes later, I flicked the light back on. Better read up about acute glaucoma, I thought. I've never taken an eye out before.

Mrs Beasley's husband pitched up at the practice just after dawn. Although he forgot to wish me a Happy New Year, he did kindly compliment me on how young I looked. It was only as he stalked into the practice that, with a double take, I understood why Mrs Beasley had been quite so shrill.

The cat, Thomas, did indeed have a bad eye. I knew it was bad, because it was protruding from the eye socket and was full of blood. Even a vet only a few days into the job can tell something's wrong with that.

'It's about time you'd see him,' Mr Beasley began.

It seemed that he was just as convinced of my gross negligence as his wife.

'Well, the thing is . . .'

'He's been suffering for days!'

Grumbling, Mr Beasley signed the admission paperwork. Thomas, meanwhile, didn't seem to be complaining. In fact, he wasn't batting an eyelid about the situation.

We took Thomas into the prep area at the back of the practice. Holly, the duty nurse, was already out back, having checked and cleaned some of the patients who had seen the New Year in at the practice. A black Labrador called Rupert, standing alert and bright at Holly's side, wagged his thick tail as I flashed them both a smile.

At least somebody liked me.

'Happy New Year, Holly,' I said, cradling Thomas and his bloody eye.

Holly flashed one look in my direction and raised her free hand to her mouth to stifle a giggle. At my shoulder, Mr Beasley stood imperiously, fixing me with a horrified stare. I could have sworn he was sniffing the air around me as well. No doubt Mrs Beasley had told him how much of a drunk I was.

'Everything okay, Luke?' Holly asked, her eyes creasing up in laughter.

I'd had two hours kip and had never taken out a cat's eye before.

'Everything's great,' I lied.

Tears started to leak down Holly's face and her body doubled over as she dissolved in a fit of hysterics. Whatever Holly was on, I needed some. I rolled my eyes at Rupert, who wagged his tail even harder. Even he seemed to be enjoying this joke.

'Was it a special tea you had last night, Holly?' I asked, slightly bemused.

'Did you get ready in a hurry this morning?' Holly just about managed to reply as another wave of hysterics racked her small frame.

I looked down at my front and blanched.

When I got dressed that morning, I had grabbed the first item of clothing to hand – a T-shirt I had picked up in a high street sale. The big black lettering printed across the front, which normally read **d o n,** was inside out and clearly visible through the cheap fabric. I had **n o b** written across my front.

I turned. Mr Beasley did not seem amused.

'Mr Beasley,' I began, proudly bearing my **nob**. 'Perhaps you'd like to take a seat while we examine Rupert?'

Without breathing a word, Mr Beasley turned on his heel and marched away.

'We'll take good care . . .' I started to call, but the slamming of a door cut me short.

Popping Rupert back into his kennel, Holly gradually collected herself and began to ready the anaesthetic.

'Definitely one way to make an impression with the clients,' Holly began, setting herself off again.

'I didn't realise . . .' I replied in disbelief, casting another look down at my T-shirt and shaking my head in despair at the whole situation.

With a heavy sigh, I pushed all thoughts of my attire to the back of my mind and focused my attention on Thomas's protruding eye – it seemed to have got even bigger. There was nothing else for it; it would have to come out. I glanced over at a thick surgery textbook that lay open on the side. The procedure looked straightforward enough – and it wasn't as if I'd never done surgery before. I'd taken off a cat's testicles once – surely this couldn't be so very different?

I looked at Holly. 'I'm going to have to remove it. Do you think I should call someone?'

Holly looked at me as if I were the village idiot.

'New Year's Day – who are you going to call?' she said.

My mouth worked like a fish. No sound came out. I had only been at the practice four weeks; I didn't want to label myself as the needy assistant and didn't relish the prospect of phoning my new bosses. But a sudden lack of confidence gnawed at me – was it fair for Thomas to have me try and cut his eye out with only an open textbook as my guide? 'What about Rachel?' I began, thinking of a part-time small animal assistant who helped out at one of the practice's branch surgeries.

Holly fixed me with a look.

'No one will be in any fit state to help you at this time. It isn't rocket science. You'll be fine – and so will Thomas.' She paused, fixing her needles. 'Follow the book and, if you get in a muddle, we'll call someone.' Usually a bundle of good cheer, Holly also had a steel streak of common sense and forthright opinions. Despite being only five-feet tall, as one of the senior nurses she had a commanding presence – and, along with the head nurse, Sheila, the two of them were the backbone of the practice.

Holly wasn't one to wait on indecision; it was clear I was going to have to get cracking on with the job. She was already gathering up the surgical kits, drapes, gloves and all the other bits and bobs we would need for the op, chatting away to Thomas as she did. Thomas, meanwhile, sat on the table idly observing her through his one good eye.

Five minutes passed as I helped Holly with the final preparations; then, proudly placing an intravenous catheter (the second ever in my career), I connected up a drip and introduced the anaesthetic.

Thomas's one good eye started to close.

Holly nodded to herself, her mouth only half smiling as she made sure I placed the endotracheal tube in the right place. It was time to begin.

Desperate to still a slight tremble in my hand, I stitched the eyelids together over the damaged eyeball and steadily dissected down to cleanly remove it. I spent about twenty minutes working my way around towards the back of the eye.

'There's something hard here,' I said as my forceps scraped something jagged.

'I would hope it's the skull . . .'

'No – it's a fragment.' I gently pulled back and, with the eye removed, several small pieces of bone followed.

A bead of sweat traced down my back.

'I think we'd better do a quick X-ray,' Holly said. For once, she was not smiling.

Gently, we lifted the deeply anaesthetised Thomas through to the X-ray room. Sure enough, there were fragments of bone all around the back of the eye. A dense object nestled just behind the eye socket; it looked as if it was just touching the front lobe of Thomas's brain.

Gradually teasing the forceps deep into the back of Thomas's eye socket and beyond, I delicately pinched what I assumed was the object in question and slowly withdrew. Holly and I held our breath.

Out it came: a crumpled air pellet.

Holly let out a little gasp of amazement as I placed the bent and blood-stained bit of lead on the table.

'I didn't see that one coming!' she said.

'Neither did Thomas,' I replied, gently cleaning the wound with a sterile swab.

'I don't envy the people in Mrs Beasley's neighbourhood when she finds out someone shot her innocent little cat,' Holly remarked with a wry smile.

'The whole town will hear about this, that's for sure! I hope she hunts them down – they picked the wrong cat to mess with!' I said with a heartfelt sense of satisfaction that there was little chance Thomas's injury would pass unnoticed by the surrounding community.

Once the pellet was out, I swiftly removed a few more splinters of bone around it and flushed the socket clean. I was in my element, now, no longer afraid.

'Hardcore healing!' Holly declared as I put the last stitch in. 'Brain surgery! I've never seen that before. Couple of eye removals, but never brain surgery!'

Being a vet was something I had dreamed of since the age of ten. It was hard to believe I was here, that all of that hard work was finally paying off – with, naturally, a whole lot more hard work. Nevertheless, this was what I had always wanted and a little thing like New Year's brain surgery would never dampen my spirits.

Young for my year, I graduated from Bristol University at the age of twenty-two, fresh-faced and clueless about life in the big wide world. Naive about pretty much everything to do with the responsibilities of having my first proper job – being a barman in a country club during my final years of study probably didn't impart the best grounding in social responsibilities – I knew I'd need a bit of mentoring as I ventured forth.

What was universally recognised amongst my more experienced colleagues was that the first job a new graduate takes is the most important of their career. Like all my friends, I'd chosen my first job with as much care as possible to set me up for the sort of career I wanted. With nearly six hundred new graduates applying for every vacancy, I knew I couldn't be picky but I'd prepared as best as possible to get the job I craved: a role in a supportive and exciting practice that would allow me to gain experience in treating all types of animals.

I applied for every job that fitted the bill, including one in a large and very successful mixed practice in the West Country. My interview with the senior partners, under the direction of the indomitable Mr Spotswode, had been intense to say the least. It seemed that at least half my year had applied for the same job as me – but what probably swung things in my favour was the fact that one of the junior assist-ants at the practice, Rob, had studied a year ahead of me at vet school. We knew each other well and, wanting to work with someone he could get along with, Rob had put in a good word for me with the management. Being a star vet student in his days at University, and someone who had taken to practice life like a duck to water, Rob's opinion carried some weight with the Powers That Be, and the job was mine.

I'd spent my first week living with Rob whilst I got orien-tated around the local area. The second week, Rob had been away so I had stayed with three crazy female bikers who were friends with Sheila, the head nurse of the practice. By the third week, a fully-patched member of the gang – but unable to ride a bike – my assigned practice accommodation was finally ready. And so, with growing excitement, I moved into a small annex attached to a beautiful farmhouse near the border between Hampshire and Dorset. It was the first time in my life I had ever lived alone.

It proved to be a pretty novel experience. It wasn't so much the freedom of being able to wander around half-dressed – we weren't shy about that sort of thing in my University accommodation – it was more the fact there was no one else's milk to borrow, no one to banter with about some rubbish TV show on in the background, and no one to have a cheeky beer with at the end of a hard day. I figured it would take a bit of getting used to and, in the meantime, set about renting the biggest TV screen I could find.

Once finally in my own accommodation, my induction period was deemed finished, and I was assigned to the out-of-hours rota. I had never anticipated the sense of dread that would accompany the harsh ringing of the practice mobile, nor the feeling of being unprepared and ill-equipped to deal with emergencies on my own. My self-confidence was ninety per cent bravado, with very little practical know-how to back it up. Although I knew the theory of how to perform a caesarean on a cow and the technical dose rates by which to anaesthetise a horse for castration, I was yet to find out if I could actually do it.

Life as a proper vet was about to begin.

Thomas had put me on a high for the New Year, but I felt a tinge of nervousness as I sat down in Mr Spotswode's office five days later. A big man with a steely gaze, Mr Spotswode demanded respect not only as the most senior partner of the biggest practice in the county, but also as a man who radiated personal authority. Partly because of his calm authoritative way – but mainly because of his famed ability as a mixed practitioner – he was the vet I wanted to impress the most.

Mr Spotswode had a story for every animal, clinical case and condition I could think of – and a thousand others I could not. Already, I had come to the conclusion that this was either because he really could heal everything and anything or else because he knocked a tenner off the bill of anyone he knew. Sheila explained to me during my induction week that senior partners could 'manage pricing' – but if I was ever in the mind to discount fifty pence off a four-hundred pound bill belonging to a one-legged pensioner whose much-loved, uninsured cat had been in an argument with next door's lawnmower, I would receive a written warning. Assistants were there to graft, nothing else.

Mr Spotswode fixed me with a smile as I sat down.

'Thank you for coming to see me this morning, Luke. I thought we might have a chat about Thomas, who you saw the other day.'

My heart sank. 'Mr Spotswode . . .'

What I was beginning to think was going to be a regular dressing-down turned out to be somewhat more sinister. Apparently, Mrs Beasley had reported Thomas being shot through the eye to a local paper – and, as the named veterinary surgeon, I was in the article.

'Have you seen this, Luke?' Mr Spotswode began.

From a drawer in his desk, he produced the newspaper. He lay it flat on the desk, spun it to face me – and there, ringed in blue ink, was a quote: 'Whoever attacked this poor cat is a "mentally challenged dwarf".'

My insides curdled. Suddenly, I remembered the call from the reporter. It was two days after the operation and I was dashing in and out of the office between consults. A man had phoned up to talk about the case 'non-specifically' and asked how I felt about the possibility that the person who had shot the cat might be laughing about what they had done. Conscious of the fact that I didn't want to swear, I had blurted out 'retarded cretin'. Now, looking at the newspaper, I saw the reporter's more literal interpretation.

It must have been a slow news week.

I looked at Mr Spotswode, not knowing whether to laugh or cry. Mentally, vertically challenged people probably have a tough enough time as it is without being targeted by animal welfare vigilantes.

'Luke,' Mr Spotswode began. 'While I agree that the perpetrator is unworthy of any form of charitable comment, we feel you might have been slightly overzealous in expressing this opinion.'

I tried to interject, but Mr Spotswode continued.

'This rather . . .' he searched for the right word, '*unorthodox* quote doesn't reflect well on the reputation of the practice.'

'Mr Spotswode, I can call the newspaper . . .'

Mr Spotswode held up a hand, folding the newspaper and dropping it into the bin at the corner of his desk.

'We've issued an apology for the rather unfortunate terminology, Luke. I suggest, in future, that you be just a little more reserved when talking about cases to anyone but the animals.'

'Even the animals?' I suggested.

Mr Spotswode nodded sagely.

I stood to leave, slightly red-faced, but before I could even reach the door, Mr Spotswode cleared his throat.

'We have also,' he began, 'had a letter from Mrs Beasley.'

I nodded mutely, certain that the sense of utter defeat I felt must be etched on my face.

'She asked me to review the policies on drinking out-of-hours. Any ideas as to why that might be?'

Without pausing long enough for me to utter a strangled

response, Mr Spotswode continued, 'Luke, I phoned her this morning to explain that we were very careful in this regard – but, if she did feel disposed to giving you a bottle of wine for the magnificent job you did on Thomas, she could be reassured you wouldn't be tempted to drink a glass on duty. The gesture, I said, would be appreciated by the whole team, who feel that you did very well with such a complicated case.'

I breathed a deep sigh of relief, pressed my hands together and smiled.

'Thank you, Mr Spotswode.'

'Mind how you go, Luke.'

Later that day, Mrs Beasley brought Thomas in to check the sutures. Naturally, I kept a low profile – there were always some injured pets to hide behind – and I emerged only when I could see the tail-lights of Mrs Beasley's motor disappearing from the car park, Thomas mewling in the back window.

When Holly found me hiding out, she reported that the wound looked great and was healing well, but Mrs Beasley had complained bitterly that I had clipped too much fur back around the eye. Then, with a sudden flourish, she revealed an expensive looking bottle of red wine from behind her back.

'What's that?' I asked, as she handed it to me.

'Your first client thank you!' she beamed. 'And from Thomas Beasley as well. Quite an achievement! I thought she really had it in for you when she was going on about how much fur you shaved off – maybe she's not so bad after all . . .'

I was on duty that night, but a glass of that wine tasted all the sweeter.

*   *   *

Vet school provides you with the fundamentals but there are things you'll never learn until you're out there, on the job, being mauled by a lovelorn donkey or running circles with a particularly truculent goose. One of the most novel bits of vetting I was to learn in my first two months of practice was that it is actually illegal to release a grey squirrel back into the wild. Not quite as interesting as the urban myth that the seemingly benign daddy-long-legs has a bite, which – if it had a mouth big enough to actually nip you, could kill a grown man in seconds – but nevertheless, still something I had to learn.

Grey squirrels were introduced to Great Britain in the middle of the nineteenth century and, being bigger, stronger and more adaptable than our native reds, they rapidly multiplied and took over many of the reds' former territories. The other big edge they have is that they carry the lethal squirrel-pox virus to which they are immune – but which wipes out reds. They are regarded by forest rangers and bird-lovers as pests because they damage trees and eat bird food – with all but the Fort Knox of bird feeders helpless in the face of their inventive attempts to get at any tasty contents within. You cannot, by law, release them into the wild, keep them as pets or import them into Britain. In fact, the biggest predator of grey squirrels is man – and, with both the Forestry Commission and National Trust constantly trapping and shooting grey squirrels in an effort to keep their numbers down, I have always found it hard not to sympathise with these sweet-looking survivors.

So, according to the law of the land, when a six-year-old boy and his twelve-year-old sister came into the surgery with a large cardboard box, whoever was on reception should have removed the box and disposed of the squirrel lying inside.

However, in reality, when the small boy walked over to Sheila with a tear in his eye and, through those tears, told the story of how he had scooped the squirrel up after it had been hit by a truck, there was not a flicker of hesitation. With predictable efficiency and kindness, she wrapped an arm around the small boy, steered him and his sister into a consult room, told them we would do everything we could – and then called me to sort it out.

Little did I know what peril lay in store.

Until I walked into that room, I had always liked squirrels. I still remember the day, when I was a child, that my parents called in a murderous pest control man to shoot some squirrels who had taken up residence in our back garden. Even then I had known it was a death squad coming to my house and today I sensed my chance to make it up to the squirrel population for my family's chequered history in squirrel rights.

The boy had a mop of spiky red hair to go with an incredibly freckly face, and his sister immediately flashed me a beaming smile, showing off a set of spectacularly large braces. As a brother and sister pair, I suspect they might not have had the easiest time of it in the hard environment of a school playground. Each clutched the other's hand – and Sheila stood protectively beside them with one of her, 'I know you'll do the right thing or I'll soon put you straight' sort of looks.

'What happened here then?' I asked.

'He got run over by a big lorry,' the sister replied.

'A big blue lorry!' the little boy interjected, nodding his head sadly.

'And you picked him up?'

'It went right over him and he just lay there.' The little boy sniffed and looked at me.

'Mummy got us a box and I put him in it,' he said with tears welling in his eyes. 'Will he be alright?'

'I'm not sure,' I said, 'but I'll do my best. Let's take a look.'

I opened the box, expecting to see the flattened form of a small furry rodent looking up at me with fixed eyes and a little rictus grin.

Now, any experienced vet would have straight away identified this as a schoolboy error but, having been caught up in the emotion of the moment, and much to Sheila's surprise, I reached into the box to get hold of the squirrel, completely forgetting to put on any gloves – or, indeed, to close the window to the adjoining office.

Another interesting fact about grey squirrels is that, not only are they super-agile, strong and adaptable but they are also super tough. It is said that they can survive a fall of thirty-feet onto the forest floor. As I quickly found out, they can definitely withstand being run over by a big blue lorry.

The squirrel launched itself from the box at the speed of light. Avoiding my futile effort to grab it, it raced around the room, knocked two pictures off the wall and jumped onto the little boy's head as a springboard before leaping across the room towards the open window.

Sheila is not a super nurse with fifteen years' experience for nothing, however. Perhaps she had been anticipating my stupidity – for, at exactly the same time as I committed the offence of opening the box, she hurled herself across the room and slammed the window shut.

The squirrel rebounded off the glass and I seized the moment to grasp it securely around the neck. It squirmed and scratched to get free. Thrusting it back into the box, I smiled at the shell-shocked children and flashed a grin at Sheila. She simply raised her eyebrows.

'You've fixed it!' the small boy cried.

I looked at the boy, unsure how to respond.

'Yes,' said Sheila, ushering the children out of the room. 'He's an amazing vet.'

As I carried the box through to the storeroom, I noticed a faint trace of blood on the lid of the box. I couldn't release the squirrel injured and, aside from having established that it hadn't broken any of its legs, I hadn't really given it a proper examination. Quickly racing back to the consult room, I prepared some sedative, painkiller and antibiotic. Shutting the door carefully behind me – and this time making sure that the room was secure – I braced myself for another look.

The little squirrel stared up at me with an appealing cheeky face and I gently lifted it out of the box. It was breathing quickly, a touch nervous but that was only to be expected; the softly, softly approach was working. I relaxed my grip just a fraction and saw the source of the blood: it had caught its nail, probably on one of the picture frames in the consult room. Debating whether I needed to inject it or not, I thought I might as well dress the wound with antibiotic and anti-inflammatory. After all, stressed animals are more prone to infection and I reasoned that he must have been a little bruised after having been run over by a truck.

The painkiller went in fine, no problem, but the antibiotic was a different story. I had injected about half when the squirrel decided enough prodding and needle poking was enough. Twisting round in its own skin, it promptly bit me through the middle finger of my left hand. I reared back – only to discover that it had not let go; the squirrel was latched to the end of my finger. Surely a bite from a great white shark wouldn't hurt as much – my scream echoed around the consult room, into the waiting room, into the operating theatre and probably into the town beyond.

Suddenly, Sheila reappeared in the doorway. Freezing only momentarily, she bolted over, prised the jaws of the squirrel apart and unhooked my finger from its curved teeth. Those fifteen seconds felt like an hour. I was pale, shaking and pouring blood as the squirrel, bemused, hopped back into the box.

Sheila replaced the lid and looked at me with a withering eye.

'You really should wear gloves when handling wild animals,' she said.

The news spread around the practice like wildfire and I was treated to a selection of my colleagues' best witticisms. 'Wrestled any squirrels recently?' 'Did he get hold of your nuts?' The only things as persistent as those jibes and grinning glances were the throbbing pain in my finger and my new fear of squirrels. In fact, when I released the beast – as promised and against all the rules – a little part of me was concerned it might turn around and come back for more.

Was I a man or a mouse? Either way, I was petrified of another squirrel attack.

Suffice to say, the partners were not impressed. I didn't want to be labelled the clown just two months into my first ever job, but it was proving difficult not to make a spectacle of myself – I had a finger three times bigger than any other on my hand. I had trouble driving, I couldn't unwrap syringes without using my mouth and, despite Rob taking huge amusement in solemnly handing me some anti-squirrel capsules – actually super-strength dog antibiotics – the infection had clearly got into the bone.

I'm a man who considers that water torture is right up

there on the list of violations of terrorism suspects' human rights but I'll say this: if you ever wanted a prisoner to talk, my tip is to unleash a squirrel. There's nothing in the Convention on Human Rights about squirrels.

Desperate for a chance to redeem myself in the eyes of the partnership, I was keen to get out on the farms. Being out and about was the real deal – no backup on hand and I would have every chance to prove myself, and put the squirrelly mess far behind me.

Driving around in style wasn't on the cards. As the new assistant at the practice, I did indeed get a car that would turn heads – but, unfortunately, only those heads belonging to scrap dealers. Even the general back-up vehicle was in another league to the ten-year-old Peugeot 205 I had to wind up to get around in. Apparently, not only was I deemed the most likely to crash but giving me a small car was also supposed to prevent me from hoarding huge amounts of medicines – a notorious habit of all new graduates.

The nightmare stories we were all told at vet school about the dangers of forgetting the scout's famous motto – and always going out on the road fully prepared – had been etched into my memory and, by the time I had finished familiarising myself with the '205 of Power', it had therefore been pimped up to spec. It now contained a complete set of large and small animal textbooks, drugs in the glove box, and a shoebox of emergency medicines under the passenger seat. In addition to all that, both back seats were jammed full of equipment to treat every ailment I could possibly dream up – from a bloated llama to a limping duck – and I was ready for action.

I'd been at the practice three months when Giles, one of

Mr Spotswode's senior partners and the practice's primary farm vet, whose most distinguishable feature was a massive bushy black beard, gestured me over to the appointment book in the office and stabbed down at a visit under his name.

'I wondered if you would do this visit for me?' he asked. 'Got another appointment here, can't miss it, and they're thirty miles apart.'

I looked at the name. Mr Tubbie from Homestead Farm didn't ring any bells, and it was not an easy one to forget. Here was an ideal opportunity to prove myself to the partnership and show them I could handle being out on the farms. I nodded enthusiastically.

'Martin will be going along with you,' said Giles. 'Wants to be a farm vet, useful lad. Nothing for him to do with me today – and he is here to see large animal work, after all.'

With a stroke of his beard – Giles stroking his own beard; I promise, I never touched it – he departed and I was left standing there dumbly staring at the appointment book.

I probably saw Giles about twice a week, but if you likened vets to grades of belt in a martial art, Giles would have been about a fifth dan black belt. In his late forties, he was rarely seen about the practice, keeping himself to himself and doing only large animal work, and – this was the amazing bit – orthopaedic surgery. If a dog had been run over and its leg shattered in eighteen places, Giles would manage to put it back together when no one else in the practice even knew where to start. Everybody referred difficult orthopaedic surgery to him, even Mr Spotswode – and Mr Spotswode was clearly the grandmaster of vets. Feeling honoured, I walked off to find Martin, get some extra gear together and look out a map to Mr Tubbie's Homestead Farm.

Martin was the work-experience student. The practice had a solid stream of them and it is something we all have to do as we chew our way up the ranks at vet school. It had been less than half a year since I was a work-experience student myself and, whilst it was appealing to have a bit of company, the idea of Martin coming along didn't fill me with joy. For some reason – not least the squirrel bite still throbbing in my finger – I didn't quite feel justified in having worked long enough to offer anyone 'work-experience'.

'Do you need all this stuff?' Martin asked as he inched his way into my car.

Martin was stocky, built like a boathouse, and a mature student, which meant he looked about forty. It was going to be a bit strange having a student along for the job when he was almost as old as my dad.

'Good to be prepared,' I replied.

'Well, I'm not going to fit in here!' he declared. 'Are you sure you need everything?'

I bit back an easy solution to the problem and started to shuffle things around. There was no escaping that the box of textbooks on Martin's seat had to go, and a mounting pile of items was hurriedly ferried back into the practice. Desperately trying to keep an eye on Martin to make sure he didn't remove anything I would definitely need, I repacked and replaced half the boxes we had removed. More than once, Martin raised his eyes skyward.

'Everything okay now?' I asked, as I finally slid into the driver's seat.

Forcing himself into the seat beside me, Martin shrugged.

At last, we headed off, weaving our way through some stunning Dorset countryside and patchwork fields of prime arable and dairy grassland. As we went, Martin began to recount his life story. I pretended to listen, but really, I was lost in the rolling hills, hidden valleys and sweeping vistas. He had worked as a farmhand for ten years before going to college and then University. 'Life experience', he knew, would give him a natural edge in practice. 'One day,' he told me, 'you'll develop the instincts to win over a farmer's trust. You stick with me – you'll see . . .'

I snapped out of my daydream, the car slewing on the road.

'How's your student debt going, Martin?' I asked.

We drove the second half of the journey in silence.

As we pulled up at the farm, having swooped in through a falling gateway flanked by dirty stone walls, I opened the door of the Peugeot and climbed out. There, waiting for us with a glowering gaze, was Mr Tubbie. He certainly lived up to his name. He was a short man with a big round belly and an angry face. On his head, he wore a tatty tartan hat, vainly trying to tame a thick mop of greasy brown hair.

'Hello, Mr Tubbie,' I began. 'I'm Luke, from Mr Spotswode's.'

Mr Tubbie walked straight past me, stretching out his hand. When I turned, I saw that Martin had already climbed out of the car on the other side. As he got to his feet, I could see Mr Tubbie nodding in approval.

'Giles said you were new,' he began, 'but you look useful enough . . .'

I hurried around the old jalopy and tried to head off the handshake but couldn't cut in quickly enough.

'I'm the vet, Mr Tubbie,' I began. 'Martin is seeing practice with me today.'

Martin looked at Mr Tubbie, holding his handshake just a little too long.

'I've still got a couple of exams to sit before I can come out unaccompanied,' he said. 'But I spent ten years working on a farm, so know my stock.'

I lowered my hand. I may as well have offered Mr Tubbie a packet of dirty playing cards, for the fleeting look of utter disgust he shot at me.

'Yes, yes,' said Mr Tubbie. They were still holding hands. 'Well,' he began, 'come and look at my cows. I've got three for you to check.' He walked on to show us the way, but threw a look over his shoulder. 'And I need you,' he said to me with a stern tone, 'to do me a *certificate*.'

There are few things more insulting than being completely blanked but it wasn't as if this was the first time it had happened to me, and I was determined not to let Tubbie know that his behaviour was getting to me. Mainly, I had received this treatment from the fairer sex, when attempting to engage them in witty banter – but this was the first time I'd had it from a farmer. This wasn't the way it was supposed to go. This was my very first farm call. I was supposed to pile into the farm with the Indiana Jones theme blasting out of the radio, ready to save a cow from certain death with a few jabs and a magic drench solution.

I opened the boot of the car to grab my wellies.

The wellies weren't there. None of my waterproofs were there. Nor were my rectal arm-length examination gloves.

I turned around. Martin and Mr Tubbie were already marching across the yard. They may as well have been arm-in-arm.

Grabbing my examination box, which contained my steth-oscope, thermometer and a few basic medicines with needles and syringes, I hurried after Mr Tubbie and Martin. I caught up with them in the cowshed. It was filthy. The deep bed of straw hadn't been cleaned out for what I suspected was the best part of a year, and my shoes instantly sunk into the soft goo. From the fence, Martin looked back and gave me a good going over with his eyes. I was beginning to think he had removed those wellies deliberately. I didn't even need to look at Mr Tubbie to know he was regarding me with utter contempt.

'Left your wellies behind?' Martin said.

At Martin's side, Mr Tubbie smirked. Struggling to maintain composure, I turned towards the farmer.

'Mr Tubbie,' I began. 'Which cows would you like me to examine?'

'Those three over there to start.' Mr Tubbie gleefully pointed to three fat beef animals loosely tied up to posts at the far side of the barn. 'But you'll need your gloves, won't you? I haven't got time to wait here all day for you to go back to the practice. You'll have to phone Giles to come out . . .'

'Not a problem, Mr Tubbie . . .' I steeled myself, looking between the farmer and Martin. This was my first farm call. I wasn't going to be defeated. I was going to be Indiana Jones. 'Gloves would be nice,' I reasoned, 'but I'm not worried about a bit of muck.'

Walking over to the three animals, rolling up my sleeve as far as it could go, I pushed my arm into each of the cows. It was warm, horrible and I looked ridiculous – but I was confidently able to tell Mr Tubbie that two of the cows were heavily in calf, and that one was not pregnant. He grunted as if he already knew, and then beckoned me towards the dark corner right at the far end of the barn. Mr Tubbie stood over a fourth unfortunate cow, collapsed against the wall. The cow, a large brown suckler, was lying on her side encrusted in muck. Her upwardly-facing eye tracked from side to side, streaked with blood. Her breathing was laboured and my heart went out to her. I should have seen her first, not at the end of the visit – she was in desperate need of attention.

I shot a look at Mr Tubbie and bent down to examine her. As I did so, I slipped and smeared muck all over my trousers and shirt. Behind me, Martin was mute. He was going to pay for the absence of those waterproofs.

'How long has she been like this?' I asked. I did not mean to be curt, but I couldn't help it.

'I'm not sure I like your tone, young man.' Mr Tubbie screwed his eyes up so he looked even more pig like than ever. 'She fell over,' he explained. 'The leg's broken.' He crouched beside me. 'I need you to sign a certificate for me and be on your way.'

I looked at Tubbie, and slowly it dawned on me what he was asking. A government scheme was in place to help subsidise farmers. In essence, it meant that, if a vet signed a certificate to say that an animal had injured itself and had to be slaughtered on farm – but was fit for human consumption – then the farmer would receive a payment for it. Few of the carcasses were reportedly checked but, still, the premise was that vets had to safeguard the welfare of animals on farms – and sick or diseased animals did not qualify for the scheme.

'I'll check her over, Mr Tubbie, but she looks more sick to me than injured.'

With a flourish, I removed my thermometer from the cow's backend. Her temperature was extremely high – evidence of a raging infection.

I stood. Underneath me, the cow lowed sadly.

'This cow is toxic, Mr Tubbie.' I held up the thermometer, as if brandishing the branch of truth. 'She isn't fit for human consumption. I'll put her down for you – but I can't sign a certificate.'

Mr Tubbie threw a look at Martin.

'*You* can see she's hurt, can't you?' he demanded, pleading to some higher authority. 'She got a bit sick this morning but she's down because of a bad leg. All bent up, it is! I'd show you but she's laying on it and we can't turn her in here.' He marched to Martin's side. 'Tell him to sign the form, would you? These new vets just don't know their arse from their elbow!'

Martin patted Mr Tubbie on the shoulder and strolled over to my side. I knelt again at the poor cow's side, rubbing the space between her eyes. Martin crouched beside me. 'Come on Luke,' he began. 'You've made your point. Just sign the form. She'll pass inspection, it'll be fine . . .'

When I spoke, it was cold and measured.

'Martin – you aren't a vet. You're a student. I don't need or want your advice. This cow is sick. She hasn't got a broken leg.' I looked at him. He eyeballed me back. 'If you were a vet and you wanted to false certify the cow, then that's your look-out.' I paused. 'But you're not and you can't.'

Mr Tubbie advanced towards me. 'Now, listen here . . .' he seethed. 'You'll get that certificate, sign it and get off my farm.'

I looked the farmer straight in the eye. 'This cow needs to be put out of her misery, Tubbie. And if you don't agree with my decision, I suggest you phone Giles right now to discuss things.'

Mr Tubbie reached into his pocket and withdrew a mobile phone. Pushing the keypad with his thick, fat little fingers, he glared at me.

'You put her down whilst I sort your incompetence out.'

He put the phone to his ear, turned his back on me and stalked – as fast as his fat little legs would carry him – out of the yard.

I looked down at the poor cow. Undoubtedly, she had been down for several days and was dehydrated. A raging fever racked her body and she was close to death. Anger welled inside me – how could Tubbie have such disregard for a creature's life? I didn't – and still don't – care for any excuses about how busy farmers are, the commercial pressures of running a viable business. Good farmers, who run successful farms, care hugely about the animals under their charge; cruel farmers are always bad ones. Getting a sick cow some clean bedding and a bucket of fresh water isn't an insurmountable task – and Mr Tubbie had neglected to do it.

Without looking at Martin, I went and got the necessary injections from the car. Back at the cow's side, I soothed her and administered the lethal injection.

I used the hosepipe in the yard to liberally wash my shoes and arms, pulled my shirt off, slipped on a spare T-shirt that Martin had failed to remove from the car, and got ready to drive back to the practice barefoot.

As I was climbing into the cab, Mr Tubbie rounded the corner, Martin trotting at his heel. His face was blotchy red and he was sweating.

'You'll need to get her out of the barn sooner rather than later, Mr Tubbie,' I began, winding down the window. 'She'll bloat and make the job a lot harder if you don't get on and do it.' I paused, kicking the engine into gear. 'Martin,' I said, eyes on the road, 'if you want a lift back to the practice, get in the car.'

Martin did not move.

'Giles is on his way,' Tubbie spat. 'He'll put you in your

place when this is all sorted out. What goes around comes around – you'll see . . .'

I nosed the car forward, kicking up dirt in the wild farmyard.

'Great stuff,' I said. 'Martin, you can wait here. Explain all my terrible mistakes to Giles, would you?'

And with that, I drove off, feeling a bit sick.

Mr Spotswode and Giles were waiting in the office when I arrived the next morning. Martin was nowhere to be seen but word had clearly spread about my adventure on Mr Tubbie's farm. In the practice common room, Rob informed me that Giles had pitched up at the farm about 9 p.m. Martin, then, had been left there for the best part of eight hours.

I entered the office and sat down. Giles's thick black beard looked somehow more menacing but his eyes were clear and I thought I detected a hint of amusement around the edges. Maybe he enjoys firing assistants, I began to think.

'So you forgot your wellies on your farm visit yesterday,' Mr Spotswode began.

'And gloves, I believe?' Giles added.

Grimly, I nodded.

'Not a great day,' I replied.

There was a long, stony silence. I closed my eyes, began to wonder if there were any jobs going at my local supermarket.

'Don't you just hate it when that happens?' Giles smiled. 'I once spent a whole morning on rounds without wellies or gloves. Had to get the car valeted afterwards.'

I couldn't handle small talk; my nerves were at breaking point.

'I'm sorry about yesterday.' The words had escaped my mouth before I knew it.

Mr Spotswode stood.

'What are you sorry about?' he began.

I looked at them uncomprehendingly.

'Forgetting your wellies and gloves is a bit silly, but you got on with the job – in difficult circumstances, I hear.' Mr Spotswode paused, took his seat again. 'We've called you here to discuss getting your Local Veterinary Inspector status pushed forward. Both Giles and I think you'll make a great asset to the farm team.'

'Would you like to do a bit more out on the farms, Luke?' Giles asked, his eyes twinkling now.

My mouth was so very dry that I seemed to be chewing my words. 'What about the certificate yesterday?'

'You did the right thing,' Mr Spotswode said in a measured tone. 'Mr Tubbie is an appalling man. Very dependable of you to stand up for yourself – not an easy situation.' He paused. 'As for the work-experience student, well, we have decided to send him on his way . . . He won't get his EMS experience form stamped by us.'

'Perhaps he'll have to false-certify it,' Giles laughed. 'That cow was in a mess, Luke, you did well there.'

It was a moment before I realised I was grinning stupidly but somehow I couldn't stop it.

'The LVI training is in Taunton – it's a two day course and then you'll need to be assessed doing a TB test out on farm,' said Mr Spotswode.

'Doing a test under ministry supervision is painful,' Giles added. 'It takes a whole day, they check all the farmer's movement records, ear tags – it really puts them through the mill. Get this first one out of the way and then, after you've done it with the ministry, I'll show you how I do them and you can learn a few shortcuts to ease things along.'

Mr Spotswode gave Giles a slightly disapproving look, not keen to condone anything that wasn't exactly by the book.

'It's almost a shame to inflict a whole team of Ministry vets on any farmer, make them go through all of their records. It's hard to know which client to single out as the Ministry always find something wrong – it can take up to a week. The farmers really hate it.'

Both Mr Spotswode and Giles were really grinning now, pleased with themselves for coming up with the idea.

I grinned back at them. 'Let me guess,' I said, peering at the list of farms due a TB test on Mr Spotswode's desk. A big asterisk was next to one name.

'Homestead Farm,' I read.

The client is always right – what goes around, does indeed come around.

2

A RIGHT PROPER SOAKING

The morning post contained a ridiculously thick envelope from my best friend Sam. Born in South Africa, Sam was the oldest of three brothers and had moved to Cornwall when he was ten years old. We'd met on the first day of Bristol vet school. My parents had dutifully driven me the three hours from our family home in the South Downs and were as curious as I was to discover what my new digs would be like. My first impression of University was actually of Sam hanging upside down from two straps fixed above a doorframe in the hallway, as I arrived. I was all fresh-faced and laden with the useless items I had naively deemed essential for my first year away from home.

If Mum and Dad were worried by the fact I was going to be living in the same house as a student who thought he was some sort of bat, they did well to hide it and with a friendly hello to Sam – as if his hanging upside down was the most normal thing in the world – they deposited my gear in a room the size of a small cupboard, and promptly departed. Whilst I had various hideous wooden masks, wall-hangings and CDs, in the frenzy of last-minute packing, I had forgotten any form of sustenance so, in a joint effort to save our limited money for the important things in life, Sam, having descended from the doorframe, heated up a couple of Cornish pasties and boiled some frozen vegetables whilst I nipped out to buy us a couple of beers. It was the beginning of a firm friendship that endured over five years of living together – and, remarkably, saw us both qualify as fledgling vets. Unleashed after long years of study, Sam had headed straight into small animal practice whilst I had chosen a mixed practice route since I craved as much variety as possible in my daily work.

Sam was interested in cardiology and was determined to focus his interests on becoming an excellent small animal clinician. With unmatched mental agility, and a knack for predicting which subjects were likely to come up in the endless exams we had to take, Sam had soared through his finals and landed himself a well-paid job in a leading small animal hospital in Kent. Now, as I battled with the likes of Mr Tubbie and Martin, Sam was on a mission to climb the ranks and establish a long-term future within his practice.

I tugged hard at the envelope, already knowing what was inside. Sam had sent me a holiday brochure of luxury resorts on the Greek Island of Samos in the North Eastern Aegean. Moderately exclusive, it was purported to be a paradise destination – and I was trying to convince Sam that it was a good idea if he accompanied me on a week's trip there. Unfortunately, the sort of holiday I had in mind was slightly different from the trip Sam was planning.

A few weeks earlier, Mr Spotswode had pulled me aside and told me how he'd met a wealthy couple who lived on the island, and who were very concerned about the number of stray dogs roaming the streets.

The couple were sponsoring a dog shelter on the island but there was no veterinarian there, and the dogs needed neutering.

'I've already been out there, Luke,' Mr Spotswode explained, upturning a small hamster to check on its stitching. 'We've even made a donation. What I need from you, however, is a little time.'

I lifted an eyebrow.

'I want you to go over there, Luke.' He popped the hamster back in its cage. 'Your mission,' he grinned, 'should you choose to accept it, is to get out there with a donation of medicine, and neuter their dogs.'

'To Samos, Mr Spotswode?'

'To Samos, Luke. The shelter is prepared to fund the flights and you may want to take another vet, just to share in the work load.' He wiped his hands clean. 'It isn't particularly pleasant spending a week just neutering dogs.'

I phoned Sam that very night. As I'd expected, his idea of the perfect Samos holiday hadn't quite chimed with what Mr Spotswode required. Dog neutering need only be one half of the equation, Sam seemed to be saying – and the holiday brochure was his way of flagging that fact up.

'My wife has webbed feet,' Mr Baffer said, his bulging eyes unblinking.

I regarded Mr Baffer with a new respect. This gentleman had come into my consult room carrying a cardboard box, his lank brown hair covering a spotty forehead and stubby squashed nose. He was short, totally unthreatening, and didn't even wear a hint of a smile. When a man can carry off an opening gambit like that and maintain a totally straight face, he deserves a bit of admiration.

Whatever was in the box was very still. Mr Baffer held it in front of him with both hands, as if he was at risk of spilling a deadly toxic liquid from a brimming glass bowl. I was intrigued; whatever was in there, it wasn't moving a muscle. Very few animals trapped in a cardboard box remain absolutely motionless – unless, of course, they have passed away. It crossed my mind that I might have found my first bona fide weirdo come to see me at the surgery. If Mr Baffer had actually come into the practice carrying an empty cardboard box, with the sole intention of chatting to me about his wife with webbed feet, Holly, Sheila and Rob would never let me hear the end of it. Not sure how to respond, an honest reaction seemed best.

'I bet she can swim well,' I said with a reassuring smile, expecting Mr Baffer to finally crack and laugh with me.

'Her hands aren't webbed,' he insisted, as if disappointed in my tomfoolery. 'It's just her feet.'

Placing the box on the examination table, he ran one of his chubby hands through his hair and looked me in the eye. Not a flicker of amusement flashed across his face.

'Both feet?' I continued, determined that this conversation would not freak me out, but unable to resist glancing down at the box.

'Yes, both feet. Just like Brian. But the funny thing is that, despite the webbing, when she goes into deep water, she sinks like a stone.' Mr Baffer was completely earnest in his reply.

'Why is that?' I heard myself say.

Mr Baffer shrugged at the obvious explanation. 'She never learned to swim.'

'Well,' I began, nodding sympathetically. 'That would explain it.'

Mr Baffer and I looked at each other, the box resting comfortably on the examination table between us. A pause hung in the air. I was aware of my hands reaching out towards the box. The moment of truth was almost upon me. If it was empty, what was I going to do? How could I treat an imaginary animal?

'Brian hasn't been eating for the last week,' Mr Baffer said suddenly, now staring sadly down at the table. 'He's just fading away.'

I took this as a massive positive step in client relations. Brian, it turned out, was indeed in the box. Reaching slowly forward, I gently lifted the flaps and peered into the dark interior.

'Mr Baffer, you've brought a giant frog to the surgery . . .'

'An African Bullfrog,' Mr Baffer replied, disdainful of my description of Brian as merely a giant frog.

'Absolutely,' I began, in a vain attempt to sound like I knew all there was to know about your typical garden pet, the African Bullfrog.

The massive amphibian filled the box. I had never seen such a big frog in my life. My dabbling in exotics was limited. When I lived with him at University, Sam had gone through a snake-owning phase. The snake had started out as a friendly foot-long rock python but grew into a not-so-friendly three-foot rock python before the landlady finally threatened us with eviction. A combination of finding the snake in Sam's room, a breeding mouse station in the bathroom and a very drunk, naked Scottish rugby player unconscious in the hall all proved to be a bit much.

That brief episode in my student history meant I had handled a snake in the past and, therefore – like all newly graduated vets, who had once touched an exotic animal at arm's length – I claimed to have had some exotic animal experience at every interview I ever attended.

Idly wondering what the frog ate, I carefully put my hands around Brain's olive-green body, heaving him out of the box and onto the table. I guessed that he must have weighed well over a kilo, and observed that, like Mr Baffer's wife, Brian had only webbed hind-feet. It was all making sense – well, that bit at least.

'When I phoned up, they said you were the exotic vet here. You're on the website. It was a long bus ride, but he means a lot to me.' Mr Baffer smiled for the first time as he looked down at his frog.

I thought Rob had been joking that the receptionist had been touting me as an exotic animals vet. I thought it was the receptionists making fun of me after the squirrel incident, counting grey squirrels as the ultimate exotics, but now it was official.

'It says you went to Cambridge as well.'

It was true. I had spent an additional year of student life at Cambridge University, doing a year-long scholarship in medicine and surgery. I didn't have the heart to tell Mr Baffer that this was in large animals – frogs, even African Bullfrogs, didn't really feature.

'I've heard you've had all this advanced training and you're an exotic vet. I suppose I was lucky to get an appointment at such short notice. I'm so relieved I could come and see you. I've been so worried about him.' Mr Baffer looked at me for some sort of affirmation that I was normally chock-a-block with examining sick frogs every day.

'What do you feed him normally?' I asked.

'Oh, he eats mice now he's all grown up.'

I'd never considered being bitten by a frog until that

moment. It isn't the sort of thing that had even remotely crossed my mind – jumping spiders, giant birds, wild dogs and, of course, squirrels, would occasionally worry me, but never frogs. Frogs were generally the good guys in every story I had read as a child, the endearing creatures that produce frogspawn and tadpoles. Brian, however, was the behemoth of all frogs and my whole childhood illusion of these sweet little amphibious creatures in the garden pond had been shattered. Brian ate mice – which didn't seem such a far removed step from eating fingers.

'What exactly is the problem?' I asked.

Brian sat immobile on the consulting room table. He didn't utter a croak.

'He isn't eating,' Mr Baffer began. 'It's his eye. Look, he's facing the wrong way.'

Mr Baffer emitted a strange cooing sound, mixed with a high-pitched squeak. Bending down, he whispered sweet nothings to Brian and, with immense tenderness, turned him around.

I peered at Brian and saw the problem – his right eye, which was now facing me, was ulcerated and infected. Eyes and exotics – both were becoming worrying themes of my first few months in practice.

'That looks sore,' I said with bewilderment. Despite my not-many years of practice, I was uncertain how frogs registered pain but it seemed reasonable that this was why he had lost his appetite. The eye was an infected mess.

Mr Baffer looked at me expectantly.

'How did it happen?'

'I think he caught it on the edge of a plastic train,' Mr Baffer replied. 'He comes out at home you see, and I have a model railway. Well, Brian likes to visit the station, and I think he thought my new Flying Scotsman was, well, edible.

He jumped forward and sort of misjudged things. He was very upset afterwards.'

Momentarily at a loss for words, I looked up at Mr Baffer.

'So when Brian tried to eat one of your model trains, he ended up banging his eye on it?'

'The Flying Scotsman,' Mr Baffer cursed. 'I've thrown it away. Can't have Brian hurt again, can I?' Mr Baffer reached down and stroked Brian, who took a little hop forward. 'I've tried everything, but the eye drops don't work and the antibiotics I got from the local vet haven't touched it. He's in agony. I went back to see my usual vet and he said he didn't know what else to do. Two hours on the bus, but he said you'd be able to help. In fact, he gave me your details.'

I made a mental note to track down this vet and poke him hard in the eye.

Brian needed to see an exotic specialist rather than a newly graduated vet who had been working for two months and whose exotics experience to date involved holding a pet snake twice during his University years and being savaged by a squirrel.

'Mr Baffer, I need to explain, I'm not . . .'

'I know it's not looking good for Brian,' he began, kneading his cap in his hands. 'But please,' he went on, 'please do your best. I just can't see him waste away like this.'

Mr Baffer's voice was thick with emotion as he looked down at Brian and I realised he had nowhere else to go.

Gently, I felt around Brian's eye, buying myself some precious minutes as I debated what on earth I might do. As I ran my fingers down the centre of his back, Brian hopped forward again.

'Oh, he likes you!' said Mr Baffer with a squeak. 'He normally only does that for me!'

I tried to smile and managed a pained grimace. Mr Baffer was now beaming. The diagnosis was actually pretty simple – the frog was in pain from an irreparably damaged eye and not eating as a result. Left in his current state, Brian would die. I had no idea how long massive African bullfrogs could go without food but, judging from Brian's size, I guessed he probably needed to eat quite a lot and, according to Mr Baffer, it had already been ten days.

Any other animal in chronic unrelenting pain from an eye that was unresponsive to medication would be a candidate to have the eye removed. But I had been labelled a frog saviour, which was, in no small way, a result of my own liberal interpretation of what constituted exotic experience – and I didn't have the faintest idea how to go about performing the operation.

'There are specialist clinics that might be able to help. They could probably remove his eye.'

He looked at me in stunned silence.

'Mr Baffer, I think that is what needs to be done. I will help you all I can but I think Brian needs to see a specialist.'

'No,' came the defiant reply. 'I want you to do it. Brian likes you. He needs help now, you're an exotic vet – I was recommended to come and see you. You have all that advanced training!'

'But . . .'

Mr Baffer looked at his watch.

'I have to get the bus,' he flailed. 'But I'll come back tomorrow. You'll look after him. I know you will!' He turned in the doorway. 'He's my best friend.'

And, before I could get any forms signed, Mr Baffer gave Brian a last smile, turned and abruptly left the consult room.

Recovering my wits as quickly as I could, I lifted Brian

down into his box and dashed out of the room in hot pursuit of Mr Baffer, who I glimpsed leaving the surgery through the main doors. I was striding towards the exit when a high-pitched scream rose behind me.

I froze. I hadn't sealed the box. Turning my head, I saw the unmistakable form of Brain hop out of the consult room into the waiting area. A thin mousey woman, clutching a small poodle to her chest, scrambled quickly onto one of the waiting room chairs and screamed even louder.

'Brian!' I cried.

'Brian?' demanded a voice.

Sheila appeared from behind the counter and, giving me the tiniest shake of her head, lifted the hatch behind the desk, strode towards Brian, scooped him up and disappeared into the consult room. Resigning myself, I smiled at the woman in the waiting area and followed Sheila.

'It's another eye operation, Sheila. I'm becoming the resident animal optician.'

After I'd briefly outlined the situation, Sheila called Holly into the room. As ever, Holly collapsed in hysterics.

'What is it with you and eyes?' she asked.

Mr Spotswode appeared to take a look at Brian, and soon every vet, nurse, receptionist, cleaner and work-experience student had nipped in and out of the consult room. Over the course of fifteen minutes, Brian was observed by about twenty people, but I was still no clearer as to how to sort the problem out.

No textbook was going to detail an operation on how to remove a frog's eye, so I went to the computer and started vague internet searches. When that yielded no miraculous cure, I phoned Sam to outline my predicament and see if he had any bright ideas. He didn't, neither did the local zoo, and nor did a 'real' exotic specialist vet in London. I was close to despair when Sheila popped her head round the door.

'I phoned a friend whose cousin's boyfriend works in an aquarium,' she began.

I raised my eyebrows.

'He uses a special drug to anaesthetise the breeding fish when they transport them long distances to other collections,' Sheila continued. 'Apparently it can be used for frogs – they absorb it through the skin.'

She handed me a bit of paper with a drug name on it, and I hastily flicked to data compendium. MS 222 (Tricaine Methane Sulphonate) was just the ticket and, after researching it a bit more, I phoned the drug supplier and ordered a batch for next day delivery. Step one was complete. I could now anaesthetise Brian.

Step Two was going to be a whole lot more difficult.

Everybody gathered in the prep room the next morning as Sheila and I readied ourselves for the big operation. As I dissolved what I hoped was the right amount of anaesthetic agent into a beaker of water, Sheila put Brian in a large plastic tray and armed herself with a syringe. The grand plan was to lower the hapless Brian into the anaesthetic solution to make him sleepy. Once asleep, Rob was to be drafted in to remove Brian from the solution and place him on the tray whilst I commenced the procedure. As I carried out the surgery, Sheila was then going to syringe the solution over him to keep him asleep.

I still like to think it was reminiscent of nineteenth-century surgeon Joseph Lister, the inventor of antiseptic surgery, who used to spray his patients' wounds with a fine mist of carbolic acid as he operated. He saved countless lives and paved the way for the surgeons of today in aseptic technique. There was only one flaw in this analogy; I was removing the eye of a frog rather than pioneering one of the most significant innovations of human medicine.

Brian looked very relaxed about the whole situation. I reached down, gave him a stroke down his back, and he did a little hop forward.

Sheila picked him up from the tray and placed him in the beaker.

'Do I submerge him?' she asked.

Stumbling block one. Brian needed to breathe but, being a frog, could hold his breath for ages – or so I assumed. I had no idea how long the anaesthetic would take to work, but anaesthetics tend to inhibit breathing in one way or another, which is why most animals and all people are intubated after anaesthetic is administered. It is the key to keeping the airways open.

'Let's try thirty seconds,' I began, groping in the dark. 'Submerge him first, count to thirty and then lift him up out of the solution.'

'We don't want him to croak, do we?' Sheila replied.

Over her shoulder, I saw Mr Spotswode watching keenly.

Twenty seconds passed and Brian remained immobile, floating under the water, Sheila's hands clasped firmly around his turgid slimy torso.

Suddenly Sheila's eyes widened. 'It's working!' she said. 'I can feel him going limp . . .'

Everybody peered hard at Brian. Slowly, his head started to droop.

'Let's get his head up and hold him there for another twenty seconds,' I said. 'Then we'll get him on the tray.'

The time inched by. Rob replaced Sheila as Brian's support

team, and Sheila set about loading syringes with the anaesthetic solution.

'He's definitely asleep,' Rob said. 'You ready?'

I nodded. Rob placed Brian on the tray in front of me and Sheila unloaded her first syringe. The solution exploded over Brian, and rebounded straight into Rob's eye. Rob stifled his cry, but didn't release his hold on Brian.

'Good job I'm not a toad,' Rob interjected.

'Bit less pressure, Sheila,' I said. 'Just gentle syringing.'

Sheila gave Rob an apologetic smile and collected another syringe. Predictably, Holly set herself off again, tears streaming down her face.

Softly, I cut around the eye, put some curved scissors behind it and lifted it out. Unsure of the exact anatomy of a frog's eye, it still seemed the most logical and fastest approach. Grabbing what I thought would be the most water-tolerant, dissolvable sutures, I threaded them into Brian's empty eye socket, bringing the freshly-cut edges tightly together.

'How does frog skin heal?' a voice asked from the back of the room.

I looked up. Giles was standing just behind Mr Spotswode, a big grin shining through his beard.

'Very fast,' I said, desperate not to sound as clueless as I felt. I looked at Sheila. 'That's it – job done. Just going to give him some painkiller and antibiotic.'

I'd opted for a dilute version of the same painkiller and antibiotics used in snakes. It had been Sam's only useful tip in our conversation. Whether snakes and frogs have similar metabolism, I had no idea but I couldn't find any books on the subject and reasoned it had to be more similar than dogs and frogs!

Brian hadn't moved a muscle. Sheila stopped syringing

and peered at him intently. A line of tiny stitches traced over where Brian's eye had been on the right side of his broad flat head.

'He didn't bleed much, did he?' Giles began, moving forward to take a closer look. 'You learn something new every day. Looks good, wouldn't you say Mr Spotswode?'

And with that, Brian took a little hop forward.

Two days later, a parcel appeared in the post.

'What is it?' Sheila asked as she handed it to me.

Ripping the package open, I looked at the card and present within.

'The card is a giant frog!' Sheila exclaimed.

'An African Bullfrog,' I corrected. Flicking it open, I scanned the contents.

'Well?' asked Rob, who had entered the office with Holly in tow.

I beamed a massive smile at the room. 'He started eating again the next day,' I said. 'Took a whole mouse. Mr Baffer says he's never been happier.'

'What's the present?' Sheila asked.

I tore off the wrapper and held it up to show the room. From the front cover of a self-published book, a picture of Brian beamed out. *How to Look After Your Bullfrog,* it read, by Mr Rodney Baffer.

Holly dissolved into laughter. 'You could have done with that two days ago,' she said.

The book rested on the tabletop between us, as Rob and I decided to indulge in an after-work pint. I was totally exhausted from being on-call and had been looking forward to this moment all afternoon.

'It doesn't really look like Brian on the front cover. How many frogs do you think he has?' Rob asked, idly flicking open the front cover.

'Ten apparently,' I replied. Mr Baffer and I had spoken on the phone at length about his frog and train collection. Catching a glint in Rob's eye, I felt the challenge of a pub quiz on bullfrogs coming on.

'How long do they live?' Rob asked me, arching an eyebrow.

'In the wild, between four and seven years,' I replied instantly.

'How far can they hop in a single leap?'

'Three to six feet,' I said smugly.

'No way – that's a huge hop!' Rob exclaimed, a wide grin on his face.

'You'd better gen up – all in the book. Could be your next out-of-hours emergency,' I replied, returning the smile.

'Ah, yes, the epic on-call. But I don't see everything and everyone who phones up!' Rob exclaimed, between sips of ale.

'What do you mean?' I replied, glancing at the mobile phone parked next to Mr Baffer's frog book.

'Luke, I'm going to give you a few basic lessons in the reality of being on-call. Not every client wants you to see their pet,' he began. 'Besides, a fair few of them can't actually afford the out-of-hours fee, and those that *do* come in will actually resent it unless their pet really is about to, you know . . .' He lifted his eyebrows conspiratorially. 'Snuff it,' he observed.

'Well, then why do they phone me at two in the morning if they don't want to see the vet?'

Rob set his pint down as he pondered my failure to understand this simplest of notions.

'Because they want to know things will be okay,' he said,

'and they have no one else to ask. There are two types of call.' Rob was warming to his theme. 'The first are from people who don't actually want to see you, just speak to you. They want to appease their own conscience, show their other halves how much they care about the family pet, but in all honesty, they really don't want to actually trudge down to the surgery in the early hours. You have the power to give them a free pass until morning comes . . .' He paused. 'And they're desperate for it.'

Rob's face broke into a broad grin. I was beginning to understand.

'Look, I used to see everything as well,' he continued. 'A cat that was scratching, a dog that was snoring too loudly, a horse that had thrown a shoe. Total waste of time: the cat had fleas, the dog should have been sleeping downstairs, the horse needed a farrier. None of them were life threatening. The clients weren't happy with the bill, the animals weren't happy at being dragged out in the middle of the night – but most of all, I wasn't happy. I needed some sleep.'

'How did you know that the dog didn't have laryngeal paralysis?' I asked. A dog having trouble breathing might have a paralysed larynx and, without emergency treatment, wouldn't last long.

Rob considered this. 'I didn't,' he said. 'If I had the call again, I would make sure I took a proper history and keep my cool . . . Has the dog done it before – as it turned out, yes, every night for about six years. Was the dog in distress? No, he was sleeping like he does every night – at the foot of the owner's bed. None of it's rocket science, but common things occur commonly, that's what you have to remember.' He paused to drink some more beer; this was thirsty work. 'The dog was keeping the client's girlfriend awake, the client felt he had to do his bit, he couldn't exactly admit it was normal for him to sleep alone with his snoring dog, so he pretended something was wrong and phoned me for a chat. If I had kept my head, I would have figured it out and been able to save us all a lot of trouble. Mr Spotswode didn't even bill the client after he heard I had seen him and the dog in the middle of night. He didn't have to say anything; I knew I had jumped the gun with it.'

Rob took a final, only-vaguely-triumphant swig.

'You've never had a night where you haven't been called out, have you?' he asked.

I shook my head wearily. The drilling of the on-call mobile hadn't got any softer as the weeks progressed. The distinctive ring tone kept on cheerfully bleeping out its irritating tune, just a little bit too high pitched. My heart rate would instantly jump and my body was becoming in synch with its wailing. Within seconds, I would be aroused from the deepest, most dreamless slumber.

'Don't get too worried about it, you'll find your way soon enough.'

'And if I don't?' I asked.

Rob took a deep, solemn breath. He pitched forward, as if to break some terrible news. 'You'll die of exhaustion in about six months.'

As if on cue, the mobile began its taunting. I reached for it – but Rob stayed my hand.

'Just get a decent history, don't rush in there,' he said, slowly releasing his hold. 'A frog that hasn't eaten for three hours may well wait until morning.'

I picked up the call. A tense voice succinctly told me the situation and then the line cut off.

I looked at Rob.

'Who was it?' he asked, arching an eyebrow.

'Hightown Farm.' I grimaced. 'There's a calving, stuck fast and they want me there right away.'

I stood up from the table, thought about downing the last of my pint, but then pushed the glass aside.

'You see,' Rob said pointedly, 'that's the other type of call I was talking about. A proper genuine, stressful emergency at the practice's biggest farm client. You want your stripes with Mr Spotswode – sort this out and you'll be there.'

'As ever,' I said, 'another pearl of wisdom. See you tomorrow.'

And, with a mournful glance at my unfinished drink, I was gone.

The evening had begun with a fine mist of drizzle, but had managed to work itself up to the bullets of icy water that now sliced through the darkness with merciless intent. I squinted into the torrents, slowly grinding my way toward Hightown Farm. The left headlight on the car was fixed on full beam, so I drove along the winding and unfamiliar country lanes, lighting up the verges and hedgerows with high abandon – unable to see whatever lay ahead on the driver's side.

I had never been to Hightown Farm but it was indeed the biggest farm client of the practice. The owner, Mr David, was a close personal friend of Mr Spotswode – and, although he was retired from the day to day running of his farm, he was an active presence about the place and I knew that whatever I did would swiftly be reported back to the Powers That Be.

Rob had not been wrong – I had to nail this calving; a good job here would really help me get on in the practice. Perhaps I was letting the thought get to me too deeply, for suddenly I saw a flash in my single headlight, something dark and brown lurching across the road in front of me, obscured by rain and ice. I slammed the brakes and the car sliced across the road but the deer, or loose horse, or creature-of-the-night, was gone. I stumbled out into the roaring rain to check the car over and then, soaked to the skin after only a few seconds, continued the interminable crawl to the farm.

Hightown Farm was massive. The pride of the farm was a large home bred dairy herd, but it also comprised an organic pig unit, a flock of sheep, not to mention a vast arable side to the enterprise. The annual account with the practice almost certainly covered both my and Rob's annual salary, with some to spare. The place was run by a farm manager who I had briefly seen when he came into the practice to pick up some medicines. He was a no-nonsense Scotsman called Mr McKara, a respected figure who brooked no argument. Overseeing a team of herdsmen, farm hands and arable workers, he couldn't afford to be anything but tough – and, as I weaved around the endless narrow bends, I hoped he wouldn't be around and that it would just be me and the head herdsman, Phil, on the job. I hadn't met Phil in person, but I had spoken to him on the phone about a calf with pneumonia a few weeks ago and he had seemed the sort of herdsman I would get along with.

It was supposed to be twelve miles from the practice, but I estimated I had travelled about twice that by the time I finally found the entrance to the farm. Turning into it, I passed a large foreboding house immediately on my left. Lights glared from the windows like the eyes from some giant skull.

Still desperately hoping that this call-out would be low-key and I'd be able to get on with it with just Phil for company,

I carried on a few hundred metres to a cluster of low-lying buildings and pulled up outside the dairy. A large figure stood silhouetted in the doorway, sheltering from the unrelenting rain. It had intensified in the forty minutes it had taken me to get to the farm, and lightning forked across the sky just as the thunder rolled. We were in the middle of the storm. My stomach lurched as I climbed out of the car.

A big man stood, quietly regarding me. Vainly, I searched his face for some flicker of recognition.

'Sorry, it took me a while to get here,' I said, patting down my drenched overcoat. 'Bit of a nightmare drive . . .'

His broad face creased around the edges as he stepped forward, outstretching his arm. For a second, I thought he was reaching out to strike me – but I managed not to flinch.

'Not so easy to find us in weather like this, Luke,' he said, engulfing my hand with his own. 'I'm Phil,' he said, hand still clenched. 'We spoke on the phone about that calf.'

I took a deep breath. The thunder boomed. The big man didn't budge, but something in me jumped. For a second, I felt like a lost little boy.

'Well,' I yelled, over the hammering rain. 'I'm here now, all set . . . Where is she?'

'She's round the side, been calving for a couple of hours. I've done my best but it's well and truly stuck.' We turned to face a tall, imposing barn. 'I'm pretty sure the calf is dead,' he said. 'I've given her some painkiller, but haven't messed around too much. Didn't want her to get sore. I probably should have checked her earlier this afternoon, but with Mr McKara leaving and the new man settling in, it's been a lousy day.'

As Phil spoke, I sprung open the boot of the car and realised, too late, that all the hurtling around the country lanes had dislodged my carefully packed boot.

'Mr McKara's left?' I blurted, as a box, pair of wellies and calving jack all spilled out onto the concrete. As I made a half-hearted attempt to contain the dropping items, I wheeled around, only to knock over a bucket that Phil had filled with warm water in anticipation of my arrival.

'Sorry!' I cried out, scrabbling to pick everything up. For a second, I was glad for the wildness of the night.

'No bother,' Phil said, chasing after the rolling bucket. 'Doubt you can make us wetter on a night like this. Yep, Mr David Junior arrived back today.'

He disappeared into the parlour to fill the bucket back up. While he was gone, I hastily slipped on my waterproof over-alls and, grabbing a few calving ropes and some lube from the car, I walked into the darkness.

The cow was behind a gate in an outside straw yard. A dilapidated lean-to offered scant protection from the elements, but the straw was deep and clean and Phil had obviously done his best to make her as comfortable as possible. The cow, clearly benefiting from the painkiller Phil had administered, seemed fairly relaxed as she stoically allowed me to push my arm full length into her without complaint.

I like calvings – it is hard to beat the feeling of introducing a new life to the world – and I eagerly searched around to find a leg or the head of the calf from which I could start to manipulate things into position. Unfortunately, all I could feel was a backbone pushed hard against the pelvic inlet. I looked at Phil.

'Transverse presentation,' I said.

'Breech,' Phil said quietly.

'Bit like a breech,' I said between gritted teeth as I tried to shift things around. 'But, with a breech, you can push them down into the uterus and get some space to re-position the legs. Transverse is different. With transverse, they're wedged horizontally across the pelvic inlet.' I stopped. It was time to stop speaking vet and start speaking English. 'It won't shift,' I breathed.

I grunted as I tried to manoeuvre the calf. I'd never dealt with this type of presentation before and, despite the cold, a sheen of sweat had formed on my forehead. As a vet student, there is no way to be trained for these sorts of situations. Bad calvings are typically emergencies, and, without any way to predict an emergency, vet students are taught the principles of how to manage a difficult birth by textbook drawings. Handy.

As I was trying to push the calf around, the cow gave a low groan and the calf moved an inch. Reaching right, I could just about feel its head twisting back on itself, compounding the jam. I slipped my fingers into its mouth and pinched the tongue.

There was no reaction. It could mean only one thing.

I pinched it again, desperate for some sign of life.

And there it was – a flicker! It was faint, but it was there.

'It's alive,' I said quickly.

'Are you sure?' Phil doubtfully replied.

I reached for the tongue again. Another pinch. Another flicker.

'Definitely alive,' I said.

'Right,' Phil said. 'You'd best be getting on with this then . . .'

I realised immediately what Phil was implying. I could spend hours trying to shift the calf into a better position and then try to calve it naturally – but the odds on the calf surviving were slim. It was already weakened from the ordeal of its birth and time was against it. The odds on me managing to turn it around without tearing its umbilicus were small and, without a vital supply of oxygenated blood from its mother, the calf would have no way of breathing inside the uterus and would suffocate within minutes.

Phil knew what needed to be done before I did.

My only option was to perform a caesarean and get the calf out cleanly. A page from a textbook flashed into my mind – *uterine viability is compromised when a dystocia has been going on for over thirty minutes*. It meant that to do a caesarean, you needed to do it within thirty minutes of the calf being stuck to stand a really good chance of stitching up a healthy and viable uterus. The longer you left it, the more friable and compromised the uterus became, making it much harder to stitch up and work with. This cow had been calving for several hours.

The cow gave another low groan.

'She's the best cow in the herd,' Phil said levelly. 'Luke, I need you to her to get through this.'

Phil seemed to be able to read the thought on my face.

'Have you done a caesarean on your own before?' he asked, not unkindly.

'Hundreds,' I replied with a smile to smooth the brazen lie.

'Can you handle it?' he asked, his eyes weighing me up.

I gave an almost imperceptible nod of the head.

'Okay,' he breathed. 'Best we get on with it then before both us and the cow catch pneumonia.'

The rain had us soaked to the skin. Releasing another discomfited moan, the poor cow looked round at me with a resigned expression. Even she seemed to know what we had in store for her.

'No way we can get her in the dry for this?' I asked.

'The barn roof got a bit battered in the wind this after-noon so we thought we'd better get the cows out in the yard until it was checked. Never expected it to rain like this . . .' Phil replied, tightlipped as the rain continued to drive into the lean-to.

Tempting fate is never a good move in an already difficult situation. As if listening in, the big yard light on the wall above us started to flicker. Blinking with frenzied intensity, it had clearly decided enough was enough. There was the fizzle of the electrics giving up the ghost, and then we were plunged into darkness.

I patted the cow and, wiping the rain from my eyes, turned to Phil who swore under his breath. Despite his immense stamina, even he was on the verge of collapse. He had been up since the small hours of the morning to do the milking, and it had undoubtedly been a day packed with action.

A thought struck me as suddenly as the lightning breaking overhead.

'I've got an idea,' I said. 'Two seconds.'

Running back to the car, I scrambled into the driver's seat and drove back around the buildings to where we were based, aiming the headlights at the cow. The left light, fixed on full beam, illuminated the whole yard.

Turning the engine off, I hastily got the caesarean kit out of the boot and set to work prepping the cow.

To her credit, the cow was amazing. She stood throughout the operation as I cut deep into her side and, with Phil's help, eased out the limp calf.

'Surely, Luke . . .' Phil said, standing over the poor crea-ture. 'Surely it isn't still . . .'

I grabbed a piece of straw and thrust it into the nose of the wet calf in a desperate attempt to trigger some sort of response and kick-start her breathing. A split second stretched into an eternity before the little calf suddenly stirred.

Abruptly, she sneezed.

'She's alive!' Phil exclaimed, like a mad Dr Frankenstein on this rain-lashed night.

I didn't have the energy to reply. We had been victorious – but the operation was far from complete. Stitching up the cow was a Herculean task. The uterus had torn as I pulled the calf and the incision extended deep into her abdomen. It felt like hours later, rain still streaming down my face, that I reached the final stitch. My fingers were numb as I checked the wound and injected the cow with a bottle of calcium to keep her strength up, and a giant injection of antibiotic.

'That was a very tidy job, Luke,' Phil said. Forcing a grin through teeth clenched together with the cold and wet, he peered over my shoulder at the side of his prized heifer. 'So, how many hundreds of them have you actually done?'

'About a hundredth of a hundred,' I replied.

A broad grin broke out over Phil's face. 'I know Neale will be pleased when I tell him tomorrow,' he said.

I looked blankly at Phil as he realised I didn't know who Neale was.

'Neale is Mr David Junior, back with his family from a few years in Australia. Mr McKara always knew he was managing things until Mr David's son was ready to take over the reins. Now his best cow is going to be okay – and a fine heifer calf to boot!' He paused. 'Look, are you alright to wash up? I've still got to check the cows in the far field on my way home. She's going to be fine here tonight – she has water and silage and the lean-to will keep off the worst of the rain. Not ideal, granted, but all we've got until I get the flipping barn fixed tomorrow.'

Phil made his farewells to the tottering little calf, and disappeared into darkness and rain. It was three in the morning, and I stood there in the freezing cold, with only the cow and calf for company. Seemingly content, with her little calf now suckling at her udder, the cow seemed to be completely oblivious to the huge wound in her side. She put her head down to take a big mouthful of sodden silage from a bucket. It was almost as if she shared our relief it was all over.

I sighed, squinted up and waited for a lull in the storm. Collecting all my things, I smiled to myself. At least I'd done it. My first cow caesarean was over, and it had gone as well as it could have. It was time to make the slow grind home and catch a couple of hours kip before the morning's emergencies started to flood in.

Hopping into the front seat of my car, I noticed, for the first time, that the blinding light on the left hand side somehow didn't seem to be so blinding anymore. In fact, it was positively dim. My stomach lurched as the realisation of what was about to happen, dawned on me. I turned the key, and the engine gave a single doleful turn before spluttering into silence. The battery was flat. I couldn't quite believe it so I tried the key again for good measure. Nothing. In wearied fury, I smashed my head against the dashboard and contemplated spending the rest of the night in the car. I was so exhausted that the thought was almost welcoming, but I couldn't let the practice down, not so soon after my wrestle with the vengeful squirrel. I was on call; I had to get the car started and I had to be mobile.

The rain sluiced down my windscreen. Phil had gone home and I didn't have his number or know where he lived. Everyone was in bed, but no matter which way I looked at it, someone with jump leads was going to have to come to my rescue. Rob was the obvious person to wake up, but I knew him too well; he wouldn't have any leads. Giles would be able to sort things – but he lived about forty minutes away.

I peered vainly around the farm. I could just about make out the silhouette of the big farmhouse through the driving rain. There was nothing for it. Resigning myself to endless ridicule and a dressing down tomorrow from colleagues and bosses, I decided I would have to wake up the new farm manager.

Doorbells can be quite abrupt, even through the noise of driving rain, but the shrill blast that followed my pushing of the button, coupled with the sound of five or six dogs going absolutely mad behind the door, was a noise that could have woken the dead. I reeled back, hair plastering my face, and watched as light after light flickered on in the farmhouse.

The whole family was awake.

With dogs baying inside, the door swung open. Standing in the doorway, the new farm manager was in his night robe. He considered me matter-of-factly, as if it was an everyday occurrence for some sodden young vet to pitch up and bang on the door at three in the morning.

'Hello.'

'Mr David,' I began, through chattering teeth. 'I'm incredibly sorry about this. But I'm the vet and have just been doing a calving on one of your cows.' I didn't quite know where to go next. I didn't quite know if he believed me or not. 'My car has a flat battery,' I rambled on. 'Phil had gone before I realised it.' Still, he said nothing. 'I'm a bit stuck. I need a jumpstart.'

Mr David looked at me.

'How is the cow?' he said calmly.

Another torrent hit the rooftop and gushed down onto an overflowing gutter to land, flat, on my head.

'I think she'll be fine,' I went on, ignoring my sudden shower. 'Went as well as it could have done. The calf was alive so we did a caesarean. Light went off in the barn so I used my car headlights – that's why I have the flat battery . . .'

'You turned the engine off, didn't you?' he said.

I nodded. This was going to go one of two ways and the next few moments were critical.

'Not the smartest move,' I said, trying not to cringe.

Mr David drew himself up to his full height. 'No,' he said. 'You should have used one of my tractors.'

Another rush of water landed on my head, cascading over my face, and Mr David smiled for the first time.

'I'm very sorry to ask you to come out in this but I'm a bit stuck . . .'

In reply, the silence lingered.

'There's not a chance, young man, that I'm going out in this.'

I looked back. I couldn't even see the car any longer; this was going to be a long night.

'Look,' I said, pleading now. 'I'm sorry, but I'm on call . . .'

Mr David held up a hand, as if to command my silence.

'It's non-negotiable, Luke,' Mr David said, evenly. 'This is my first day back. You must understand – if I'm to live up to the fearsome reputation of Mr McKara and take over the mantle from my father, I can't be seen going out in this. You're a smart lad. You see why I . . .'

'Mr David!' I implored.

Mr David turned suddenly over his shoulder. 'Will!' he yelled.

The heavy tread of feet bounding down the stairs echoed

out the doorway. I took a step back as a six-foot, solid figure loomed in front of me with a disgruntled look upon his face.

'It's at times like this that my son pays his rent,' Mr David said.

Will shot his father a resigned look, then fixed me with an accepting expression and headed silently out into the wet darkness.

Too tired to say anything further, I nodded gratefully and went off to jumpstart the car.

As Mr David closed the door, I swear I heard him chuckling.

3

WILD DOGS AND ENGLISHMEN

I returned from Hightown Farm more bedraggled than a stray dog, and it wasn't long before news of my exploits there started to spread. Fortunately for me, the trip to Samos was on the horizon. There were only five working days before Sam and I we were due to leave – only one working week to get through without marking myself out for further ridicule.

Thankfully, the week passed by in a blur of dogs, cats, rabbits, and a pair of sickly goldfish and, before I could take breath, I found myself sandwiched next to Sam on a plane as we embarked on the first leg of our trip of power.

Sam had taken the responsibility of booking our tickets and seemed certain we would make the connecting flight in Athens. Sixty minutes didn't seem a huge amount of time to me as we scrambled from concourse to concourse, but Sam assured me that this exact combination had been recommended by the airline itself. It was, apparently, a regular connection.

Naturally, we missed it.

We'd never stood a chance. Trying to make a connecting

flight in under an hour is a challenge in any airport in the world – and, in Athens, managing to do it in less than two would require an act of God.

'What is it with you and metal detectors?' Sam asked as, once again, I set off the alarms as we trudged through another security checkpoint. 'This is the third one you've set off – have you picked up some sort of magnetic charge as we flew over the Mediterranean?'

'I'm feeling electric,' I replied, struggling under the burden of our bags.

'You're feeling the hands of a lot of Greek security guards,' Sam replied. 'You do realise us missing this connection is entirely down to whatever metal object you've stuffed down your trousers?'

'The blame surely has to lie with the fool who booked us tickets that virtually overlap in time,' I said, grimacing as the guard frisked my buttocks, clearly testing Sam's implication that I might have something tucked into my pants.

'An hour should have been fine! You deciding to get felt up by every man carrying a gun and dressed as a soldier, that's what's caused us issues. We now have five minutes to get on a plane which has already stopped boarding and is probably taxiing to the runway . . .' Sam stopped. Even he could tell he was beginning to whine. 'I need a drink.'

'We need our bags, and we need a plan!' I replied. 'That's what we need! Someone called Joeri is meeting us at Samos airport in an hour – we need to contact him, let him know when we'll actually be arriving and get there!' I paused. Sam was still pouting. 'Then we can both have a drink,' I finally relented.

Backtracking to the baggage hall, at last we spotted our motley collection of rucksacks and a big square box, neatly stacked up by the side of the carousel with stickers indicating they were supposedly in transit on their way to Samos.

'Lucky for us, looks like our bags weren't going to make the flight either. Nice box by the way,' Sam said giving it a slap on the side.

'Contains a couple of surgical kits, clippers and a whole host of hardcore anaesthetics.'

'And the legality of you bringing in a box loaded full of animal medicines – otherwise known as drugs – to Greece?' Sam enquired.

I shrugged. 'I'm not worried.'

For a second, Sam stood back, seemingly aghast.

'What?' he began. 'You aren't seriously smuggling them in are you?'

'Not exactly . . .'

Sam looked at me quizzically.

'I checked in the box under your name,' I finished.

Sam's jaw dropped as I laughed.

'Well, if I go down, I am not going alone!' he railed, heading for the bags. 'I've got enough on you to put you away for a long time – don't think for a second I won't use it!' He paused, heaving a rucksack onto his shoulder. 'Maybe it's a good thing our bags didn't travel on without us,' he sighed.

Rifling through the top pocket of my rucksack, I dug out a scrap of paper with the charity's contact details. Hastily tapping the number into my mobile, I groaned at Sam as a solid tone blocked the call.

'I'm barred from international calls,' I said.

'How come?'

I gave a sheepish grin. 'I haven't always been the best at, you know, *bills* and things . . .'

'Brilliant,' Sam muttered, reluctantly reaching into a pocket and handing me his mobile. 'It's going to be a cheap call – international ones always are, right?'

'Pennies,' I replied.

I swiftly dialled the number again – and, when there was no reply, rattled out a text to tell Joeri of our change of plan. I hoped he wasn't already waiting at the airport for his two intrepid English veterinarians – he would be in for a long wait.

Sam and I headed over to customer services to try to work out the best way to get to Samos.

The ever-helpful member of the airline's customer service team must have been having an off day. The person behind the counter was the silent type and Sam's quips about transit times and connecting flights fell on deaf ears. After receiving a series of shrugs, we were finally dealt the devastating news.

'When is the next flight to Samos?' Sam asked, stressing each syllable as if he was speaking to a little child.

The face behind the desk grunted and checked his computer.

'Two days time, sir,' he said. He seemed to take delight as he rolled the last word around his mouth.

Sam and I beat a hasty retreat to consider our options. Two days in Athens was too much to waste when we only had seven days in total to get the job done.

'Islands by definition are surrounded by water,' Sam ventured. 'How far is it the old-fashioned way?'

'It's too far to swim,' I replied with a smile.

'Let's go with trying to find a boat for the time being,' Sam said. 'We'll try swimming when that fails.'

Locating a travel information booth, we thankfully found a much friendlier member of our EU brethren. It transpired that there was an overnight ferry that left the harbour in a couple of hours and would get us there by dawn. Phileas Fogg had nothing on us.

Adventure beckoned. Outside the airport, we loaded our packs – smuggled veterinary medicines included – into a taxi and rode down to the docks of Athens. The port was bright and beautiful, and the sun arched overhead as the driver chattered at us in a language neither Sam nor I understood.

Arriving at the port, we made a beeline for a large grey building which seemed to be a hive of activity and, after some chaotic weaving from office to office, and abrupt conversations in broken English, we somehow managed to procure a couple of ferry tickets. Grinning from our triumph against (admittedly, self-made) adversity, we made our way toward what we were promised was a luxury liner.

'Hope you brought your own life raft,' Sam said as we approached the vessel.

I stopped dead on the jetty, letting my packs fall at my feet.

'This can't be the right one . . .' I said. 'This is a container ship!'

The boat had seen better days. It was a huge steel structure, dirty grey with liberal rust patches on its sides, and it lolled against the harbour wall with a tilt that made me slightly uncomfortable.

'Does it have a boat name on the ticket?' Sam asked.

I held the tickets up: two green tabs of paper with a single dash on each of them.

'Not the most detailed ticket in the world.'

'Have we just been totally taken for a ride?' Sam enquired, not unreasonably.

There was only one way to find out. I swerved towards the walkway that would take us up to the deck of the big ship. A burly Greek sailor in jeans and a loose blue coat took an idle glance at our green tickets before reaching over and taking them off me, gesturing with a casual wave towards the deck.

'How to disappear without a trace,' Sam muttered.

Our allocated area was on the open deck, with about fifty other passengers. Rapidly, we realised that we'd made our way aboard a cargo ship that took a few travellers on its decks and stairwells for a bit of extra cash.

Angling towards a bench at the fore of the deck, Sam and I swung down our backpacks and rolled our eyes. An old lady had come aboard and settled opposite us. She glowered in our direction as the dog she had brought with her – a large white boxer – promptly lifted its leg against the railings and jettisoned a thick stream of urine which pooled around its feet before starting to run back across the deck, directly towards our bags.

'How about you sleep here and I'll find a hammock some-where?' Sam asked as I grabbed our bags and whipped them from the path of the spreading pool.

Arriving at the port in the eerie light before dawn, we were exhausted. Between us we must have had about forty minutes sleep all night. The rolling motion of the ship had left us both queasy and, as we dragged ourselves down the quay, I was grateful that neither of us had thought to bring breakfast.

The sun was already starting a steady climb into the sky and it was abundantly clear from the people out and about on the streets that Samos was a Mecca for the rich and beau-tiful. Sadly, not fitting into either category, we called Joeri, the shelter manager, to tell him that we had arrived.

'Yar,' came the thick Dutch accent through the crackling static. 'I am here. Where are you?'

I mumbled directions down the phone. 'How will we recognise you?' I asked.

The voice just laughed. 'I'll find you, don't worry.'

In a matter of moments, a huge blond man strode up the quay, the throng of passengers parting before him like the waters of the Red Sea. His hair was peroxide blond, wild and unkempt, almost dreaded at the tips, which extended down to his shoulders. Wearing a large silver nose ring, his weathered face was complemented by a torn T-shirt, ripped shorts and big heavy boots.

I knew straight away that he was Joeri.

'English vets!' the voice boomed 'Come here! We go this way.'

Picking up our backpacks, one in each hand, Joeri surged ahead and led us towards a tiny red car badly parked right outside the main port entrance.

'Are you allowed to park here?' Sam asked.

'No matter, they know me,' Joeri replied with a deep laugh.

Pulling one of the front seats forward, he threw in our backpacks and ushered Sam to climb into the tiny confines of the back of the vehicle. From the boot, a large Husky looked at us with a cool reserve.

'Houdini – be good!' the big Dutchman barked, contorting himself into the driving seat. The dog took the hint and sank down to its paws, as if begrudging the fact it could not confront these two insipid English vets.

Before we knew it, we were hurtling through the tiny side streets of the port, rising at last to climb up the side of one of the mountains.

'We go first to the shelter and then to the house,' Joeri declared.

Too shell-shocked and exhausted to say anything different, Sam and I just nodded and took in the surrounding scenery. Considering Samos was the ancient home to Epicurus, Pythagoras and Aesop, I didn't think Sam and I could add much to the island's history – but we were the first English vets to go there and work, so in our own little way we were doing our bit. I wondered what the ancient philosophers would have thought about our mission – all the money, effort and resources that had gone into getting us out here to help the dogs, when there was so much human suffering in the world.

The narrow roads that weaved through Samos town were soon left behind as we climbed steadily further and further up, to overlook the harbour.

'It's a beautiful place,' I began. 'Is the shelter far?' I gazed out of the window at the town below us, framed by mountains and set neatly against the waters of the sparkling Mediterranean.

'People don't want barking dogs around them so we are high up!' Joeri boomed.

After driving a couple of miles parallel to the coast below us, away from Samos Town, Joeri abruptly turned off onto an unmade road.

'We go along here. Lot of dogs here.'

The sea disappeared from view and suddenly we were careering along a crude dirt track, jumping in and out of potholes and swerving around huge areas of landfill. The stench was overpowering. I cast a look at Sam, who glared at me from the backseat with raised eyebrows.

'It's at the rubbish dump?' I asked.

'Ya. That is where we got the permission. Hard for water! We have to get a tank filled every other week but we are mostly left alone up here which is good.' Joeri paused. 'Lot of dogs live in the landfill though. Bad, bad dogs.'

Joeri pulled up outside a seven-foot wire enclosure.

'Welcome to the shelter!' he declared. 'Come meet the dogs!'

We were in the middle of nowhere, surrounded by landfill and the stench of rotting rubbish. The perfect picturesque streets of quaint Samos Town seemed a million miles away, not just down the mountainside.

The enclosure was makeshift and the top of the fence sagged around the perimeter, which extended in a large rectangle about a quarter of the size of a football pitch. As the dust settled, I noticed a breeze-block hut standing just outside the shelter, crumbling and dilapidated. It had no door but the outside had a cheerful coat of white paint – a stark contrast to the surrounding grey wire and brick. Joeri saw me looking at the hut and gestured towards it.

'The office,' he said with a big hearty laugh. 'I paint last week in your honour.'

'Very smart,' Sam chipped in. 'Is that our centre of communications?'

Joeri seemed to completely miss Sam's gentle jibe.

'Yes, it is nice. I paint the kennels last month but it fades very quickly. No phone here though – we use the house for calls.' He looked at us earnestly. 'Come to meet the dogs.'

'If he kills us and feeds us to the dogs I wouldn't be the least bit surprised,' Sam muttered under his breath as we followed in the wake of the big wild man.

Directly behind the office, the enclosure stretched back about twenty-five metres and was divided into three strips. The area on the far left was an open dirt pen in which a multitude of dogs, all different shapes and sizes, began barking excitedly. Bounding up to the flimsy fence, they jumped at the wire expectantly and clamoured for Joeri's attention as he started to unlock the thick padlock.

The middle and right-hand side of the enclosure was subdivided along its length into a line of ugly breeze-block kennels and adjoining runs. Four or five dogs were kept in each enclosure, with the exception of only two of the kennel areas, which just had one big solitary animal in each. As Joeri inched open the gate and waved us to follow him, Sam and I exchanged surprised glances as the cacophony of the shelter dogs increased to a frenzied intensity.

By the time I turned back, Joeri had been totally swamped by the dogs jumping all over him. They clearly loved him and his affection for them was evident as he ruffled hairy coats and spoke softly to many of the dogs by name.

'You need some ear defenders to work here!' Sam yelled.

'What?' Joeri replied, turning his attention back to Sam.

'You need ear defenders here, for the noise!' Sam repeated.

Joeri was clearly confused. 'Why would you wear them?' he asked.

'To block out the sound!' Sam replied earnestly.

'But you couldn't hear anything!' Joeri called back, dead-pan serious. 'How would we talk?'

Sam looked at me and raised his eyes upwards. Joeri, it seemed, was not talking about us. He was talking about talking to his dogs.

'With our ears blocked we would have difficulties,' Joeri went on, pausing for a response.

'Yes,' Sam finally conceded. 'You're right, silly idea.'

'Yes. Not good idea.' Joeri nodded, satisfied, and looked at me to make sure all was well.

'It's great, Joeri, I think Sam was just saying it was noisy!' I shouted.

'Yes,' Joeri patiently said. Turning back to Sam, he smiled and nodded to make sure he understood. 'The dogs, you see. They're barking.'

An involuntary laugh escaped my lips as I caught Sam raising his eyebrows in disbelief. That laugh almost got me into deep trouble, as, suddenly, a pack of the dogs looked up and began to bound over, an unstoppable tide of fur and slobbering jaws.

'How many dogs do you have here?' I asked, the animals clustered all around my legs. I was staggered by the volume of animals in such a desolate and desperate spot. It was achingly hot and we were in the middle of nowhere, exposed to the sun.

'We are very over full,' Joeri replied. This time he did not laugh. 'More every day,' he said. 'About eighty here and we are supposed to have forty-five.'

'Where do they come from?' I asked.

'We get called by tourists to go and pick up injured ones. If I see one on a chain in the sun, I also take it. Up here people also dump them. This one . . .' He bent down to a lean-looking mongrel with big, doleful eyes. 'This one was tied up to the fence yesterday morning when I arrived. They don't care.'

'You just take them?' Sam interjected.

'Yes, on a chain, no water in the sun all day. If I see it, I take it,' Joeri repeated, speaking a little slower and, once again, smiling at Sam encouragingly.

Sam looked at me, exasperated.

'He was just wondering how you can do that legally?' I said, relishing my role as the mediator.

'Is it legal in your *country* to chain a dog in the sun all day with no water?' Joeri demanded.

'Well, it's not your dog . . .' Sam replied.

'I don't care! I take the dog!'

'What happens if they love their dog?' Sam continued.

Joeri looked at him for a moment. Then he drew himself tall, gesticulating wildly and responding in an overly exaggerated way, as if Sam was about three. 'They chain the dog in the sun with no water all day!' he declared, mimicking a chained-up dog. 'Sometimes the dog dies.' He looked suddenly mournful, his lips turned down like a sad circus clown. 'They don't love the dog, so I take it and bring it here!' As he finished, Joeri again nodded at Sam to make sure he understood.

Sam just raised his hands in the air.

'Don't mind me; I'm going to howl into the wind!' he declared.

Joeri nodded and smiled sympathetically. 'Yes, dogs will like the howling, that's good.'

'What if they want it back?' I interjected, certain that Sam could not go on.

'They never want it back,' Joeri replied simply.

'What about the dumping – who dumps dogs all the way up here?'

'People who don't want the dogs. The wives bring them up here.'

'The women bring them up here?' Sam asked, battling off a scraggly lurcher.

'Yes, often women,' Joeri replied.

'Now you're talking!' Sam said.

This time, it didn't take long for Joeri to understand.

'Yes,' he said. 'The women, they are often in the bikinis.'

Sam flashed me a big grin.

'How often do they come here?' he asked.

'They come all the time. Sometimes,' he said with a conspiratorial wink, 'they are even naked . . .'

'Naked?' Sam repeated, a little nonplussed. 'You mean topless from the beach?'

'Naked! They are completely naked, the women with their dogs!' Joeri boomed, but Sam just looked at him agog. At last, Joeri looked at me, his big face split in a huge smile.

'Your friend is very funny, ya! He thinks naked women come here to a dog shelter in a landfill! Very funny!'

I took delight in joining the laughter. For once, Sam was on the receiving end of a joke and the big Dutchman had handled him masterfully.

'Can but hope!' Sam interjected.

'We all hope!' Joeri agreed, giving Sam a big slap on the back, which sent him forward a couple of paces.

'Come,' Joeri eventually went on, 'you say hello and then we go to the house. All these ones here you need to sterilise. We start this afternoon.' Joeri gestured at a row of kennels, each one containing five or six dogs.

'What about the two dogs by themselves at either end?' I asked.

'They fighting dogs. They kill the other dogs. That one there . . .' Joeri gestured to a big tan and white animal which looked at us with his tail wagging slowly, 'he very nice to us but he has killed three dogs in here.'

Joeri said it very casually but it didn't seem casual to me.

'How did that happen?' I asked.

'He was dumped over the fence one night into the large pound. He killed two dogs there. I found them in the morning. I separated him but one dog managed to crawl under the wire and into his pen.'

'And that was that,' put in Sam, walking up to the pen and stroking the killer dog through the wire.

'Ya,' said Joeri.

'Will he ever be re-homed?' I asked.

'I don't think so,' Joeri replied. 'He stay here with me.'

Joeri moved about the enclosure with ease, chatting away. He was totally accepted by the dogs as he walked down the line of kennels, checking his beloved charges.

'How did you come to be here?' I asked.

'I travelled here and helped the people trying to save the dogs. I like dogs. They had a house for me so I stayed and looked after the dogs.'

'What about your job back home?' Sam asked, walking over to stroke a small black dog that was lying in a shallow hole it had burrowed into the dirt.

'Haha! I lived in squat in Holland. I do activist work. I come here, I stay!'

It seemed to be all the explanation we would need. The Dutchman threw us another maniacal smile and gestured for us to follow him to the car. It was time to head back into Samos so the hard graft could begin.

The house was perched halfway up the hillside on the outskirts of Samos Town. Within walking distance of the harbour, it had sweeping panoramic views of the houses below and the ocean beyond. A terraced construction, it belonged to a German expat resident of the island. He had founded Animal Care Samos and both he and his wife were ardent dog lovers. Moved by the plight of the dogs moping in and around the town, and especially the fate many of them suffered out of the tourist season, they had formed the charity and arranged for a parcel of land to be donated from the municipality for the purpose of sheltering and re-homing the street dogs. Influential in the local government of the island, they had smoothed the waters and paved the way for Joeri to set things up and enabled us to come over and work legally under the umbrella of their organisation.

Ensconcing Joeri in one of their spare houses, they had created a central base of operations from which the charity could grow and develop. Split over three storeys, the kitchen and lounge area on the ground floor backed onto an open yard, which was bordered by a high fence. The kitchen was to be our operating theatre, the yard our recovery area, the lounge our drug and equipment dispensary, leaving upstairs free for our accommodation. Joeri and Houdini occupied the middle floor. Meanwhile, at the top of the house there were two adjacent rooms, each with a large mattress on the floor and nothing else; our living quarters for the week.

'Where are we supposed to do this magical healing?' Sam asked as we stood in the kitchen, trying to figure out how best to set up the operating theatre.

Looking out through the double French doors leading into the yard, I could see a few puppies playing with a piece of string in the dirt and numerous larger brown shapes dotted around the fence line, presumably our intended patients for our first afternoon's work.

'You do it here!' Joeri announced, as if such a thing was patently obvious.

Not for the first time, Sam raised his eyebrows at me.

I knew what he meant. There wasn't even a table – we couldn't exactly operate on the floor.

'There's a picnic table out there,' I said, gesturing towards a filthy plastic table in the yard, its surface encrusted with a thick layer of dirt.

'But where will we eat lunch?' Sam replied, the hint of a smile playing on his lips.

'Eat much later, first we do the dogs!' Joeri said loudly. 'I get table. You sort out medicines.'

As Joeri bustled outside, Sam looked at me. 'Honestly,' he whispered, 'you are going to owe me for this one. Next time I pick the holiday, okay?'

'We're in the business of saving lives, buddy,' I replied, organising the medicines we had brought with us.

'We do that forty-eight weeks of the year. I had different things in mind for the other four.' Sam paused and heaved a box of medicines out of his pack. 'Like finding those women in bikinis that Joeri was talking about.'

'Believe me; your sense of achievement will rate much higher working with the shelter dogs.'

Sam didn't have the chance to offer me yet another acid reply. Suddenly, Joeri reappeared, dragging the table into the room.

'We wipe it and perfect!' he declared. 'Just like home?'

Sam shook his head and then headed out into the yard himself.

Joeri looked at me questioningly.

'A law unto himself!' I said as Sam came back into the room, clutching four bricks to his chest.

'Modified hydraulics – got to consider health and safety in these sorts of situations. This table will now be the perfect height and fully compliant with all EU working regulations,' Sam said, carefully placing a brick underneath each table leg.

'Now he gets it!' Joeri boomed with a big laugh.

The first day flew by, both of us immersed in a world of working out injectable anaesthetic dose rates, guessing dog weights, and generally getting caught up in the mayhem of the work. The banter between the three of us flowed and we spent a lot of time over the next few days, laughing and joking as we steadily worked through Joeri's list of dogs. Local restaurants delivered us meals and, as word spread throughout the town, residents began to drop by to see exactly what we were up to.

On the fourth day, we woke to see a collection of cars lined up outside, a variety of dogs peering out of the windows at us, as if even they were intrigued. Joeri pointed outside.

'You two,' he said. 'You are island celebrities now.'

With no vet on the island, the rumours of our presence had clearly spread. Even when Joeri was not with us, people began to wave and say hello. They also began to arrive at the dogs' shelter with various pets in tow.

Joeri kept nipping off for a few hours each afternoon. Neither Sam nor I had any idea what he was up to, but I just assumed it was standard charity canvassing work.

'Where does he go?' Sam asked one evening, as we strolled to the quayside to grab a bite to eat and a cold beer. The evenings were fantastic and there was no better place to finish up the day than sitting on the quayside, watching the water lap against the shore.

'Hopefully it's to try to arrange more dogs,' I replied. A stray was eyeballing us from an alley. 'We've almost finished the ones in the shelter. You see – it only takes a couple of superheroes like us to neuter a billion dogs. By midday tomorrow, we'll be twiddling our thumbs.'

'You'll be twiddling your thumbs,' Sam muttered. 'I can think of a million things to be doing on this paradise island should the opportunity present . . .'

Sam did not get a chance to finish his sentence, for a big

brown shape shot across the street in front us, quickly followed by four or five other dogs hurtling in pursuit.

Sam and I exchanged glances as another couple of dogs suddenly appeared and chased after the others. The stray in the alley suddenly pricked up its ears and joined the pursuit, disappearing into a dark backstreet.

'Now that,' Sam said, 'is what I call a bitch on heat.'

'It takes one to know one.' I grinned.

Sam was right. The brown shape that had darted in front of us must have been a bitch in season and all the other dogs were street dogs in the area, drawn to her scent and desperate for the chance to have their wicked way. A few growls emanated from a couple of streets over, followed by the cry of what we presumed to be an angry waiter.

'That's what causes all the problems,' I said. 'Those dogs will chase her all night, growling, barking, fighting and being a general pest. Especially around the restaurant area.'

'That's why locals poison them out of tourist season,' Sam replied, hearing the waiter giving another cry. No doubt he was waging a war with one of the energetic mongrels. 'But they can never kill enough and each litter can number nine or ten puppies – so, come summer, when an amnesty on street dogs prevails so as not to upset the tourists with too much dog slaying, the population surges back to record levels.'

I paused, pondering this. 'We should target the area local to the house. That pack are a pain. If we can neuter them now, show the locals that once they are sterilised and back on the street they'll be a stable population, they'll be a lot less trouble and they won't breed more dogs.'

Sam looked at me with a grin more wolfish than those of the runaway dogs.

'Great plan . . .' he said, 'but how are we supposed to get

those dogs back to the house? Leave a trail of pizza? If you think I'm sharing my dinner with a pack of street dogs, think again!'

At last, we reached our chosen restaurant for dinner. It was a nice Italian with a wooden veranda and the promise of a filling meal and cold beer.

Taking a seat opposite Sam, I stared into the darkness, down towards the sea. A shape darted past, just out of the periphery of the immediate lights. I twisted round in my chair to look in the direction of where the dogs were now scrabbling around on the sand.

'I was thinking more Pied Piper rather than Hansel and Gretel,' I said.

Sam looked at me, openmouthed.

It has to be said that the Pied Piper of Hamelin was not a great guy. The story, dating back to around the thirteenth century, tells of a man, dressed as a piper, who lured away rats plaguing a small town in rural Germany. The townsfolk didn't pay him for the job, as they had promised, so he piped out a tune and lured all their children away to their death. He wasn't exactly an inspiration of social responsibility – but, undeniably, he had come up with a cunning technique for getting rid of the unwanted rodents. Neither Sam, nor I, had a magic pipe, but we did have the next best thing – and even better was the fact that the children of Samos would be in no immediate danger.

'That bitch is red hot,' I said.

'You're kidding me?' Sam replied. 'We'll get arrested or sectioned – or both! You can't swoop up a bitch in heat and use her to bait a pack of street dogs! She'll bite you for a start.'

'She might not . . .'

'Well, while you ponder the odds, I'm going to eat a giant pizza.'

'Make it a meat one and save a couple of slices,' I replied.

Sam shot me a look like daggers. 'Why?' he moaned.

'Something's got to lure her into range.'

Racing through the narrow streets of Samos carrying a twenty-kilogram dog in your arms, being chased by a pack of street dogs, is the sort of surreal experience you might have in a dream. The reality was no less exciting.

Despite Sam's warnings, the bitch in heat had proved to be an incredibly friendly black cross breed that was presumably very used to scavenging along the picturesque waterfront. She first appeared just as we were served our meals, at a restaurant adjacent to ours. Scampering away from the waiters who materialised to wave a broom in her direction, she moved from table to table, her black tail wagging at the customers dotted in clusters on the candlelit verandas who, more often than not, tossed her a bit of warm bread. As she moved towards our restaurant, a slice of Sam's pizza won her over in seconds.

Whilst Sam settled the bill, I tempted her over with the promise of more pizza.

'Come on, girl,' I whispered, looking into dark soulful eyes. 'Come on, girl – I won't hurt . . .'

Just as she was beginning to trust me, snuffling at my hands and licking the grease off my fingertips, I struck. I was a python. I was a lion. I was, above everything else, an idiot. I scooped her up into my arms and, crashing through the tables as I went, set off.

The rest of the dogs in the pack had not been so bold down on the waterfront. Whilst the waiters had made a half-hearted attempt to keep the bitch away from their tables, ultimately they had indulged their customers by allowing a sweet little black dog to slink among them, hovering for scraps – but they weren't letting any of the other dogs even close. The big male harbour dogs were feared by both locals and guests. With long, scarred muzzles, thickset hairy bodies that moved in the shadows of the waterfront, and deep-throated growls, these were not dogs meant to be petted by anyone. Whenever one dared to venture into the periphery of the eating areas, two or three waiters would appear, a pack in their own right, and chase the dogs away with shouts, sticks and stones.

Yet, once we left the restaurants behind us, the dogs started to appear. One after another they came, slinking out of shadows and alleys, snouting forward for the bitch in my arms. We careered along a narrow lane of cobbles and a mutt looked up from the rubbish bins. If I were prone to melodrama, I would have seen its glowing, knowing eyes fixed on me.

Somewhere, I swear, a howl went up.

We reached a broad thoroughfare and began to hurry up the hill. A pack of dogs, of all shapes and sizes, was following us already. The bitch sensed the trouble she was in and snuggled down, deeper into my arms. Carrying a female dog in heat felt a bit like driving through the African plains with a big juicy steak tied to the back of my car and hoping that the lions would come and have a nibble. You sort of hope they do – and a little bit of you hopes they don't.

'This is totally crazy!' Sam cried as we started our trot a mile uphill. 'We're going to be exhausted before we get half way – and your feral friends are going to be all over us.'

'If any of them get too close, shoo them off,' I breathlessly replied. 'This bitch is mine, remember?' I was already feeling the burn, and couldn't even laugh at the ridiculousness of our predicament.

'Great!' Sam remarked. 'So, I get to chase off the shaggy monsters whilst you have a little cuddle with your new best pal.' Sam cast furtive glances all around us.

We didn't really have a plan, but I was sure things would fall into place. As we neared the house, Sam would open the gates, he'd hide, I'd go in, the dogs would rampage after me – and then Sam would race inside the house to the kitchen and let me and the bitch inside. That was how it went in my head, anyway.

As we ran, chased by the hounds, we worked out the kinks.

'What if the dogs decide you aren't carrying the hottest bitch on the block after all?' Sam asked.

It was a question that I didn't need to answer. A sharp bark from the shadows was like a bugle call and, suddenly, four dogs materialised from a narrow road just up ahead. We sprinted as hard as we could to get in front.

'There are another two behind them,' I said, seeing two dim shapes appear out of the dusk.

'We're sure this is safe?' Sam said.

'I'm pretty sure we're safe,' I said, cuddling the dog in my arms. 'It's her we have to be worried about.'

As we got closer, Sam somehow summoned the strength to rush on ahead and open up the house to take me straight into the yard at the back. As I was still panting my way up the hill, the shaggy tide of dogs in close pursuit, he readied about ten dog bowls with food and scattered them around the enclosure. With the bitch out of the equation, spending the night in the house with us – I was beginning to like that bitch – our theory was that the pack would then settle for the night. We weren't going to kennel the dogs individually – there wasn't the space for that – but we simply wanted to get them all in there, shut the doors, and then, come the morning, go in and start the neutering.

I glanced down; the dog in my arms was being incredibly good and seemed to be enjoying the ride. I think she knew that being carried was a much more peaceful option than running on the streets with the horde behind us on her tail.

The dogs were getting nearer and nearer as their bravery increased. I guessed that it had to be most of the males from the harbour pack. The lead dog was a large grey animal – a Weimaraner crossbreed – but it wasn't its imposing size or pale green eyes which gave it a menacing appearance; it was the fact its ears had been hacked off by a pair of scissors. This would have been done when it was a puppy; someone had clearly had aspirations for it as their guard dog, but it had either been abandoned, or escaped for the night. Either way, it looked like the top dog in the pack and it steadily trotted behind me, scenting the bitch that cuddled tight against my chest.

I slowed my pace to let the dogs draw close as I turned and entered the yard at the back of the house. It was empty except for Sam and the food bowls. The large grey dog hovered uncertainly at the entrance. Sam ducked behind the gates, and I kept my back turned to the entrance, having walked as far into the yard as I could go. The other dogs clustered behind the grey one, feeding off their leader's uncertainty. One barked, and then another joined in; soon, the hound pack was in full cry.

Whether it was the lure of the food or the smell of the bitch, at last, the grey dog couldn't resist and walked into the yard. As the others followed, Sam quickly swung the door shut and, with a whoop, raced into the house to let me and the little black dog into the sanctuary of the kitchen.

'I love it when a plan comes together . . .' Sam began as I walked into the kitchen.

Just as he did so, the grey dog, realising I was disappearing inside the house with the bitch, made a rush for the gap. Suddenly huge claws were scrabbling at my back, as it desperately tried to barge past. I managed to block it and Sam shut the door in the nick of time.

'Joeri is going to be in for a surprise in the morning!' Sam said, crouching to eyeball the captured mutt.

I turned to the window. The shadows were massing.

'I think he'll know about it long before the morning . . .' I said. I rubbed my hand against the condensation that fogged the glass. Out there, the dogs howled in chorus.

Morning came in the blink of an eye. I awoke with a jolt to find that the little black bitch had edged herself onto the end of my mattress. Joeri stood over me, gesticulating wildly with his arms.

'You crazy English! Where did all the dogs come from?'

I shrugged. 'It's her fault,' I said, putting a protective arm around the little dog.

Joeri paused, longer than seemed natural. I couldn't tell if he was about to laugh or explode.

'You get it!' he declared in a big booming voice. 'You get it! You and your funny little friend get it!'

'Get what?' I groggily replied.

'You get it!' he boomed again, beaming down at me as I rallied into consciousness. 'Come on! We have lot to do . . .'

We started with the little black bitch. It's never ideal to spay a dog in season, but we'd had no choice in this situation, and she was doing well. As Sam and I began to work through the rest of the dogs, Joeri strutted back and forth. Neutering community dogs, he explained, was a fine line.

'This little dog . . .' Joeri began, patting the recovering form of the bitch, 'everyone know her. She would not get poisoned!'

'So?' Sam said.

Joeri looked at him with anger that might even have been real. 'If this little dog not goes well, then everyone would hate us.'

'What do you mean, Joeri?' I asked. 'She's a lovely dog, but . . . does that mean everyone in the community claims some ownership of her?'

'Ya!' the big man replied. 'You get it! People already ask me first thing this morning if she okay. I tell them your plan and they all laugh. Funny only if she goes well.'

We paused, thinking back on that mad dash up the hill.

'Well,' Sam finally said, 'it did go well. She'll be back out there in a couple of days.'

Joeri remained silent, checking the bitch over. 'We see if it works!' he boomed. 'But ya, I think this could be very good thing for Samos.' He stopped, shaking his head wistfully. 'I like the idea! I wanted to try it with the big grey one with a cat.'

'What?'

'What? You think only crazy English have this idea? Once, I saw the big dog chase a cat and I wanted one to lure it here. Only problem: I just couldn't find a good cat.'

Sam realised he was once again falling for the bait, and ventured a laugh.

'Ya, hard to find a good cat.' Joeri laughed too and slapped Sam on the shoulder. 'I need to go,' he said. 'Back later.'

'Where are you going?' I asked.

'To the shelter, job to do, then back.'

Our surgeries were done for the morning so I decided to leave Sam to keep an eye on the recovering dogs and tag along with Joeri. He initially seemed a little reluctant to let me come along, but as soon as he realised Sam was staying behind to keep an eye on things, he brightened up.

'Just call me nurse,' Sam replied acidly. 'I'll be sure to make your bed while you boys are out having fun.'

'Hospital corners on the sheet – no mattress on the floor is complete without them,' I said, waving Sam a dainty good-bye as I followed Joeri to the car.

As we drove up to the shelter, we chatted about the charity and Joeri's plans to turn things around. Joeri hoped to spend a good few years on the island, living on a tiny stipend donated by the charity supporting the animals. He had no insurance, no official job and his visa enabled him only to work as a carpenter – but, still, he was one of the happiest people I'd ever met.

'Why do you do it?' I asked as we pulled up outside the pens.

'I love the dogs. They nice to me and I look after them.' He looked at me, his great big nose ring catching the sun.

'What about family, friends, job?' I asked.

'I have this job. My friends, they can come visit. I left home long time ago.' When he laughed, he seemed slightly uncertain.

'Don't you get lonely? You can't speak Greek!'

Joeri seemed to consider this a long time. 'I have Houdini,' he said, with a heartfelt conviction that things would turn out well. 'And now you come. You will send others. They all come and help.'

We drifted on. No doubt, back at the makeshift surgery, Sam was having a good moan at the freshly castrated dogs.

'What are we here to do?' I asked.

The shelter was cleaned, scrubbed and the animals had been fed and watered first thing in the morning. Joeri kept nipping up here in the middle of the day and he had, so far, always been a bit evasive about exactly what he was doing. Now it was time to find out.

'This not good job but has to be done,' he said earnestly, looking me square in the eye.

'What?' I said.

He breathed softly. 'We put down the puppies.'

I couldn't believe what I was hearing. 'You mean you take them away?' I asked.

'No, nowhere for them to go,' he said, no longer looking me in the eye. 'I kill them all. Very sad but every day puppies come. Dumped or a bitch has them here.'

I suddenly realised why there was such urgency to neuter all the shelter dogs. It was virtually impossible to separate off all the males from the females and, invariably, some dogs would have slipped between pens despite Joeri's best efforts to prevent it.

'You can't do that!' I exclaimed. 'We're in the business of saving the dogs, not killing them!'

But Joeri was not to be deterred. 'Ya, no one must know about this. But why do you think we are not with puppies everywhere?'

I looked around. It was true; the shelter wasn't overrun with puppies. In fact, I couldn't see one. It had never occurred to me to question this, but of course, there were puppies on every street corner in town, but none up at the dog shelter.

'I just assumed that people took in puppies . . .' I said, though perhaps I didn't even believe it myself.

'No, sometimes the litter gets dumped here – I find whole

litter in box yesterday outside the gate. But if they get in the pen, other dogs will kill them.' He paused. 'Also the parvo sickness big problem. Within one week, they all die here.'

I looked into Joeri's eyes. He spoke in an anguished tone and this decision to euthanise all the puppies was clearly something which tortured him. I also suspected it was something he had had to instigate himself as no animal welfare group would ever condone the recurring euthanasia of lots of healthy puppies.

Joeri could read the doubt in me. I couldn't believe a dog shelter would do something like this, round up puppies and kill them all – it seemed to almost support the extermination campaign of the community. It was probably the reaction Joeri feared and the one he expected. It explained why he had been so vague about his afternoon visits and the fact that, when he got back, he was never his normal cheerful self.

'How do you mean they all get parvo?' I asked. It was a pointless question, but a drowning man will grab for reeds. 'Can't you quarantine them? Surely they would all get homes very quickly?' The question died on my lips as I looked at the makeshift wire pens within the enclosure: the hard breeze-block walls dividing the kennels and the dilapidated shed in the middle of a landfill site on a hillside in Samos.

'There is just me,' Joeri said quietly.

Neither of us moved. We stood, looking at the dogs in the enclosure playing, sleeping and seemingly at peace.

Running a quarantine facility was intensive. Many of the dogs dumped with Joeri were sick, the diseases they carried sometimes very contagious. Many of the older street dogs had invincible immune systems – but puppies wouldn't last two seconds in an environment endemic with disease. Parvo virus is something people vaccinate their dogs against all over the world and something to which young dogs are incredibly susceptible. It destroys their gut lining and they develop horrendous bloody diarrhoea, fever, and vomiting. Worse still, there is no treatment. While some dogs can survive it, it has an eighty per cent mortality rate.

'You have parvo here?' I asked.

'Yes, put puppy in here, it will either get into a cage with one of the big males who will kill it or it will get parvo within a week,' he said. Then, softly, 'I cannot do it.'

'What about a separate re-homing pen for puppies?' I said quietly.

'No money. No help. I can't keep it clean enough. Also, the dogs that have been here for a year. They need a home and we will become known for supplying puppies which will then get thrown back on the street when they grow older. People then just come for another puppy . . .'

I didn't know what to say. It was a vicious circle, a situation I had never envisaged. The prospect of nursing one puppy through parvo in the UK caused minor panic in a well-run veterinary practice, let alone dealing with an outbreak through a shelter.

'Every day they come. If I don't take them then people will drown them.'

Joeri was desperate for me to understand. Perhaps he just needed someone to understand. I wondered if I was the first person he had told. He had devoted his whole life to the dogs and to helping them; putting the puppies down must have broken his heart on a daily basis.

'And today?' I finally ventured.

'One of the dogs has given birth last night,' he said. 'Today, I take her away and put down puppies.' He hesitated. 'It is hardest thing I ever do.'

Suddenly I was jealous of Sam, stuck back at the house with the recovering dogs. Both of us had been having such a good time on the island, but we had only seen the rosy side of helping the shelter. We hadn't even scratched the surface of what was actually involved in running things in such a desperate situation.

'You can stay here,' Joeri said. 'I be back soon.'

But I couldn't let him go alone.

'I'll help,' I heard myself say.

Joeri looked at me hopefully and, together, we walked over to the pen where the bitch had had a litter. Handing me the bottle of the drug with which to inject the puppies and a needle and syringe, I didn't even consider how Joeri had managed to get hold of such a lethal medicine – which was undoubtedly difficult for him to get. Reflecting on it, it showed the efforts he must have gone to in order to smuggle the medicine up to the shelter to ensure the puppies had as painless a passing as possible.

We worked in silence. The dog was a beautiful German pointer. She wagged her tail as both Joeri and I walked into her pen. Joeri stroked her gently and she was very relaxed as Joeri looked at each puppy, before he gently took her by the collar and led her away from her newborn pups. She hesitated by the door, not wanting to leave them, but not wanting to offend the man who she trusted so implicitly. She looked straight at me, sensing that something wasn't quite right. I felt my heart rip as Joeri dragged her through the door and I stood there, looking down at the mewling little perfect puppies at my feet.

Bordering on tears, I picked each puppy up and injected it. They hardly made a whimper as each went limp. I couldn't speak and my hand was shaking by the time I finished. I looked at the six little bodies lined up by my feet. Still and quiet.

Joeri placed a hand on my shoulder as I left the enclosure.

'What about the dog?' I asked, the words forced out between clenched teeth.

'She be sad for couple of days and then she go back with others. Next time you come, you spay her,' Joeri said softly.

We drove back to the house in contemplative silence. Only now did I truly begin to realise the extent of Joeri's sacrifice; working in the dirt and heat to try to protect dogs that the community reviled. The daily torture he put himself through staggered me and I realised that my work in animal welfare in England was really just a token gesture compared to his altruistic dedication. What I had done felt wrong – but, deep down, I knew it was right; each of those little pups would have had a horrible death. I cursed the lack of funds for Joeri's shelter, the lack of help, the total apathy of the community about this problem.

That night, I told Sam what we had done. We stood at the window, looking out over the beautiful island, and for a long time, neither one of us could speak.

'But you need to remember, Luke,' he finally said, breaking that interminable silence. 'You need to think how many children are in insufferable conditions around the world.' He punched me, softly, on the shoulder. 'Keep it in perspective.'

'I know,' I replied, though at that moment I couldn't make myself. 'But we're vets,' I said, 'not doctors.'

The shadow lingered over me throughout our final day and into the next morning. As we bid a fond farewell to Joeri, I felt a guilty relief that it was him staying to deal with all that new day's problems and not me.

'But what more can we do?' Sam said as we climbed aboard the boat and the shoreline disappeared.

'We can help,' I replied.

4

FOOT IN MOUTH

'You need to get this suture as tight as you can,' Mr Spotswode said, peering intently at the leg on which I was operating.

I removed the needle and rethreaded the suture material to get a bigger bite of joint capsule.

'That's right,' Mr Spotswode went on, spectacles perched precariously on the bridge of his nose. 'Nicely imbricate it. Like that, yes – horizontal mattress sutures, overlap those edges . . .' Mr Spotswode stood back to inspect my work at a distance. 'Sheila,' he said, 'give me a call when you're done here, I'd like to see the finished masterpiece. Well done, Luke.' With a genial nod to Sheila, Mr Spotswode left the operating theatre and I started my final layer of stitches.

'Mrs Hazel is going to be so pleased,' Sheila said. 'She dotes on this little dog.'

I looked at the form lying on the table. It was a West Highland white terrier called Arthur and Mrs Hazel had brought him in a few days previously, very worried about his back leg. He was prone to bouts of sudden lameness and, after a bit of gentle probing and feeling of his knee joint, I'd diagnosed him with a luxating patella. Arthur's kneecap kept slipping in and out of place and, whenever this happened, he suddenly couldn't bend his leg properly and became very lame until it popped back in. Expecting the surgery to be done by Giles, I had been pleasantly surprised when Sheila came to tell me that my name had been put down for the operation – under the supervision of Mr Spotswode himself.

'You've got to get these things under your belt,' Mr Spotswode had said. 'I'll be around but – best you get on with it . . .'

I'd spent the previous night reading up on the surgical techniques, how to position the leg, cut into the knee joint, chip away a sliver of bone to deepen the groove in which the knee cap would sit, and then reposition it. The final stage had been to overlap the edges of the joint capsule – imbricate them – to tighten it all up and provide stability for the joint to work.

'We'll put up some good pain relief for Arthur but I'm over the moon with that,' I said to Sheila, tying off my last stitch.

'See, I told you, you could do it,' Sheila replied, giving Arthur a reassuring pat and me a big smile.

Since coming back from Samos, the haunting images of putting the puppies to sleep were still raw in my subconscious and, although part of me wanted to forget that particular incident, I knew I shouldn't and couldn't push it away. Somehow it defined the struggles that people like Joeri must be facing all over the world, determined to do a job which was much more difficult than my own. I couldn't help but wonder, on a daily basis, how Joeri was getting on. We'd exchanged weekly emails and Joeri had told me that a German charity had offered to take a lot of dogs from the shelter and re-home them in Germany, which would help his workload immensely. I was glad that things were looking up, and it was nice to keep in touch and offer him what advice I could about some of the cases he was treating.

My confidence in my own abilities had surged. The banter with Rob, Holly and Sheila made every day something I looked forward to and even my onerous on-call duties some-how seemed easier. For the first time since starting work, I went to sleep easily with the on-call phone balanced in the hallway, knowing I would wake up and not fearing the emer-gency that probably wasn't going to happen.

As these thoughts flickered through my mind, Mr Spotswode reappeared to have a final look at Arthur and nodded his approval.

'Very good,' he said. 'Looks excellent.' He paused. 'Luke,' he went on, 'would you mind nipping out to Martin Hootle's farm for me? Old friend of mine, got an emergency, been with the practice since the dawn of time. He's given up milk-ing but now has a big suckler herd. Got a problem with one of his steers and he needs someone there right away.'

As Sheila walked past, carrying Arthur off to his recovery kennel, I stripped off my operating gown and threw my gloves in the clinical waste.

'No problem,' I said, racking my brains as to the common things that go wrong with young castrated bulls. 'What's the . . .'

Suddenly, I was cut off by a blood-curdling shriek. Holly flailed madly into the prep room outside, Rob hot on her heels. A bearded collie hung in his arms.

'I'm covered in poo!' she cried, waving her arms wildly in the air.

True to her word, Holly's dark green uniform had a large

smear of brown all down its front. Mr Spotswode raised his eyebrows and looked at Rob.

'You can't walk around in that,' Rob said mischievously. 'What will the clients think?'

'It will have to come off,' Mr Spotswode mused, with a twinkle in his eye. 'I'm sure we have a plastic apron somewhere.'

Mr Spotswode joining in a joke was as rare as snow in summer. He looked at the still visibly distressed Holly with a wry smile.

'Right,' he said, 'I have to go. Luke, if you could sort that steer out, we had best leave everyone to get themselves organised.'

With another – this time rather bemused – look at Holly, he marched out of the prep room.

'Martin Hootle,' I said quietly, wondering what on earth was wrong with the steer.

'Martin Hootle?' Rob replied, his ears pricking up to my mutterings. 'You are going to love this one. Normally a Mr Spotswode client – never been there myself, but met him once at the surgery. Real character.'

'Does anyone know what is wrong with the steer?' I asked.

Naturally, Holly was too engrossed in her own problems to answer but Rob took one look at me and held open the door.

'Only one way to find out.'

For once, the farm was easy to find. Perhaps, I wondered as I left the main road to follow a surprisingly-pothole-free dirt track, something was kicking in inside me. I was a born again natural navigator.

As I approached the farmhouse, I saw a smart Range Rover parked to one side and a tall lean figure approached me as I got out of the car.

'Right you are. Nice to meet you. Martin Hootle's my name,' he said in a quick-fire, thick Dorset accent. 'Got a problem with a steer. You didn't have any trouble finding us did you?'

'No trouble at . . .'

'Glad to hear it. Are you keeping well? Don't think we've met before. Call me Martin.' He extended a strong arm for a handshake.

Mr Hootle was in his seventies but exuded a vibrant energy. He had sparse, scraggy wild white hair, sharp blue eyes set in an open face and hands like spades, one of which was currently crushing my own.

'Luke,' I just about replied before Mr Hootle was talking again.

'Right you are, Luke. You got here just in time. Got a problem with this steer.' He paused, shaking his head as if at odds with the whole wide world. 'I think,' he went on, 'it's a potato.'

Unsure what Mr Hootle meant, I looked at him slightly baffled. Surely he didn't think his steer was a potato? Was this what everyone meant by saying he was a character? Did they actually mean he was barking mad?

'A potato?' I repeated as I followed Mr Hootle round a corner at the end of the barn.

'I love potatoes,' he replied. 'The problem is – they love potatoes too.' He paused on the threshold of the barn, hand on hip. 'You can see why that would be a problem, can't you?'

I could see only that he wasn't making any sense but, all the same, I nodded eagerly.

We rounded the corner. In the barn, the unfortunate steer stood with its mouth agape, drooling saliva. The animal, only ten months old, was a young castrated Simmental cross and was feeling very sorry for itself. It looked as if it was fit to burst from a hugely overblown abdomen.

'It's them damn potatoes,' Mr Hootle said, sadly. 'I been feeding them potatoes for years. It finishes them off good and proper. You can really taste the difference with a cow finished on potatoes.' He approached the steer, but the steer backed away, in obvious pain. 'This one just likes his potatoes so much. He's got itself stuck, hasn't he?'

Cautiously, I approached the steer, whispering for him to calm down.

'Tight as a drum, isn't he?' Mr Hootle rattled on, his cheerful disposition unwavering as he contemplated the beast in front of us. 'Poor boy, been like this for about an hour now, saw him in the field struggling a bit and got him in. The potato must be stuck hard in his pipe. He won't last much longer like this.'

It was true; the poor animal was so bloated I doubted it would be able to cope for much longer. Although able to breathe, it couldn't release the gases from its stomach – and these were building up and up inside the abdomen. Trapped wind is a horrible thing in people – but, sometimes, in animals, it can be deadly.

'They die quite fast when they're this bad,' Mr Hootle happily observed. 'Lucky you got here in time . . .'

The steer wouldn't explode but as the rumen expanded outside, it would squash all the internal organs, compressing the diaphragm, which would eventually prevent the poor animal's lungs being able to expand. If that happened, the steer would suffocate. And all on account of a hastily gobbled-up potato.

'Have you had this before?' I asked as I felt underneath the steer's throat.

'Not for many years, happens every now and again. Used to run a dairy, didn't feed so many potatoes then. Had one of the first automated parlours in the country – milked a herd for forty-five years, didn't have a day off in forty of them. Milked on my wedding day, can you believe? Decided to stop it five years ago and change to beef. It's a young man's game is milking.'

'You milked on your wedding day?' I remarked incredulously, as the steer gave a low groan as I prodded down the underside of its neck.

'Oh, the wife knew what it was all about. No one else to do it, you see. Got up, milked the cows, got married, nipped back for afternoon milking and then went back to the wedding.' Mr Hootle was beaming with pride at his achievement. 'You wouldn't see that happen at many farms nowadays, would you?'

I shook my head in disbelief.

'I can't feel the potato,' I said. I was growing concerned. 'It must be jammed deep in the pipe.'

'Right you are. Look at that stomach – never see them that big do you?'

The rumen did indeed look huge. I had a momentary panic at not having the slightest idea what to do. Perhaps I could stick a trochar – effectively a giant hollow pin – into the steer's stomach and release the gas; it would buy me a bit more time – but, either way, shifting that potato was the only solution to getting things back on track. But how on earth was I supposed to remove a potato from halfway down a steer's neck?

'I'll just race to the car and get a few things,' I said.

In truth, it was just a stalling tactic – but I couldn't stall for long. As I ran, I tried to figure out exactly what I would need. There was no way I'd be able to pull the potato back up the throat, so my very roughly formulated plan was to try and push it down into the stomach. I caught sight of a bottle of drugs lying casually in one of the boxes crammed into the car. It was a horse drug used for colic, but, although the steer was not a horse and it didn't have colic, I knew the drug reduced spasm and relaxed smooth muscle – and it would work on the oesophagus. It could be a real help for the poor animal I was there to save; I just didn't know if it could be used on a cow.

I glanced at my mobile – thinking of phoning back to base for a bit of advice. No reception.

I heaved a thick book out the back of my car.

'I think it's in trouble!' came Mr Hootle's cry from the far side of the barn. 'Never seen one so big!'

I hastily started to leaf through the pages, desperate to find some reference to the drug being used in bovines.

'Everything okay?' Mr Hootle chirped away. 'Do you need anything? I've got a bucket of water.'

In my hurry I ripped a page in the book as I tried to turn it. Realising the futility of trying to look up a drug dose for an animal on which it wasn't supposed to be used, I took a deep breath and sighed. I would just have to get on with it. Thrusting the drug bottle into my pocket and clutching a cattle mouth gag and a big thick stomach tube, I raced back to the steer.

'Right you are then,' Mr Hootle nodded, still – for some reason I couldn't quite fathom – beaming. 'Have you got all your gear? Nick of time I would say!'

He was right. In just the five minutes I had been away, the steer had deteriorated. It stood there, rolling its eyes and emitted a low moan. As I tried to thrust the plastic gag into the side of its mouth, the poor animal, clearly unimpressed with my idea to ram a giant plastic tube down its throat, promptly tossed its head and knocked me to the ground.

'Oh,' Mr Hootle tutted, 'you need to be careful with these animals. Still got a bit of fight in him hasn't he?'

'He certainly does,' I replied, picking myself up off the ground.

I repeated my effort, this time with a little more success. The gag wedged between the steer's upper and lower molars, I steadily introduced the tube. The steer emitted an exhausted bellow of protest.

'He doesn't like that very much, does he?' Mr Hootle pointed out.

Concentrating hard on feeding the tube down the steer's throat with my right hand, whilst using my left arm to hold the beast's head, I didn't reply.

'Oh, it's going in okay isn't it? That's good. The potato must be lower down. Almost there are you?'

No sooner had Mr Hootle spoken when the tube came against the blockage.

'It's a fair way down,' I said. 'I'm right up against it.'

'How you are going to get that out then?'

'It's not coming out,' I replied, straining to gently push the potato further down the throat. 'The plan is to push it down into the stomach.'

No matter how much pressure I applied, the potato wouldn't budge. I sighed, I was going to have to put the trochar in, release the pressure and try to figure out another plan. Maybe time would soften and rot it down – but I had no idea how long a steer could cope with a potato stuck in its throat. For a start, it wouldn't be able to eat or drink.

As I stepped back and lent against the crush to collect my

thoughts, I felt the horse drug in my pocket dig into my side. It was surely worth a go. I stepped forward.

'I'm going to try a special drug, Mr Hootle.'

'Special drug, eh? That sounds like a plan. We haven't got long.'

'It's a horse drug actually, not really supposed to use it on cows . . .' I paused. I wasn't sure how Mr Hootle was going to take this. 'But I think it will help relax the oesophagus.'

Mr Hootle rocked on his heels, full of thought.

'If a horse drug can help us, so be it!' he declared. 'Off licence, right you are. I know what you mean. Not going in the food chain for a long while yet, so no problem there. Great idea!' Mr Hootle grinned. 'Just one question,' he said. 'Will it work?'

I pressed the syringe to the steer's neck and located the jugular. 'I hope so,' I said, injecting a stallion-sized dose.

Pausing long enough to recover my strength and let the drug work its way into the steer's system, I reached for the gag and started to feed the tube down the throat one more time.

As I again nudged against the potato, I teased the tube forward. Miraculously, it started to shift.

'I think it's going down!' I said breathlessly as I eased the tube further and further down the throat.

Suddenly, a huge amount of gas shot out through the end of the tube. Mr Hootle staggered back, as if caught in a sudden storm.

'You've done it!' he gushed. 'By Jove, you've done it! Knew you would! Young man, you've just saved a life!'

'Well, until . . .' I began.

'Well, precisely,' Mr Hootle chirped. 'But the abattoir's a little way off, you know.'

The gas continued to flow out of the tube as the stomach steadily deflated, much to the immense relief of the steer. Within seconds, it seemed to be righting itself. It stood properly again, and the death rattle was suddenly gone from its throat.

I stood there, a big grin on my face, holding the tube and beaming back at Mr Hootle.

After I was certain the steer was unharmed, I cleaned up and Mr Hootle and I tramped back to my car. As I threw my instruments back into the boot, Mr Hootle clapped his hands delightedly and grasped my own.

'Good job, young man!' he exclaimed as I dropped into the car and started the engine. 'And I sincerely hope I shan't be seeing you again very soon!'

I had no idea what he meant. Perhaps it was just Mr Hootle's strange way with words, but something in me started to niggle. I wound down the window and peered up.

'What do you mean?' I asked.

'Well,' Mr Hootle went on, 'didn't you hear about the Foot and Mouth this morning? Couldn't believe it myself! Heck of a business, back in '67 – horrible times! They found it in Essex, at an abattoir, bunch of pigs. What a drama. Who would have thought it?'

I stopped the car and climbed back out. It was the first I had heard of the news. Foot and Mouth disease was eradicated years ago – or so I thought, in my naive way.

'Are you okay, Luke?' Mr Hootle asked. 'You look like you've seen a ghost.'

'Foot and Mouth?' I repeated. 'Are you sure?' Instinctively, I reached for my practice mobile, left lying on the passenger seat. A solitary reception bar had appeared and I had three missed calls, all from Giles.

'Oh yes,' Mr Hootle said, shaking his head sternly. 'All over the news at lunchtime. Big drama. Must have been imported somehow. Right mess for the Government to sort out that will be!'

I must have been distracted, because Mr Hootle still looked concerned.

'Is everything alright, young man?'

I dropped into the car, kicked the engine into gear, and snatched up the phone.

'I hope so, Mr Hootle . . .'

A week later, and I was, if not exactly lulled into a sense of security, at least wondering whether Dorset might be spared the Foot and Mouth outbreak that was affecting other areas of the country. We had all been watching the news avidly but so far the disease had not affected any of our clients. In the meantime, there was the everyday business of healing to be done.

'I just think you need to do it quick. Don't try and make friends with him, just inject and be done. He hates men.'

I looked at Sheila with an arched eyebrow. 'Do you want me to wear a dress?' I asked.

Before Sheila could reply, Rob came through the door.

'I think miniskirt,' he said, looking me up and down.

'You'd look good in one yourself,' Sheila responded.

'How are you getting on with your neighbours?' Rob asked her, clearly uncomfortable with delving too deeply into his choice of skirt length.

Sheila had just moved into a flat in town and was having trouble with an old BMW that persisted in parking across her garage.

'I've left notes every day for the last week,' she replied. 'It's driving me mad. They park just a foot across the door so I can't open it.'

'Have you spoken to them?' I asked.

'I never see who it is,' Sheila sighed. 'I think it's the flat below me, but I can't be sure.'

'Then they'll be in for it,' Rob laughed as Giles walked through the doorway.

Giles looked grave. 'Luke and Rob, Mr Spotswode and I need you in his office.'

Without waiting for a reply, he turned on the spot and disappeared. For a moment, the three of us stood there, hunched over the unfortunate dog.

'You know what that's about, don't you?' Sheila whispered.

'I've got a feeling,' I said.

Sharing a quick look of consternation, Rob and I went after Giles. In the office, Mr Spotswode sat behind his desk with a pile of papers ranged in front of him, Giles at his side like a trusted General. Wordlessly, he handed Rob and me the top page, which turned out to be a copy from one of the most important textbooks that we'd spent years slaving over.

Foot and Mouth: *An extremely contagious, acute viral disease of all cloven-footed animals clinically characterised by fever and vesicular eruption in the mouth, on the feet and on the teats. Rarely fatal except in young stock but because of the speed with which it spreads, its effect on milk production and the growth of animals and the trade sanctions that are imposed on countries in which it occurs, FMD is one of the world's most important diseases.*

'We've had a call from the Ministry today,' Mr Spotswode began. His tone was sombre. This was not a mission we could choose to reject. 'Giles and I have discussed it and we are going to send you to the Exeter MAFF headquarters to help with the national crisis.'

Rob and I both stood there, a bit dumbfounded.

'You mean go there on secondment as a Ministry vet?' Rob asked.

I'd often fantasised about secret work as an agent for the Government when I was a boy, but I hadn't thought it would be like this.

'Exactly,' Mr Spotswode replied. 'I know the lady who runs the Exeter office. Jan Svelton. They're desperately short of competent vets with farm experience. They're phoning around the practices and she got in touch today. Giles and I have considered things, and we recognise we have a national duty to perform here.'

'The farm work is at a standstill with all the restrictions and I can handle things here,' Giles said.

'We'll need to live down there?' I asked.

'The Ministry will put you up in a hotel,' Mr Spotswode replied. 'I'm sure it will be very comfortable, compared to your little place here, Luke.'

'How long are we being seconded for?' Rob asked.

Mr Spotswode looked sidelong at Giles. 'I hope not for long,' he began. 'I dearly do. But . . .' He paused. 'We shall see,' was all that he could say. 'As things stand, you're to be there for four weeks.'

'It depends on how well the National Crisis is managed,' Giles chipped in. Mr Spotswode, anticipating what Giles was about to say and always disapproving of any open criticism of the Ministry, shot him a cutting look. 'At the moment,' Giles went on, unwavering in his belief, 'they're totally out of their depth.'

Rob and I simply nodded, not sure what to say.

'You're to report to the Exeter office at dawn on Monday morning,' Mr Spotswode finished, handing us our forms. 'You need to fill these in when you arrive for your induction.'

As Rob and I turned to leave, Mr Spotswode called us back with a word of caution.

'This may be quite difficult,' he said. 'Look out for those farmers and their cows. Remember to keep your wits about you.' He tapped the phone on his desk. 'And boys,' he finished, 'we're only at the other end of the line.'

Rob and I strode into the large brick building, fifteen minutes early and eager to report for duty.

'You realise this is as close to National Service as we're ever going to get?' Rob said.

'My Grandpa used to tell me stories about leading a regiment of Gurkhas on secret jungle missions in Burma during the Second World War,' I replied.

'Well, your grandchildren are going to hear about how you visited a lot of farms on Dartmoor,' Rob replied.

'The riveting tales of Grandpa Gamble – the one who wasn't in the Special Forces.' I grinned as we approached the reception desk.

The first two hours saw us issued with our induction pack. We didn't exactly receive rifles but we did get a pack of standard-issue disposable body suits, a few sets of waterproofs and a pair of Ministry green wellies. Straining under the weight of an armful of massive lever arch files, each one crammed full of bullet-point infested sheets depicting various sub-clauses, rules, regulations and standard operating procedures we were supposed to adhere to, I marvelled at how complicated it could be to go to a farm, check over some cows for Foot and Mouth and leave.

Rob and I were split up almost immediately. We hovered with a whole clutch of fresh vets, most young graduates, around a huge open-plan office, where our names were called out. These were then written on cards and posted into slots on a large board, allocating us a corresponding technician and a team name.

My name was called out first and, before I knew what was going on, I was labelled as Team 34 and my assigned technician was at my side, ushering me out of the door and to our allocated vehicle – an impressive silver pick-up.

'Now this is a farm vet truck!' I commented and received a flat stare in response.

One of the techs I worked with, Sandy, was in her late thirties and a fully-fledged member of the core Ministry establishment. It rapidly became evident from the first five minutes of being in her company that she had absolutely no sense of humour.

'This is a Ministry vehicle for Team 34,' she replied, totally deadpan.

It crossed my mind to banter about the practice car back home but I decided this approach was not going to win Sandy's favour.

'How long have you been doing this for?' I asked, heading for the driving seat.

'I'll drive,' Sandy said, bustling past.

We sat in silence for ten minutes as we weaved our way out of the car park and headed west towards Dartmoor and our targeted farms.

'So how long have you been doing this?' I tried again.

'I've been working with the Ministry for fifteen years,' came the reply.

'I meant Foot and Mouth?'

'Since the outbreak. Mobilisation of staff was very swift within MAFF.'

'So you must have a good grasp of all the information in those files then! Paperwork gone mad, isn't it? Someone got the short straw having to compile all that lot – most tedious job on earth I'd imagine!' I gestured towards my induction pack on the backseat.

'It was very interesting,' Sandy said icily.

'Absolutely,' I said. 'Just must have been hard work.' My last words petered into silence and I looked out of the window. For a long time, the frosty silence lingered.

As a 'clean' vet and tech team that hadn't been on a farm that had Foot and Mouth, we were deemed low risk of spreading the infection ourselves. We were off to inspect various farms around the county of Devon for evidence of the dreaded disease. All the farms within a huge radius of a contaminated farm had to be inspected, whether the farmers liked it or not.

Our first call of the day got us off to a great start. We weren't supposed to drive directly onto a farm; instead, we were meant to park outside each farm, don our protective bodysuits, disinfect our boots, and then approach by foot. Our first job was to inspect a smallholder with twenty sheep, a few pigs and a couple of goats. Having phoned the owner, I was told that we could park at the end of the lane where there would be a bucket of water outside the gate.

I relayed the information to Sandy, who received it with an almost imperceptible nod of her head.

After one of the longest thirty minutes of my life, we pulled up outside a gate where a small black bucket of water had been placed, and climbed out of the truck.

'Isn't it a bit ridiculous for me to disinfect all this stuff when I've just taken it out of the packet?'

At first Sandy did not reply; she was far too busy pouring disinfectant into the bucket.

'No,' she said. 'It is the proper procedure. Disinfect your waterproofs and then put on a disposal bodysuit.' She paused. 'What risk is this farm?'

'This farm has been identified as medium,' I said, scanning the paperwork.

'You need to wear your hood.'

'Sandy,' I said, 'cut me some slack! I'll pop it up once we've got near the farm – we can't even see the buildings!'

Sandy said nothing. Instead, she pulled her phone out of a small plastic bag tucked inside her jacket.

I watched as Sandy held it up to her ear.

'This is Sandy Elswit,' she said. 'I'm on a medium risk inspection and I'm having trouble with the assigned vet. Can I speak to head of veterinary ops?'

Sandy turned and glared at me as she spoke. Challenge blazed from her eyes.

I mutely shook my head and raised the hood over my head.

'It's okay,' she said. 'I have the situation under control now. Thank you.' With a flick of the wrist, she hung up.

'There are no shortcuts here,' she said. 'This isn't a game. We are doing everything according to the protocol because, if this farm does have Foot and Mouth, we will be responsible for ensuring that correct procedure is followed. I will report on you every day – and if I feel you are not performing adequately, you will be replaced. The Ministry are not playing with this.'

Winning Sandy over was going to be akin to reaching the summit of K2. Considering that one in four people who attempt that challenge, dies in the process, I wasn't sure that making friends with Sandy was worth the risk.

With a final dip of our boots into the bucket, we started down the track onto the farm. The hill was long and steep. Dressed in a shirt, trousers, plastic waterproofs, oversized wellies and a disposable bodysuit with the hood up, before we had gone a hundred metres I was hot as a furnace. Ministry vets were obviously made of sterner stuff, because Sandy was marching ahead like one of the Imperial Guard from Napoleon's army – only a foot shorter. A mile and a half later, I was gasping for air.

Finally, having crested the brow of the hill, I saw a lonely bungalow sat deserted on the left of the track and two neatly fenced fields on the right. Each field sloped away and a barn was tucked into the corner of the furthest field. Squinting at the barn, we could just about make out the silhouette of what looked like a wizened old man toying with a pitchfork outside it.

Walking along the boundary of the field, I bellowed out the name of the farmer we had come to see. The old man stirred but didn't respond other than to twirl his pitchfork.

'He must have heard me,' I said, muffled through my hood.

She shrugged. At last, Sandy too was red-faced and out of breath to speak.

I yelled again and, this time, the old man raised his fork to rest it over his shoulder, and waved us over. Sandy needed no further invitation and briskly strode into the field with me following in her wake.

It was the wrong field, belonging to the wrong farmer – and the old man was completely confused as Sandy started to question him about holding numbers. It transpired that his brother owned the sheep and he lived on the farm next door. What the old man did have was a barn full of wild beef bullocks.

Sandy stood stock-still. 'And you didn't think to mention this when we phoned?' she demanded.

The old man was befuddled. 'I thought you could just do me while you were here, I'm right next door to my brother,' he said.

Sandy was about to explode. As the old man went to his bungalow, I turned to her. 'Can't we just check these?' I asked. 'It'll save someone an epic walk . . .'

Sandy's face, already red, turned a vivid scarlet.

'You don't have a holding number, stock information or map reference!' she thundered. 'You can't just walk onto a random farm – it isn't on our list! Our movements need to be traceable! You should have checked the details with him much more carefully on the phone. I am going to report this,' she fumed. 'You have no idea. How old are you, exactly?'

'But I can check these bullocks quickly,' I said, 'and save another team the bother. They need to be checked by a clean team and we're right here.'

To me, the logic was irrefutable.

'We need to phone head office,' Sandy said.

There was no mobile reception so high on the hill. I looked back down the slope that had almost conquered me. We would have to go halfway down to use the phone.

'Off you go,' said Sandy. 'Explain your mistake and tell them what's happened.'

I looked at the farmhouse. 'Could we just use his phone?' I asked.

'And risk a contamination?' Sandy barked, purpling with rage. 'Off you go, Luke!'

Pleased to get away from Sandy, I headed back down the hill until I managed to get a crackly line through to the headquarters. Explaining that we had wandered onto the wrong farm on my very first call wasn't the easiest thing to do, but thankfully, common sense prevailed and I was directed to continue with the inspection and then get back to our list.

When I reached the top of the hill again, I was delighted to break the news to Sandy.

The bullocks were clear, as were the sheep on the neighbouring farm and, gradually, the day got going. As we drove from farm to farm, Sandy took to imparting me with tedious information about the documents in the files she had helped to compile.

'Form A's impose quarantine of a premises and are for suspected IP's.'

I was thrilled to hear it. 'IP's?' I asked.

'Infected premises, Luke!' she trilled, her minuscule reserves of patience clearly at an end. 'Form C's are issued for confirmed cases. They're issued depending on whether the clinical signs are unmistakable or if blood results come back positive. Form B's reverse a Form A and Form D's are given to premises that may be at risk because of proximity to an outbreak or a tracing.' Sandy lectured like this throughout all our journeys, but it was better than frosty silence and she seemed to be easing up a bit. 'You taking this all in, Luke?'

'A tracing?' I asked, trying not to stare out of the window. 'Say a milk tanker passed through a particular farm after going to an IP the day before it was confirmed. Form E's lift a Form D. Got it?'

A Form B reversed a Form A and an E lifted a D. I had it down pat!

'How long does a Form D last for?' I asked. Sandy launched into a long explanation, and I settled back for the ride.

The final farm of our day was much larger than the others we had visited. A two-hundred-strong dairy unit, it also had six hundred lambing ewes and a beef suckler herd to boot. I had to serve a Form D – which was clearly the highlight of Sandy's day.

Without exception the farmers had been very friendly and the most difficult challenge had been getting on with my technician. Despite a few moans about how the disease seemed to be spreading in their direction, most farmers were hopeful that they could weather the storm. They could still bring in food from a non-restricted area and they all had a good laugh at the silly outfits we had to wear.

Much to Sandy's disapproval, I finished the day with a boundary check of a sheep field on the back of a quad bike. No doubt it broke some sort of Ministry restriction on safety in the working environment and I would have to be served with a Form QF#4 myself.

'You should try it,' I said, as we waved goodbye to the final farm. 'It's exhilarating.'

'My work is exhilarating enough,' said Sandy, and ordered me into the passenger seat as we headed back to base.

Two days later, after our third day on the job, Rob and I managed to catch up for a beer and a bite to eat. We hadn't spoken since that first day we were split up; the Ministry had exhausted us both, and there was no time for anything else.

'So how is it going?' Rob asked.

'Painful technician,' I replied. 'You?'

'Painful technician,' Rob agreed. 'Agonisingly slow about everything. They've allocated all the old-school, hardcore Ministry staff to non-Ministry vets.'

'Luke Gamble!' bawled a voice behind us. 'How the hell are you?'

The voice had caught me unawares. I turned round. A huge man with black bushy hair stood holding a pint glass in a gargantuan fist.

'Dave,' I said, recognising him at once. 'Good to see you!'

Dave was a final year student from Bristol and although a couple of years below me, I had once known him fairly well. He was outgoing and a regular on the social scene at University.

'What are you up to, Dave?' I asked, enduring a bone-crushing handshake.

'It's this Foot and Mouth thing, Luke. I'm in it up to my neck, same as you . . .'

I shared a look with Rob. So final year veterinary students had been drafted in as well? The crisis was obviously deepening more quickly than we'd realised.

'We've all had a terrible few days,' Dave went on, draining his pint in one last gulp. 'We're all just desperate to get on with it.'

'Get on with what?'

'What's coming . . .' Dave mysteriously said.

'What do you mean?' Rob asked.

'Diplomacy has never been my strong point,' Dave went on, 'but a few of us, we've been having some trouble with our lovely EU brethren.'

Rob and I looked at him blankly.

'We've been paired with some visiting Spanish vets who basically can't speak a word of English,' Dave explained. 'It's achingly slow.'

Rob stood up and looked Dave square in the eye. I recognised that twinkle; I'd seen it one too many times.

'We'll just have to come up with a cunning plan then, won't we?' he said.

'What do you mean *reallocated*?' Sandy demanded.

'I don't know, Sandy,' I replied, as innocently as I could. 'But your name is next to another vet's and someone called Dave's seems to be next to mine.'

Sandy walked up to the board and stared at it intensely.

'I think they've moved the more experienced technicians to the newer vets,' I said.

'You've been here four days!' Sandy tersely exclaimed. 'You *are* new!'

'Sandy,' I said, managing to keep a straight face. 'You are one of the best techs they have. You know the legislation inside out. There will be a good reason why they reallocated you.'

Rob appeared at my side, peering at the board with an apparent look of confusion on his face. Aside from a cursory nod of hello in my direction, there was no acknowledgement we were friends.

'I can't believe they've changed my tech!' he exclaimed to no one in particular.

'Me too!' I said.

'This is ridiculous. I don't want to get stuck with some idiot!' said Rob, flouncing off.

Sandy watched him go and looked back at the board.

'Looks like we're not the only team to be split up,' I said.

Sandy didn't reply.

A familiar voice rose behind us. When I turned, Dave was moving toward us like a huge bear. His frame seemed to fill the corridor and Sandy peered up warily as he loomed over us.

'Excuse me,' he said, squinting at the board. 'Are you Luke Gamble?'

I nodded and shook him by the hand.

'I'm Dave,' he began. 'Looks like I'm assigned to be your tech today.'

'Seems to be a bit of confusion,' I said. 'My tech is normally Sandy.'

Rob reappeared, sidling into view around Dave's massive frame. 'They've reallocated a whole bunch of us,' he said. 'Typical idiocy! Who the heck is Tom Waterworth?'

'And who on earth is Ignacio Mendoza?' Sandy suddenly demanded. 'And how am I supposed to find him?'

In unison, the three of us shrugged – and Sandy stormed away, screaming out the name Ignacio at the top of her voice.

'I can't believe you did that,' I whispered, trying hard not to laugh and turning to Rob. 'Who on earth is Ignacio Mendoza?'

'He's one of our newly arrived Spanish brethren who speaks about three words of English. Trust me, Sandy will love it.' Rob grinned. 'Have a good one today, Luke! And get to the right farm this time, won't you?'

Dave couldn't have been more of a contrast to Sandy. Aside from being a lot more talkative, he was about six foot four and seventeen stone, totally uncomplaining about the long hours and keen to get on with the job as practically and efficiently as possible. He rapidly proved himself to be an absolute grafter and we formed a good team, disinfecting on and off each farm and checking through the stock. The farmers liked him, respecting his size and strength as well as his willingness to help and whilst we still both looked ridiculous dressed in our Ministry costumes, we invariably got offered cups of tea – something that hadn't happened once when I visited the farms with Sandy.

We spent our first day together chasing the trail of a milk tanker that had been to a farm that had subsequently been declared a quarantine zone. On the assumption that Foot and Mouth had been on the farm when the tanker visited, it was possible that it had been contaminated and then trailed through the Devonshire countryside, spreading the disease at various dairies along the way. Dispatched in its wake, Dave and I careered around corners, foot hard on the accelerator, checking farms in her wake. From there on, though, we had been out and about examining stock on foot and the strain was starting to show.

'The hardest farms are the sheep ones,' Dave said as he contemplated our list for the eighth day on the job. 'Epic walking up and down these tors – I reckon we trekked about eight miles yesterday afternoon on just that one holding.'

'Dressed in our special costumes,' I agreed. 'The ultimate diet plan.'

'It's a nightmare,' Dave said as we trudged along. 'It's impossible to examine every single sheep and lamb for lesions. For a starter, if we try to round them up we'll stress them out. Most are in lamb – we'd cause a miscarriage storm!' Dave paused. The hills were wild around us. 'What if we miss one?'

The particular strain of Foot and Mouth virus that vets were locking horns with across the country didn't affect sheep as badly as it did pigs and cattle. That was good news for the sheep – but less good for us. It meant that infection was more difficult to spot from only a cursory exam. We'd had to think on our (thankfully not cloven) feet.

The plan I adopted was to talk to the farmer and ask about their lambing mortality and general health, check all the animals in each group, ensuring that we looked at any obviously lame ones and that we also picked up any animals that had wandered away from the main flock. We tried to boundary walk each field, looking for the ones that had got away – but this proved a challenge when we were faced with the roving stock that inhabited Dartmoor.

That day was a case in point. It was blustery over the heights of the moor, and Dave and I trekked around twenty-eight acres of near-vertical Dartmoor hill, tasked with checking twenty sheep for any signs of infection. By nightfall, we'd still only found eighteen of them and had sullenly given up stalking the remaining two.

We plodded wearily back toward the farmhouse but by now, even that downhill walk seemed like a Herculean labour.

'I think two must have escaped,' the farmer began, bemused at our futile efforts to trek round his boundary.

'Fencing is a bit of an issue in parts of those back fields, isn't it?' I managed.

The farmer smiled. 'They'll come back!' he said. 'Do you want me to send Bess out after them?'

Quickly, the farmer whistled. Within moments, a small collie appeared at his side, beating its tail with frantic excitement.

With a minimal wave of his hand, the farmer sent Bess off to round up the sheep. The eighteen we had already checked clearly knew the drill and came trotting towards us as soon as they saw the dog galloping across the field. The farmer promptly tipped some nuts into a shallow feed trough and they all tucked in as Bess disappeared out of sight.

She was gone for about fifteen minutes as the three of us stood expectantly scanning the horizon. Then, she reappeared – herding two other creatures as she came towards us.

'She's got something there,' the farmer said with a twinkle in his eye.

Dave took a huge stride forward, hand cupped to his eyes as he watched the animal procession approach.

'Some big sheep she's got, isn't it?' he said, puzzled.

I looked at the forms trotting towards us and clapped a hand on Dave's shoulder.

'I don't think Dartmoor ponies are on the list,' I said.

In the middle of the field, Bess stood triumphant, with the pair of small brown Dartmoor ponies standing thoroughly confused behind her.

The farmer whistled out and Bess came bounding over, beating her tail happily.

'She means well,' the farmer said, bending down to pet her.

'I think those two sheep have gone on a holiday,' Dave remarked, shaking his head at the two befuddled ponies.

'I wonder what form we need to fill in for that?'

When I woke the next morning, I already knew the day was going to be sour. There was a heavy feeling in the air, and a heavier feeling in my stomach.

Sure enough, when we arrived at work, we were assigned to visit a farmer who had sheep stuck out in a field about three miles away from his heavily waterlogged farm. The lambing ewes were now trapped outside, with newborn lambs choking on the mud. The farmer was desperate to bring them into his barn for lambing but couldn't, due to the restrictions of a Form D prohibiting the movement of his stock down the road. It was an impossible situation. Forbidden from moving his lambs, he could do nothing but wait for them to die.

At the farm, Dave and I tried to explain – but I've always had trouble explaining away the inexplicable. The farmer bawled after us as we turned to disinfect and leave. 'You're killing my sheep!'

'I'm sorry,' I replied, suddenly ashamed to look him in the eye. 'There's nothing I can do.'

Disinfected and back in the Ministry truck, the silence stretched between Dave and me.

'It is so frustrating,' Dave finally said. Anything we could say seemed so facile compared to the reality of what the farmers were going through.

'I hate it that it makes sense,' I said.

Dave didn't reply, but I knew that he felt the same.

'If the Ministry allow one movement on a farm under restriction, they'll have to allow a thousand,' I said, kicking the truck uselessly up a gear, 'and we won't have a chance of containing it.'

'Still,' Dave said. 'Luke, that's his livelihood . . .'

I didn't want to turn into Sandy, but I had a creeping suspicion that I was about to. There were no right and wrong answers in this. I thought suddenly of that dog shelter on Samos, and the terrible decisions Joeri had to make every day.

'There have to be rules,' I said. 'The buck has to stop somewhere.'

'And never mind that someone has to suffer?'

He was not accusing me; he was accusing the world in general. It was hard to justify not being able to help the farmer and his poor sheep but the restrictions had to be enforced or more livelihoods and entire farms' worth of animals would be at risk.

By midday Dave and I had finally recovered our sense of humour. We'd virtually completed our list and were parked outside a fantastic country pub with the prospect of lunch for the first time in three days. Duty bound, I quickly phoned back to base to report in and ask for a few more farms to visit that afternoon.

The operator disappeared off the line and I assumed she was getting the details of our next visits.

'Hello,' echoed a completely different voice, a man this time instead of the friendly young woman. 'Team 34?'

'Yes,' I replied, detecting the change in tone.

'There's a report case just come in,' the line crackled. 'Not all that far away from you – frothing bullock, no . . . frothing *bullocks* – you may have hit the jackpot with this one.' The voice paused. Jackpot? He had to be joking! 'Hang on, let me get a map reference for you.'

The voice had a particular tone to it, sharp and commanding like a stern father – or a benevolent dictator.

'This is a case in a new area. If it is an outbreak, it will spell bad news. Please report back to me as soon as you have examined the suspect animals.'

As I rang off, a barmaid ambled over to our table carrying a couple of lovely fat menus.

'No, thanks,' I said, hearing my stomach rumble.

As she disappeared, Dave almost clamoured a food order after her. 'Luke!' he said. 'I'm not sure I can . . .'

I stood up, truck keys jangling in my fist. 'It's a report case, Dave,' I said, feeling a slight surge of adrenaline.

Suddenly, Dave's hunger seemed to dissipate. 'This could be it,' he said quietly.

'We'd better get going.'

When we arrived at the case, I surveyed our surroundings. A straw barrier had been positioned between two solid gate-posts with the gate lazily resting open, propped against an ancient stone wall that bordered the farm entrance. Two farmers appeared behind the gate; I sensed tension oozing from them before a word was spoken.

'Hi Mr Tocker,' I said, resisting the urge to extend my hand. 'My name's Luke. I'm the vet and this is Dave, my technician.' I spoke with a smile, trying to put the men at ease. 'I'm afraid I'm here about the report case you called in.'

Both men looked from me to Dave. With a measured pause, the taller of the two creased up his face, which emphasised his sixty-odd years, and spoke in a heavy Devonshire accent.

'I don't mean to be rude,' he said, 'but do you know what you're looking for? You both look a little *green . . .*'

'Don't worry,' I replied, knowing already that I could do little to reassure them. 'In fact, you've almost got two vets for the price of one – Dave's a final year at Bristol and is going to be sitting his exams in a couple of months.'

As I surveyed the farm where I dreaded we would come face-to-face with the disease, Dave explained that, although we hadn't been on an infected premises, we were both well schooled in the clinical signs. I muttered something about previously working in a big mixed practice and doing a lot of cattle work and the two farmers nodded, still very tense. We hadn't eased their fears tremendously, but in this situation nothing would.

'So what have you got?' I asked. 'A frothing cow?' I collected a sampling kit and thermometer from my car and put on my plastic gloves.

'It started this morning with just one,' the tall, lean one said. 'But it looks like four or five now. You know, if it wasn't for all this we'd just let 'em go on for a few days but, you know, thought we'd better get them checked out. Don't want to be any trouble and all that!'

His brow, already furrowed with worry, developed a muddy smear as the farmer kneaded his forehead.

'You're sure you ain't going to bring it onto the farm if we haven't got it, are you?' he asked anxiously.

'Absolutely not,' I promised. 'We're completely disinfected. The Ministry can't send dirty vets to potentially clean sites so there's no chance of that.'

'Alright then,' the tall farmer quietly said. 'Best be on with this.'

The two men proceeded to lead us down the drive adjacent to the main farmhouse. As we followed, for the first time I fully appreciated the Ministry clothing and the reassurance it must give farmers. I suddenly didn't feel ridiculous and, with the future of this farm in the balance, I was glad to be wearing so many layers with a hood over my head. I would have worn three times as much if somehow it meant this farm wouldn't have Foot and Mouth.

'What a lovely little farmhouse,' Dave commented as we walked past.

It was utterly picturesque. Almost removed from reality and tucked away in a self-sufficient valley, the freshly-painted windows gleamed in stark contrast to the warmth of the old worn brick and I guessed it was at least a couple of hundred years old. The lane outside the drive was only just about big enough for a tractor, unmarked and unused by almost everyone except the local farmers. A lawn bordered with flower beds sat in front of the house and, on the right, a gateway led to fields where picture perfect ewes and lambs frolicked on the pasture. To the left of the house the driveway sloped down into the farmyard. Holding areas were dotted between the buildings, which were all in good solid working order.

A couple of dogs barked as we walked past the stables and, in classic West Country fashion, some foxes' feet were nailed up on the stable door.

In a yarded enclosure next to the parlour, there stood eight beef cattle. They looked like a mixture of crossbreeds: a few Limousans, a Friesian-cross-Hereford, and a few with Angus blood in them. Four of the beasts were standing hunched and tucked up, the other four lying down on the concrete between smatterings of dung that stained the grey floor. Almost every one of the animals was salivating profusely, a thick layer of froth pasted around their mouths. On the edge of the yard, I stalled. Dave looked at me; the same thoughts were clearly stirring in him.

'Right,' I said, swallowing down my fear as I pointed to the nearest upright animal. 'Let's get that black-and-white in a crush and have a look.'

I felt sick as Dave and I shepherded the animal into the crush. Even before we began the examination, I knew we were in trouble. The reality of the situation crashed around me as I noted the bullock's raging temperature and then opened its mouth. Inside, there wasn't so much an ulcer; the cow's tongue was almost sloughing off. Blisters grew like fungus all over its gums.

Dave crouched down to look at the cow's feet. Sure enough, there were deep, raw ulcers, so thick and terrible between its claws that it could barely stand. I tried to imagine how much pain might be involved in having the entire surface of my tongue removed, but I just couldn't.

Dave and I stood back. The cow lowed softly, but didn't have the energy to make anything other than a whimper. In silence, we flickered looks at the other cows still awaiting our inspection. We knew already what we were going to find; we had been fortunate until now, two green vets doing Ministry work, whining about overcoats and pedantic Ministry techs – but there could be none of that any longer. This thing was bigger than all of us. Suddenly, I wished Sandy was with us.

I motioned Dave to look in the bullocks' mouths. Our faces must have said it all as, with terrible resignation, the shorter farmer slumped against the wall.

'Oh Christ, no,' he said softly.

'Are you sure?' the tall farmer breathed. Then, before I could reply, his face fell, sobbing into his arms, his body slumped against his brother's.

Dave and I were silent. For perhaps the first time in my life, I didn't know what to say.

'This can't be happening,' said the older brother quietly, his body starting to rack in silent sobs.

I looked at Dave, still crouched by the cow. He seemed almost as shocked as the farmers. It dawned on me with a horrible clarity that I was the most experienced vet on show – and I'd never seen anything as desperate as this, not even on Samos.

I tried to console them, but my words sounded hollow. I knew I had to take control, steer everyone through this, but it was hard to comprehend that the horror that was being broadcast on television every night was now going to visit their idyllic home.

'What will the neighbours think?' Harry, the tall farmer, began, finally able to speak again.

'The neighbours?' I asked. For a moment, I was confused; idle gossip was the least of this farm's problems.

'They'll think it was our fault. Where could it have come from?'

'It was our Grandfather's farm . . . They're all going to go, aren't they?'

Their questions leapt around them, garbled and confused. I didn't know where to start.

'Harry,' I said, desperately grasping at straws. 'We'll get through this. The neighbours won't blame you. We'll figure it out, but there could be a whole range of reasons; none of them are your fault.'

It was a parish in which no other cases had been reported, over three miles from the nearest infected premises and the farmers were desperate to know where it might have come from – but, like them, I had no idea and no answers.

I'd put down family pets in heartbreaking situations, pets that were loved as children – but I always knew it was for the best of that animal and that it was only one animal at a time. I'd consoled grown men in tears over their lost dogs but I was cut to the core trying to support these two farmers, both old enough to be my grandfather, strong, capable and infinitely wiser than me. I couldn't hold my head high and tell them they were going to be okay; they weren't. I thought the puppies in Samos were as bad as it could get, but this was on a different scale. Powers beyond my control had dictated the impact that these lesions were going to have on this family and, indeed, the whole parish for miles around. It was up to me to instigate them.

It was up to me to start the killing.

Leaving the farmers to their silent grief, Dave and I began to collect the necessary samples from a few of the animals. I then asked Dave to have a walk around the herd to see if anything else looked clinically suspicious and get any additional blood samples as backup. As he went about his grim task, fully expecting to see the disease spreading before our eyes, I asked Harry to accompany me into his utility room. It had started to rain and I needed to do lots of paperwork and make phone calls to get things in motion.

Harry stared blankly at the stack of papers I had pulled from a file. I needed to work out the exact boundaries of the whole farm, identify how many stock he had and where they were kept. As he slowly stared to leaf through some of the forms we had to fill in, I rang up headquarters.

'This is Team 34,' I said grimly. 'We're on a report case at . . .'

'What is your job number Team 34?' the voice crackled in reply.

'I don't have a job number; it was a report case we were called to,' I said.

'Wait and I'll give you a job number.'

I steeled myself against making a curt reply.

'Your job number is 190,' the voice came back after a short pause.

'Great,' I breathed.

'Where are you, Team 34?'

'At the Tockers' on a report case,' I said, giving the address. The line crackled again as the voice on the other end looked something up.

'That's job number 190,' he said. 'Go on.'

I didn't know where to start. Harry looked up at me from the mountain of paperwork with a horrible look of resignation.

'The bullocks here are exhibiting clinical signs of full blown Foot and Mouth,' I said. 'They've got it pretty bad.'

'Hang on,' interrupted the voice. 'Let me put you onto the duty vet.'

Sure enough, the man I'd spoken to earlier echoed down the line.

'Team 34?' he began

'Hello,' I began. 'This is Luke Gamble, out at the Tockers, job number 190. You sent me on this report case about two hours ago.'

A hint of exasperation must have been creeping into my already stressed voice, but I struggled to suppress it.

'Well,' I said, 'they've got it. About eight bullocks . . .' I was about to start listing the clinical signs, but the man quickly cut in.

'I thought it sounded ominous,' he said. 'How many stock has he got?'

'About one hundred and twenty cattle,' I replied. 'Forty-nine are a dairy herd and unaffected, the rest beef. All of them are housed in buildings behind the main farmhouse. He also has about nine off-premises scattered around a three mile radius with about eight hundred sheep and lambs dotted over them.'

The voice was still. 'How often does he visit the sheep?'

I looked at Harry, whispering the question.

'Usually, twice a day,' I said back into the receiver.

The voice hissed out a string of curses. If Harry drove all over the Devonshire countryside twice a day, visiting numerous flocks of sheep, the implications were potentially disastrous. The disease was on them in the yard and perhaps they had carried it all over.

'Have you phoned Page Street?' the man suddenly asked.

Page Street was the address of the main Ministry office in London. It hadn't occurred to me to call them.

'I've only phoned you . . .' I began, confused.

'It's written in your induction files, Team 34. You must have missed it.' He paused before parroting back the information, as flatly as Sandy had once done. 'Upon finding a suspect animal you must notify Page Street first and then notify us here. Have your telephone report form ready,' he went on. 'They'll ask a lot of questions – CPH number, contiguous premises on all the lands owned by the farmer, map references, exact numbers of stock and where they are, where he has been in the last twenty-one days, who's been on the farm . . .'

The list went on and on. By the time I put down the phone, my head was buzzing with the information. I looked back, through the utility room window, catching sight of the infected cows once again.

The man's final words rang in my ears. 'Good luck,' he had said. 'Notify me when things progress.' For the first time in my life, I felt completely abandoned. I wanted nothing more than to pretend it was all a terrible mistake, get in my car and go home.

Through bleary eyes, I saw Harry watching me carefully. I had no idea how I was going to handle this but he was looking at me, searching for an answer.

'Harry,' I said. 'I'm sorry. I've got to do this.' I paused. 'And I'm going to need your help.'

We were on the phone with Page Street in London for longer than an hour, all the time grilling Harry about his farm. His mind must have been in turmoil, for the numbers kept changing on each off-premise he tried to describe – and suddenly he'd remember another field somewhere and we'd have to start again. At last, there came a question even more difficult than those that had come before. The Ministry needed a list of all those farms that bordered his, farmers whose livelihoods would also be ruined by the disease found on this farm, and Harry bravely battled his way through. In the end, we had a list of about twenty farmers who had properties next to all of his various fields.

'What about the sheep?' Harry suddenly asked, moments after the Ministry had hung up.

'Well, we have them listed – do you have more?'

Harry paced the room, despair quickly turning into something worse: a feeling of utter helplessness. 'No,' he said, 'they need feeding. They're due a feed this afternoon.'

I paused. I couldn't let Harry or his brother Jonathan leave the farm, and Harry knew it. Everyone and everything was under restriction.

'Harry,' I said, 'the police will be here soon. They'll stand on guard outside the gate.' I paused. 'We're not leaving this farm,' I said quietly.

Harry stood and stared. 'They need their feed . . .' he whispered.

'They'll have to go hungry tonight, Harry. They have grass . . . they'll be ok.' I didn't know what else to say.

'What if I phone Jeremy to go and check on them?' he asked, reaching out for the phone.

Jeremy must have been a neighbouring farmer. I lay my hand on the receiver.

'On no account must anyone else go and visit those sheep,' I said. I was desperate to be as sympathetic as possible, but I had a job to do as well; the two things strained at one another inside me. 'If they have it too, anyone going near them could spread it back to their own animals.'

The door to the office swung open and Jonathan and Dave walked in, wet and bedraggled from the rain.

'Need to go check on the sheep,' Jonathan blurted, his face strained as he looked at me expectantly.

Dave stood behind him, grim faced. He raised his hands in a small gesture of helplessness.

'Jonathan,' I said, 'I'm sorry, we can't leave the farm. No one can come or go.'

'What about the sheep?' he said again.

Harry turned to face the wall, his face set like stone.

'What about Elsie?' Harry said between clenched teeth.

'Elsie?' I asked.

'Elsie's our sister. She's here to do the cleaning. She comes on Wednesdays. She's in the house . . .' Harry paused. 'She needs to go home.'

'She'll be finishing soon!' Jonathan echoed.

Suddenly the phone rang and, for some reason, it startled me out of my skin. I let it ring and Harry gestured for me to answer it.

'Nick Seggot here,' a shrill voice said. 'Independent valuer. Are you the owner of the farm?'

Alarm bells went off in my head as I handed the phone to Harry, just as an elderly lady with a kind face joined us. Jonathan introduced us all to Elsie, and as I explained the situation to her, she nodded and remained remarkably calm. Once she had digested all the information, she placed a reassuring hand on Jonathan's shoulder.

Her hand still resting there, she looked up at me. 'I already knew,' she softly said. 'You'd have been gone by now if it wasn't here. The phone in the house hasn't stopped. Neighbours have been phoning for the last half an hour.' She paused. 'Don't worry Jonathan,' she said, 'I've taken care of everything.' Again, she paused, as if there was only one thing she could say next, only one thing to make everything alright.

'Why don't we all go into the kitchen and have a nice cup of tea?' she asked. 'I've made some pasties.'

Leaving Harry to his phone call, we followed Elsie back into the rain and to the farmhouse kitchen, where a modest spread had been laid out on the big wooden table. Rain still blew in gusts against the glass; somewhere, out there, the cows were in terrible pain.

'Elsie,' Jonathan began. 'You'll be needing to go home now.' He eyeballed me as he said it.

'Don't be silly, dear. I'm staying here tonight. These gentlemen will need some tea and you have enough on your plate.'

I took a seat, but I didn't want to touch a thing. Next to me, Dave sipped at a cup of black tea.

'Luke,' Elsie began, still fussing around her brother. 'What happens next? When are you going to put down those poor animals?'

Before I could answer, the door slammed and Harry trudged into the kitchen. I was thankful for the reprieve; it was a question I didn't want to answer.

'That was the valuer,' he said, eyes fixed on me. 'They want to come and value the farm.'

I knew what he was saying. It wasn't my fault the disease had come to his farm, but somehow I felt like it was. The value of his life was plummeting, even as we sat and ate a snack.

'Let's go through what's going to happen,' I said collecting my wits and pulling out a large file.

Harry snatched up a pasty. It crumbled between tense fingers.

'We're going to take this step by step,' I began. 'We won't start anything drastic until we have everything in place and we're all prepared.' I hesitated. 'We know, now, that we have

Foot and Mouth – it takes two days to confirm the samples, but based on these clinical signs, the cull will be actioned immediately.' I paused to collect myself. It was the first time I had mentioned culling out loud. The word was easy to say – but we all knew what it meant.

'Everything?' Jonathan said softly.

'Everything,' I said, lifting my hands. 'Jonathan, I'm sorry. Everywhere you go every day, where there are animals, they will need to be culled.'

I found it hard to meet his eyes but forced myself to do so.

'Next door?' Harry asked.

'The farms with animals immediately next door to this part of your farm will be culled within forty-eight hours,' I said.

'You can't do that!' Jonathan exclaimed, catching his breath. Elsie stepped forward, as if putting herself between Jonathan and me.

'It isn't his fault, dear . . . it's the law.' She placed her hand reassuringly on Jonathan's arm.

'We need to hear this so we can prepare ourselves.'

I waited for Jonathan to acknowledge her before going on.

'The cows in the yard are at their most infectious,' I said. 'The blisters have burst – it's in the air; it's everywhere, Jonathan. We're infected, the Land Rover is infected, and your boots are infected. It isn't anyone's fault, neither you nor Harry are to blame – but we have to do everything we can to stop it spreading.'

Jonathan grabbed a chair and sat down, clearly in shock. Neither he nor Harry spoke and, as if to dispel the terrible silence, Elsie cleared away some of the cups.

'It's even in our hair, Jonathan,' Elsie said matter-of-factly. 'We need to stay put and get it contained or it will happen to other farms.'

In that moment, I knew that Elsie was a godsend to all of us. I wasn't sure how Jonathan and Harry would have coped without her. I wasn't sure how *I* would have coped either.

The phone rang again. This time, Harry picked it up and I couldn't help but overhear the word 'valuation' crop up in the conversation. Harry rang off fairly quickly and looked at Jonathan. 'It was another valuer,' he said. 'They also want to value the stock.'

I looked at him, feeling confused.

'Apparently an independent valuation needs to be done before you start doing what you do?' Harry asked, stressing the last word like it was a curse.

The phone rang again. This time, Jonathan picked it up.

'Harry,' I began. 'You've got to . . .'

Jonathan looked up from the phone, cupping a hand over the receiver.

'Is Jeremy going to lose his sheep?' he yelled across the room.

Turning from Harry, I saw Jonathan clutching the phone to one ear and looking at me expectantly.

'Jeremy's your neighbour?' I asked, remembering his earlier concern.

Harry chipped in. 'He has sheep next to ours at Daggons.'

I recalled Harry suggesting Jeremy might be able to check on the sheep and remembered the map; Daggons was an isolated field about two-and-a-half miles away from the holding.

'I don't know,' I admitted. 'It depends if your sheep there have Foot and Mouth.' I stopped, realising what I'd said. 'But on no account must he go and look at your sheep to find out.'

Jonathan repeated what I said down the phone. I could hear the consternation crackling back through the receiver.

I turned back to Harry.

'Harry, the . . .'

'Jeremy wants us to go and check those sheep!' Jonathan shouted again.

I stood, battling to keep myself from snapping out. 'Jonathan, we can't go *anywhere* anymore. If we start going to other fields we'll spread it there . . .' I paused. 'And then Jeremy will *definitely* lose his sheep.'

'But you said all our sheep were going to be culled anyway!' Harry interjected.

Suddenly, I felt cornered; it was hard to explain. I wasn't sure I understood it myself.

'It could be that if those sheep don't have the infection, they'll just be culled as a contiguous premises,' I floundered to explain. 'It means Jeremy will be served a Form D and only placed under restriction.' I silently blessed Sandy for her endless lecturing on forms and rules.

Jonathan turned back to his call and I turned back to Harry.

'Harry,' I said. 'About these valuations . . .'

The Ministry had a responsibility to value everything on an infected farm before the process of culling began. That way, farmers could be recompensed – in theory – for their losses. While payment could ease the pressure on a farmer financially, we all knew it could do nothing to ease the psychological burden of a livelihood being erased.

I guessed that, somehow, the news had got out about the farm's infection. These independent valuers were like vultures, hoping to get some business out of farmers who were at loggerheads with the Ministry and wanted an independent valuation instead.

'Jeremy wants to know what a Form D is!' Jonathan barked, again cupping his hand around the phone.

'It restricts movement.' I paused, trying not to be exasperated. 'Harry,' I went on. 'Your stock does need to be valued – but independent valuers . . .' I was finding it hard to disguise my distrust of these vultures; Page Street must have an active list of infected premises on the internet and they must have added the Tockers to it immediately. Somebody was obviously keenly monitoring those sites. 'The valuers will promise you the world,' I said, 'but they'll take a huge commission. I can't advise you the best course of action – but if you use a Ministry valuation . . .' I stopped; I was losing the thread of my own argument, trying desperately to do the best by these poor farmers whose stock we were about to destroy. 'Look,' I said, 'the Ministry figures are very generous in terms of the value of stock. It really is a favourable deal to farmers. There is no commission deducted and they even offer a set amount for any beef animal under thirty months – so a day-old calf is worth the same as a twenty-nine-month-old calf.'

'But is a twenty-nine-month-old calf worth the figure they're offering?' Harry asked.

I had to admit that it wasn't. The Ministry figures were generous but they would undeniably be different to those that Harry could have expected for individual animals on the open market. But that market was closed now – and, for this farm, always would be.

'Harry,' I said, 'it's your decision. I just don't want you to lose . . .'

'Lose out?' said Harry, rising again to look out of the window, where his cows were waiting to be killed. 'No,' he said. 'How could we possibly ever lose out?'

Just as Jonathan slammed the phone down on Jeremy, it started ringing again. Harry left my side and snatched up the receiver.

I sat at the table and rubbed my eyes. Valuations on infected farms, it seemed, were a Catch-22. All the Ministry figures did was effectively push the value of stock up – making it even more appealing for independent valuers to force their way onto farms, and for farmers to opt for them. Five more phoned in the next half an hour, promising vastly more money than the Ministry figures allowed. I could see poor Harry and Jonathan getting more and more confused as to what to do.

'Luke, what do you want me to do?' a steady voice said to me.

All this time, Dave had been sitting in silence. I looked over at him now, buried in a mountain of paperwork as he tried to work out the logistics of how we were going to manage things.

'Sorry,' I said. 'We're waiting for a slaughterman and hopefully a back-up vet. With all the fields dotted all over the place, it's a huge farm . . .' They should have been here by now though. Perhaps the delay was only because the Ministry was still trying to work out how best to deal with it all. 'Grab another cup of tea,' I said. 'You're going to need your strength soon enough.'

Dave pulled his chair over to me. In a whisper, he said, 'There have been three other outbreaks today . . . I think head office is snowed under.'

'Really?'

'One of the valuers told Harry and I heard him tell Jonathan.'

I was suddenly aware of a deathly quiet in the kitchen, no more questions and whispering from Jonathan or Harry. Dave must have sensed it too, for we both turned slowly around. Jonathan and Harry had stepped outside, Elsie had disappeared deeper into the farmhouse – and we were alone.

I stood up and peered out the window. The rain had stopped but the sky was still dark and foreboding. Out in the yard, Jonathan and Harry flanked a tall man with a hooked nose and greying hair. He moved with an easy arrogance and I flashed a look of consternation to Dave before pushing through the kitchen doors to find out what was going on.

'Excuse me,' I said hurrying over and struggling to keep calm. 'What's going on?'

I couldn't believe another person had come onto the farm, and seemingly with the collusion of Harry and Jonathan. This was a plague town now; anyone who came in could not go out.

Harry and Jonathan looked at me sheepishly, not really sure what to say. The tall man stepped forward and held out his hand.

'Neville Snatter,' he sneered. 'Independent valuer. I am here to represent the interests of my clients, Harry and Jonathan Tocker.'

Anger surged through me. This ridiculous man had just strolled onto an infected premises in a bid to line his own pocket. Lives were at stake, histories were being destroyed – and now I had to face this clown.

'How did you get on the farm?' I demanded.

'I arrived to discuss valuation issues with Harry and Jonathan and have been invited on the farm to conduct an independent valuation – to which they are legally entitled. I prefer a face-to-face discussion than a cold call,' he responded airily.

My face was red. I took a deep breath. I felt Dave looming behind me, silently backing me up.

'You turned up and walked onto the farm – an infected premises?' I demanded. 'And you didn't stop to think what that meant?' I paused. Along the farm trail, I could see blue siren lights and headlights approaching. 'Do you know what's happening now?'

I pointed so that he might see. The police had arrived at the end of the trail, and a man in uniform was beckoning me over. I didn't have time for Neville Snatter and his over-hyped valuations.

'This farm is sealed,' I said. 'And you can't leave now. You need to stay here until I get back.'

I turned to stalk away, to where the policemen were gathering.

'I will start my valuation as is Harry and Jonathan's legal right . . .' Snatter began.

I turned, only able to control my anger because I caught sight of Dave.

'You will stay there and not move! According to the law, I need to validate all your paperwork.'

Dave, sensing the dark way this thing could go, stepped forward. Six foot four, seventeen stone with a face like thunder, he nodded at me. 'I'll stay here with Mr Snatter,' he said firmly.

For the first time, Mr Snatter looked a little unsure of himself. Jonathan and Harry looked at me apologetically – but, although I didn't blame them in the slightest, I didn't have time for apologies now.

The two brothers slowly went into the house. Elsie, who had been watching from the window, opened the door as they approached it and I saw her embrace them both as they went inside. I thought suddenly of all the time this family had spent on this farm, and how it would be from this day on.

Dave stood directly in front of Snatter. He didn't say a word and Snatter, his arrogance gone, stood there in silence, fiddling with his phone. Meanwhile, I rushed over to the policemen just as, blessedly, another few vehicles arrived and figures climbed out, donning Ministry protective clothing and starting the laborious process of disinfection.

I glanced at the sky. Daylight was beginning to be a concern – it was already half past five in the evening and we still had to begin the slaughter. Quickly, the police got themselves in place to prevent people like Mr Snatter coming onto the farm; the end of the lane would be sealed off for the next twenty-four hours and the gateway was to be guarded around the clock.

'You must be Luke,' said one of the new arrivals in a soft Southern Irish accent as he proffered a hand. 'How are you doing there?' Sharp eyes met mine, then swiftly scanned the layout of the farm behind me. 'I'm Dermot,' he said. 'This is Nick my tech and this is John . . .' He paused, saying the next words sadly. 'The slaughterman.'

I nodded at all three, suddenly overwhelmingly relieved that help was at hand.

Dermot and Nick, it transpired, had been in my situation yesterday – and, having culled one small farm, Dermot had been asked to come straight away. John had driven separately, having been assigned the job direct from headquarters. Confident, capable and reassuring, Dermot went through all the details with me.

'Who's that man with your lad over there?' Dermot asked, gesturing in Dave's direction.

It was going to be a difficult one, but Mr Snatter was here now, and he could not be ignored.

'The vultures descend,' Dermot cursed after I explained. 'I had them heckling my farmer from outside the gate. No stopping them,' he said. 'They inflate the price, lie through their teeth – they're a plague.'

Together, we looked at the sky.

'Light's fading fast,' I said. 'It'll be a late one.'

'It seems to be the nature of the business,' Dermot said wearily.

We walked back toward the farm and, all of us ignoring the insidious Snatter, I introduced the new arrivals to Dave. Inside, Harry, Jonathan and Elsie were waiting in terrible silence, broken only by the offer of yet another cup of tea. We left Snatter outside, ignored by all of the team – except for Dave, who watched him like a hawk.

'Harry,' I asked, 'have you had a think about the valuation?'

Elsie interrupted before Harry could answer.

'Mr Snatter's promised figures are much higher than the Ministry ones,' she said calmly, resting a hand on Harry's shoulder. 'We don't want to be difficult but . . .'

Much as I hated Snatter and wanted to deny him this commission, my feelings were still with the poor farmers. 'Elsie,' I said, 'it is really no problem. I'll work with Snatter on this; he needs to go round all the stock before we start . . .' I paused. I didn't want to say it, though everyone knew what I meant. 'Dermot, Nick, Dave and John are going to get things ready,' I lamely continued. 'I'll go round with Snatter and we can agree the value of the herd.'

'You have to agree the value?' Harry asked, suddenly surprised.

I nodded, slowly. 'We have to do that to ensure that the prices are fair – some valuers aren't very honest,' I said. 'They add on animals, inflate prices . . .'

My words were falling on troubled ears, and I wondered if they were getting through. Harry didn't have to worry – I was on his side, but I was honour bound to make sure Snatter was doing his job properly. It looked like he simply had too much to worry about now, to care what I had to say.

While Mr Snatter and I walked around the yard, counting all the animals, the rest of the guys got things organised. The plan was to cull all the housed animals immediately. It would mean working late into the night and probably the early hours of the next day but it was imperative that we did all we could to stop the spread of the virus into the rest of the parish.

We decided to use the parlour, an old-fashioned abreast, which held six cows standing side by side at any one time. The design allows cows to enter and leave the parlour individually and although slower for milking than the more common Herringbone parlour found on many commercial dairy farms, it suited what we needed to do perfectly. The plan was that the placid and docile dairy cows would go in as if for milking and we'd then inject them in the muscle with a sedative before walking them, one by one, over to a concreted, partially covered yarded area which doubled as a silage clamp at certain times of the year. Bedding the far end of it with straw, the cows would walk towards it and, as the sedative kicked in, they would lie down. John would then walk up to them and, there, it would end.

I wasn't going to argue over details with Snatter. I had the farmers' interest at heart and I simply made sure that his count was accurate and his figures didn't exceed the boundaries. I doubted Harry and Jonathan would be better off once he had taken his cut of the price, but I was glad to get it done and it seemed to reassure them that someone else would be dealing with the Ministry paperwork relating to compensation.

An hour later, I rejoined the others. In the yard, Snatter

took signatures to his papers and began to make his fare-wells. Dave and I eyeballed him carefully. 'Where do you think you're going?' Dave asked bluntly.

'Home,' Snatter replied, glaring back. The old arrogance was suddenly back in full force, no doubt fuelled by his commission. 'Where do you think? I'll see you back here at 8 a.m. to go round up the off-premises.'

'Not in those clothes, you won't . . .' I began.

On the other side of the yard, Dermot, Nick and John paused in what they were doing, eyes drawn to the altercation.

'You walked onto this farm in those clothes,' I said, 'but you can't leave in them. They're infected with Foot and Mouth.'

Dave gave a half smile for the first and only time since we had arrived.

'So here's what we're going to do,' I said, grim faced. 'We are going to walk to the gate, you'll take your clothes off so we can incinerate them, you'll disinfect yourself – and *then* you can cross the barrier and go home.'

I bit back my laughter. It would have been nice to revel in some petty pleasure on this horrible day, and I was looking forward to sending this odious little man marching naked into the hills, but there was killing to be done – and this wasn't the time for cheer.

Mr Snatter's mouth worked like a fish, outrage on his face. Dermot silently handed Dave a bin bag and turned back to what he was doing. Nick and John turned back to their work as well, readying sedatives, cartridges and pithing rods. Dave stepped forward and started to escort Snatter to the straw barrier at the entrance to the farm. A policeman posted guard there watched us from his car. Dave halted Snatter and held out the bin bag.

Snatter looked around him. Suddenly, he realised how serious we were. Knowing we couldn't follow him over the barrier, he seemed to contemplate a mad dash for it – but, seeing the glint in Dave's eye, he thought better of it.

'My shoes?' he trembled, sounding like a little boy.

'We can disinfect your shoes by dipping them in the disinfectant,' I said. 'You'd best keep your underpants on too – they've been protected by your outer garments.' I stopped. 'But everything exposed to the air goes in the bag, Snatter. Your shirt, your trousers, your . . .'

'You can't do this!' he hissed. 'This is an expensive jacket!'

'It's our legal right,' Dave replied evenly.

The policeman over the gate had wound down his window to hear the exchange. I looked at him for approval to continue and he nodded silently back. People like Snatter were the reason he had to spend the night outside the farm listening to the sound of cattle being slaughtered. There would be no sympathy from that quarter.

Snatter placed his clothes in the bin bag and soon stood there in his underpants, pallid, weak and cut down to size. I had made an enemy for life – but I wouldn't have had it any other way.

'See you tomorrow morning,' he said with as much dignity as he could muster.

Dave handed him his pair of shoes, each one dripping with strong disinfectant.

'Tomorrow, Snatter,' I said and walked back to the yard.

Within ten minutes, the slaughter began.

I can't remember the first shot that night. I remember the first shot the next morning because, after two hours' dreamless sleep, I was back on the farm and the killing continued. The sharp crack made me jump in my skin and is etched in my memory. I remember Jonathan crying, tears streaming down his weathered face, Harry hugging him; Dave, a power-house of strength, working relentlessly to ensure the cows were calmly herded into the parlour; Dermot and I drawing up sedative and injecting each animal. We worked in silence, steadily focused on the horror of what we had to do.

Nick had the worst job by far. As John shot each cow with a captive bolt, firing a metal rod into the animal's head, which then retracts itself, Nick had to pith the poor creature. Pithing involves inserting a plastic rod down through the hole of the captive bolt to destroy the base of the brain. It is the most gruesome and most dangerous part of the process because, as you thread the plastic rod down the hole – although the animals are stunned beyond the point of recovery – the nervous system is triggered, causing them to thrash out with all four legs. It looks horrendous but, truth-fully, the cows can't feel anything and the captive bolt has, ninety nine times out of a hundred, already killed them outright. Pithing is an insurance procedure only required for cattle, but it had to be done.

I vividly remember the pet sheep in the garden, the mother and her baby lambs shot, lying between the feet of a beautiful jersey cow who had protectively stood with them even after they had been culled. She was a family pet who lived in the backyard and wasn't part of the herd, and the brothers couldn't watch us shoot her. I could barely watch it myself – but I made myself stand there as she was dispatched. Each cow in the herd also had a name; every animal was known to the brothers and had been bred on the farm. It was a genera-tion farm, had been in the family for over a hundred years. Jonathan kept whispering to himself, praying for us not to shoot his dogs. His dogs were always going to remain unharmed – but as the bodies mounted up, blank sightless eyes, trusting cows being led to their death, so too did everyone's confusion at this terrible tragic waste of life.

I had met slaughtermen before but never worked with them. They have to be accurate, fast and conscientious about what they do but, more than that, they have to be utterly fearless. Any hesitation causes mistakes and gives the animal the chance to react. Their job is violent and hard. John had grown up surrounded by death and gore. He told me he had been in and out of slaughterhouses since he was six years old; his dad was a slaughterman and he'd entered the trade straight from school.

'Gotta be kind to the animals,' he grunted at me, gently teasing the head of a ewe into position for the deadly shot.

Looking at John, it struck me that he was exactly the sort of bloke that in normal circumstances, you'd never want to have a gun in his hands. He looked impervious to feeling, his eyes direct and his big frame moving from animal to animal with practised ease. I watched him work with meticulous attention to detail. Never cruel, angry or frustrated with the animals, he was a consummate professional; you just wouldn't want to meet him on a dark night.

It took us four days to cull the entire stock on the farm. We averaged eighteen hours a day and Dermot left us after day three, exhausted at having worked twelve days on the trot with two consecutive slaughter jobs. He had qualified only a year ahead of me, but his strength and guidance had been invaluable during the traumatic time and, on the final day, we all felt his absence keenly. Nick, his tech, stayed on and the four of us finished in silence, the carcasses of the last flock of sheep lying crumpled in the corner of a field.

John had brought an extra gun with him because there

were so many sheep and we needed an extra slaughterer. The sheep didn't need pithing, their skulls being so much smaller than cows, so Nick and Dave calmly corralled the sheep into a makeshift pen whilst John and I worked our way through them. As they dropped, the sheep next to them hardly stirred. There was no sense of panic; it was just calm, relentless slaughtering.

I'd spent my life learning how to heal and prolong life; to take it away was an alien concept. The first time I took the gun in my hands, something made me pause.

'No hesitation!' John yelled as he painstakingly watched me shoot five sheep. 'You have to cross to the other side.'

I shot again and again, watching them dumbly fall.

'Any fool can shoot an animal,' John said, pride in his voice, 'but it's how you shoot it that counts. Takes years to be a good slaughterman. Many of the new ones in the trade are scared of it, you can't show no f*****g fear, they can sense it and that's when you're in trouble, see?' He paused to watch me shoot another row of sheep, stepping over their carcasses to carry on killing. 'That's better!' he said. 'You're getting it. A couple of thousand and you'll be a f*****g pro.'

That night, saying goodbye to Harry, Jonathan and Elsie, was the first time I cried during the Foot and Mouth epidemic. Tears silently leaked down my face unbidden. Now that it was over, I couldn't stop thinking of the terrible way I had just spent four days of my life. Beside me, Dave was also crying. As we prepared to disinfect and disappear forever, Jonathan and Harry threw their arms around us, grown men imploring us not to leave them to the cleanup team who were, even now, marching upon the farm to take away the carcasses.

As we finally made our way, Elsie gripped our hands.

'Thank you, so much,' she said.

I couldn't speak. No words would come. How could we be thanked for doing something as horrible as what we had done?

Nick was stony-faced and John respectfully turned his head, pretending not to see the shining tears on my face as I walked to the car.

'Some f*****g way to make a pound' he said quietly, unpacking his cartridges.

Two weeks later, after another relentlessly gruelling day, I slumped on the bed in my hotel room, too tired to get up and turn the light off. The phone made me jump with a piercing shrill. I almost let it ring itself out, but eventually, I scooped up the receiver.

'Hello,' I said flatly.

'Luke, how are you?' It was Rob. 'Sorry about the late call, been one of those days. I've been meaning to touch base with you since I came back and Mr Spotswode also asked me to phone you,' Rob said. 'He'd appreciate a call to know how you are – but didn't want to be, how shall we say, over-protective about his young protégé . . .'

I let the phone hang at my ear for a moment. Rob had been called back to the practice and though I couldn't begrudge him that, something in it certainly riled. He hadn't found any infected premises and Mr Spotswode had needed him back at the surgery to cover a sudden sickness amongst the other vets. I hadn't spoken to him for a fortnight – and it had been the longest, worst fortnight of my life.

I couldn't stop myself. It all spilled out, everything that had happened in the last two weeks.

'A slaughter team?' Rob repeated. 'You have got to be kidding me!'

After leaving the Tockers, the Ministry had decided that they needed more slaughter teams to deal with infected premises once they were diagnosed. No longer were green vets and techs expected to deal with it; a specialised slaughter team would move in and take over after an IP was reported to Page Street. As a ready-made unit, Dave, Nick, John and I had been assigned as one of the first slaughter teams to take on this role. The Ministry favoured young, unattached men for the job – and our little group was the perfect fit.

It had been a fortnight from hell. I had lost count of the animals I had shot; we had worked every day, sometimes eighteen hours and never less than twelve. We had developed a system of killing that felt like a factory – we were good at it, and I hated myself for that. We were always two guns now; it was much faster and our system worked well. We'd visited five infected premises and the forms, logistics, valuations were now second nature. We arrived, the vet and tech already on site inevitably breathed a huge sigh of relief, and then we completed our task with frightening efficiency. The dynamic of the whole process changed; the army had been mobilised to assist with sealing off farm entrances and, on numerous occasions, I sealed off a road by posting a soldier at one end of it. Theoretically, I was supposed to get the Highways department and the council to issue a written order but there was no way I was going to risk a family driving past and seeing piles of dead animals. Besides, no one questioned a road being shut when an armed soldier was standing at the end of it.

I saw Sandy with a vet at one IP. She was white as a sheet as we arrived, the vet unable to explain in simple English what was going to happen to the farmer's animals. Too shell-shocked to be of any assistance, Sandy and her vet left and we took over. On that site, we culled over three thousand sheep. The vet had misdiagnosed Foot and Mouth, thinking that the oral ulceration on the sheep was the dreaded disease instead of orf, a common pox virus endemic among many UK flocks. I couldn't even bring myself to talk about it; nothing could be done. The fact that my team had arrived on the premises guaranteed the flock would be infected with Foot and Mouth – even if it wasn't before we arrived. It was a horrific situation in which we had to kill three thousand animals because of clinical incompetence.

The problem was compounded by a new official policy. The Ministry was battling to get on top of the epidemic so a policy of SOS (slaughter on suspicion) had been instigated. It meant that no vet could be unsure – if there was any possibility that Foot and Mouth was present, that was it, there was no waiting three days to see if samples came back positive; by then all the animals were culled. The trouble was that whilst Foot and Mouth was glaringly obvious in cattle, it was harder to spot in sheep and required a knowledge of everyday farm animal diseases.

While I sympathised with the vet, his lack of experience was typical of many of the locum vets who had arrived to cash in on the crisis. With the locum rates so high, vets flew in from Europe, New Zealand and South Africa to swell the ranks and sign on. Just as I had talked up my exotic animals experience when applying for my first job, half the vets patrolling Devon had talked up their farm experience to get on the Ministry payroll. The Ministry, short-staffed and in desperate need of vets, wasn't too fussy and as a result, many of the vets on patrol had absolutely no idea what they were looking for or, more importantly, how to distinguish Foot and Mouth from much more common conditions. Like Sandy's vet, many had never seen orf or interdigital dermatitis, so they didn't know any better. It was no use railing against the injustice of it all; by that time, it was already too late.

'You need to come home,' Rob said, clearly shocked by what I was telling him. 'It's Sunday tomorrow – have a break, this is ridiculous . . .'

'I can't go anywhere,' I replied, wearied. I was trapped – by disease, by my own instincts, by this terrible conveyer we were all on. 'I'm breathing Foot and Mouth.'

'Look, as long as you don't go to any farms or for a walk in the countryside, you'll be fine . . .'

'Rob,' I said, 'I live on a farm.'

'Well, there is that,' Rob conceded. 'Look, come and have lunch tomorrow – it's only an hour and a half drive. Pop down, let's have a proper Sunday lunch . . .'

'I'll have to bathe in disinfectant.'

'Luke,' Rob said, 'you always did need a good wash.'

I mumbled agreement and headed off for a fitful night's sleep, visions of dead animals in my mind.

'Luke, how are you?' Mr Spotswode asked kindly as he joined us.

My invitation for lunch had been carefully orchestrated and Giles, Mr Spotswode, Sheila, Holly and Rob were on a mission to pick my spirits up. Mr Spotswode was horrified to learn of my duties; his concern was touching and I appreciated it more than I realised at the time.

'Well,' I said, 'it's not the greatest job in the world . . .'

'Is it a quick death?' Holly asked.

'We sedate all the cattle first,' I said. I saw it only too vividly when I closed my eyes. 'Then we shoot them away from the rest of the herd.'

'What about the sheep?' Sheila asked.

'We round them up in a pen and dispatch them. They don't get stressed, it's so sudden . . .'

'What happens if you don't shoot a cow properly?' Holly asked.

I paused, momentarily reliving one horror. A farm we had been to the previous day had called us back because one of the cows we had shot was standing in the yard. It was inconceivable, every animal was shot, pithed and checked – but, somehow, there she was, still standing, a hole in her head. When we returned to the scene of the butchering, she seemed calm despite the carnage around her. One in a thousand, John had said. The poor animal . . . All of us were dumbfounded and desperately upset. It was probably one I had shot where I hadn't dropped my wrist enough. The image haunted me as I contemplated Holly's question. There was no real excuse for it, it was totally unacceptable and yet, somehow, everyone at headquarters had accepted it, said it was a minor incident.

Not for the cow, I thought.

'They're all pithed and checked,' I replied, monotone.

'I've heard all sorts, cows being missed, escaping, attacking each other . . .' Sheila chipped in.

To my immense relief, Giles deftly turned the conversation away from Foot and Mouth and it was wonderful to chat about other things. Mr Baffer had been back to the surgery to show off his newest frog to everyone, promising to come back when I returned to duty. Mr David Junior up at Highwood Farm was proving to be as firm as Mr McKara had been but was universally accepted to be a very fair and well liked boss. The cow I had caesared had made a full recovery and was back in calf. Mr Tubby, meanwhile, was in trouble for not properly ear-tagging his cows and Trading Standards were after him. It was great to know that there was still some normality in the world.

'So what do you do in the evenings down in Exeter?' Sheila asked.

'Chat about the day's murder and go to bed,' I replied, allowing myself a tight smile.

'No different to home then,' Rob quipped.

'I can't wait just to vaccinate something!' I said.

'Even a frog or a squirrel?' Holly giggled.

'Especially a frog or a squirrel!'

'You look thin,' Sheila observed.

I looked at Sheila dryly. 'First time in twenty years.' Sheila, too, looked a little weary. She rubbed at her eyes. 'Are you okay?' I asked.

'The BMW car is still parking across her garage,' Holly piped up.

'Still?' I laughed. 'It's been six weeks! I'm surprised you haven't sorted him out.'

'I've tried,' Sheila seethed. 'Notes, letters . . . I even went round and had a quiet word.' She paused. 'He doesn't seem very receptive.'

'What about the management of the block of flats?' Rob asked.

'I've written to them,' Sheila replied. 'He moved it for one day then started doing it again.' 'You need to call the police,' Mr Spotswode interjected.

There was a moment of lingering, awkward silence.

'Luke, we're going to welcome you back to the practice like it's the return of the prodigal son!' Sheila announced.

'A big party!' Holly added, giggling.

I grinned. A party was exactly what we needed.

'And when you get back you need to do something to take your mind off all this,' Giles commented.

'Something totally unrelated to being a vet,' Mr Spotswode added.

I wondered where all this was going.

'We've enrolled you in Italian night classes!' Holly shrieked, unable to contain her mirth any longer.

I froze for a moment. Around me, the smiles were spreading, the grins growing until they took over whole faces. I wasn't sure I could bear it. 'Mr Spotswode, what's all this about?' I couldn't help it, I sounded mildly irritated; my sense of humour had failed me persistently these past weeks.

'Luke, you have three more weeks on Foot and Mouth and then I will need you back,' he said. For me, it couldn't come a moment too soon. 'And we decided you needed a little welcome back present, so we had a whip round.'

'You always said you wanted to speak another language,' Sheila laughed.

This much was true; I always said I wanted to talk to the animals, learn all their languages.

'And let's face it,' Rob interjected, 'you don't have a girl-friend – so it falls to us to sort something out . . .'

I looked across at Giles, who simply raised his glass. 'Ciao foot and mouth,' he said.

I raised my glass. 'I'll drink to that.' For the first time in long weeks, I wasn't thinking about slaughter.

Driving back, I was in good spirits. The idea of me spouting out Italian at night classes was bizarre but it was such a thoughtful gesture that, suddenly, there seemed hope after all the horrors.

As I started to weave my way out of town, I realised I was passing Sheila's block of flats. Casting a quick glance at the entrance I noticed the BMW parked in the communal car park. Before I knew what was happening, I'd turned into the driveway to take a closer look.

Sure enough, the beat-up BMW with tinted windows and sports trim was parked with its bonnet across Number 4's garage – the one belonging to Sheila's flat. I sat in the truck and stared at it for a moment. There was no need for the thoughtlessness of that driver; it was petty spite that had driven him to it, and after all I had seen in the past few weeks, I didn't think there was room for pettiness in the world anymore. Suddenly, a horrible anger bubbled inside me. Sheila – our Sheila, who worked incredibly hard, lived by herself, minded her own business, was simply a great person – didn't deserve this idiot making her life difficult. There are a lot of little injustices in the world, I decided, and precious few that anyone can do anything about.

I glanced up at the block of flats from behind the steering wheel of the big silver truck. I wondered which flat he lived in, if he got his kicks out of watching Sheila come home each night and trying to get in her garage. I didn't know who he was; I couldn't knock on his door. I banged the steering wheel and looked back at the car.

I was going to drive away, but somehow, I couldn't leave it. A cold rage was upon me. My friends had been so kind to me that afternoon, dragging me from the horror of my last month, and none of them deserved this. Enough was enough. If I couldn't talk to him, then he could come and talk to me.

I was vaguely aware of driving forwards and then reversing right up to the back of the BMW. As the back of the silver truck nudged the BMW, I gently pushed my foot further down on the accelerator. The truck hardly noticed the difference as I shunted the car twenty feet, across the row of garages, off the tarmac and half into a large laurel bush. The screech of the shunting was horrendous. I shifted the truck into first and drove forwards into the middle of the car park, facing towards the block of flats.

I got out of the truck and I waited.

It was already twilight and the blood rushed in my ears. I figured there was every chance he was watching for Sheila's return.

Curtains twitched. I waited – and they twitched again. Fleetingly, I saw a face silhouetted behind the glass. The curtains fell back but the silhouette was still there. At last, he retreated into his flat. I knew where he was now. If it happened again, I would know where to come knocking.

I climbed back into the truck and wrenched it around the car park to drive away. I was due on shift at eight in the morning. Tomorrow, I would have to kill again.

5

PICKLE IN A PICKLE

'He shot his finger off?'

I looked wearily over the dashboard, as Sam's voice filled the car through the hands-free phone. It was my first day back at the practice and despite being a little tired, it felt fantastic to be driving through the familiar country lanes on routine calls. I soaked up the feeling of doing something I loved.

'Yes,' I repeated. 'He didn't mean to, he was trying to shoot a lamb . . .' I was so fed up of this question. It had been the hot topic around headquarters for the last ten days before I finally left.

'I thought you were supposed to inject lambs into the heart to finish them off?' Sam asked.

'It was a big lamb,' I said. 'You know, Sam, it's a much kinder death to be shot than being injected into a contracting muscle with no sedation.'

'Except it costs fingers rather than pence,' Sam chuckled.

It was hard to argue. John had shot his finger off and, being immune to pain, he hadn't said anything. It had taken me a while to realise the extent of his injury.

'What did you do?' Sam asked.

I shrugged. 'I took him to hospital,' I said.

At first, I hadn't noticed. In hindsight, I remember him sort of shaking his hand in irritation – but at the time I didn't even register he'd done himself any harm. It had been the copious amounts of blood that gave it away and, as much as he tried to disguise it and keep working, not even John was normally covered in that much fresh blood. Once we made him stay still, I realised that his finger was hanging by a thread. We frog marched him off the place straight away.

'What did the farmer say?'

'The farmer laughed,' I said.

'I'm surprised you didn't shoot *his* finger off.'

'He just didn't know how to deal with any of it. I think us leaving halfway through the job was the straw that broke the camel's back,' I replied. For the first time I had understood what people meant when they said that if they didn't laugh, they'd cry. 'He was left with a half-slaughtered flock.'

John's finger had been stitched back on by an extremely capable trauma surgeon at Exeter Hospital within two hours of us arriving. After multiple pins had been inserted into the many fragments of bone, John was given a hospital bed and effectively signed off from the Ministry. Shouting 'Gunshot wound!' and being one of four blokes covered in blood charging into A&E is clearly a good way to grab attention.

The conversation paused as Sam pondered the scenario.

'So what happened after John's accident?' he asked, finally sobered by the conversation of slaughter.

It had been another turbulent three weeks. After John's accident, Dave went back to University and Nick went back to work but, somehow, I found myself staying on, now a veteran of the slaughter. I was assigned a new crew. I couldn't gel with them, felt myself growing increasingly estranged and, when one of the new techs decided to needlessly beat a cow around the head with a piece of plastic piping, the cold rage I had felt on that night outside Sheila's garage just bubbled over.

'What did you do?' Sam asked. 'Did you throw your stethoscope at him?'

I said coldly, 'I had him thrown out of the Ministry.'

Sam took a long, deep breath. 'Nothing like a half-measure. I bet the rest of his team were loving you after that!'

'Honestly,' I said, 'I couldn't care. I'd do it again in a heartbeat. The last thing a farmer wants to see is the slaughter team beating up his cows before they kill them.'

'And you had no big Dave to watch your back so I'm guessing you spent the last few weeks hiding in a cupboard – which would explain why you didn't phone me?'

'No,' I replied, 'I didn't phone you because I was assigned to another slaughter team and finally put on the duty vet desk for the last week.'

'The ultimate accolade!' Sam sighed.

The last few days had seen me taken off frontline work – for which I was thankful. The slaughter teams had all been disbanded as the crisis had finally been brought under control and, too contaminated to do any routine patrolling, I was now the voice on the end of the telephone answering questions from confused vets and frustrated technicians.

Unable to move their stock or bring in food, but forced to open up their footpaths for the summer hordes descending on the county, there had been a feeling of deep disquiet among pockets of the rural farming community. Despite the strong stance of the National Farmers Union against vaccination, many farmers felt that the decision to cull rather than vaccinate infected stock had been politically motivated by anxieties about potential trade sanctions in the future. Some felt that they deserved more solidarity and back-up from the Powers That Be but, instead, they found themselves under movement restrictions whilst holidaymakers strolled carefree all over their farms. The result was that Ministry vets doing routine checks were being given an increasingly hard time – and my role as duty vet was to try and resolve disputes between farmers and vets about examining stock.

It was a difficult call for the Government; the lobbying from the tourism sector was intense and it was impossible not to feel for the owners of the numerous empty B&Bs dotted all over Dartmoor. Although the farmers had borne the brunt of events, the ripple effects of the national disaster were widespread and potentially devastating for many small rural businesses.

'To the point,' said Sam, for the first time conjuring a smile out of me, 'did your position as a top-rated killing machine and font of all Foot and Mouth-related knowledge help you get a girlfriend?'

'Oh yes, plenty,' I replied. 'In fact the women were all over me. They couldn't get enough of the stench of disinfectant . . .'

'You have got be to be kidding me!' Sam exclaimed.

I laughed. Sam's gullibility could always make me laugh. 'Surprisingly,' I said, 'the farms I visited weren't exactly geared up for finding girlfriends. It wasn't really at the fore-front of my mind.'

'You are such a tool,' Sam said. 'How can it not be on your mind? You've been single since we qualified . . . Don't forget, I lived with you for five years – I know how your mind works!'

'If you'll remember,' I replied, '*you* were the one with your pants constantly on fire. I was just the hapless sidekick on your unsuccessful forays . . .'

'Well, rather my forays than catching dogs in heat in the backstreets of some Greek island,' Sam retorted. He paused, a thought suddenly occurring to him. A lightbulb may as well have started flashing above his head. 'Let's book another week off,' he said. 'This time – I get to pick the destination . . .'

I glanced at the phone on the dashboard as the hands-free went dead. The reception had cut out but I had no time to call Sam back as I was almost at the call. I was due to see Pickles the donkey, on my way to heal some poor creature instead of to kill it.

Pickles looked at me from inside the stable. He didn't blink, just eyeballed me and twitched his long grey ears.

'He wasn't himself this morning,' Mrs Sinclair began. 'It really isn't like Pickles, he normally is so perky when he eats breakfast. I was very worried about him.' She sounded a little embarrassed. 'Thank you for coming so promptly.'

'No trouble at all, Mrs Sinclair. Did he eat any of his breakfast?' I peered at Pickles, who was still standing there regarding me with the kind of curiosity only a donkey will ever have.

'Oh yes, but just not with – how shall I describe it? – his normal *gusto* . . .'

'I know how he feels some days,' I said with a smile. 'Was it his normal breakfast you offered him?'

'I made him one of his favourites this morning – chopped apples, and some Ready Brek mixed in with his nuts . . .' She paused. 'And, of course, his morning cup of tea.'

'Cup of tea?' I asked.

'Oh yes, Pickles has a cup of tea every morning. He did drink it this morning, but it took him longer than normal and he didn't seem, well, you know, *cheerful*.' Mrs Sinclair began to wring her hands, obviously perturbed.

I noticed another small brown-and-white shape behind Pickles in the far corner of the stable.

'Is there someone else in there with Pickles?' I asked.

'Oh, yes. Harriet never leaves his side,' Mrs Sinclair replied. 'She's a bit down this morning but she always gets that way if Pickles is a bit sad. She did eat her cucumber sandwich though.'

'Cucumber sandwich?'

'Harriet loves her sandwich; she has it when Pickles has his tea. I know it sounds a bit silly, but they really are part of the family.'

Mrs Sinclair stopped, her eyes furrowed. She gave me a look, as if seeking reassurance that this was all perfectly normal.

'It sounds like they have five star treatment,' I said. 'Nothing wrong with that, I'm sure . . . I take it Harriet isn't a donkey, though? I can't really see her behind Pickles but she looks like a . . .'

'British Toggenburg,' Mrs Sinclair said.

'. . . goat,' I said, at exactly the same time.

We stood and looked at each other for a moment.

'Ah yes, a British Toggenburg goat!' I exclaimed. 'My favourite type!'

'There's a goat farm down the road and they make wonderful cheese,' Mrs Sinclair explained. 'Mr Smyth, who owns the farm, helped me get Harriet when she was just a kid. She bonded with Pickles from day one, they're totally inseparable! I know donkeys love to be in pairs, but they sort of fell in love and I didn't want to upset things once they were so settled . . .'

After the horror of the past few months, this logic of love was undeniable.

'Well, they seem pretty happy in there together,' I said. 'Can we get Pickles out so I can take a look?'

Mrs Sinclair was suddenly taken-aback. 'Oh no,' she said, 'we can't do that.'

I hesitated before opening the stable door and looked at Mrs Sinclair in surprise.

'Pickles doesn't like to come out of his stable before noon,' she began. 'He likes a bit of a lie in. Couldn't you . . .' She paused, looking worried. 'Couldn't you see what is wrong with him from here?' she asked.

I stood in silence for a moment, a little lost for words.

'I need to take Pickles' temperature and perform a thorough examination,' I said. 'He's going to have to come out a bit early today. Do you have a halter I can borrow?' I slid back the dead bolt and flicked the kick bar to swing open the stable door.

'Oh dear, they really won't like that!' Mrs Sinclair sighed. 'But I suppose desperate times call for desperate measures.'

As Mrs Sinclair went to get a halter, I eased myself into the stable. Pickles was a small donkey and Harriet was a small goat – it wasn't exactly life-threatening stuff to get him out of the stable. Pulling the door shut behind me, I walked over to try and make friends.

As I approached, Pickles watched me with a look of what can only be described as contempt. I ran my hand down his shaggy neck, but he didn't respond in the slightest. As Mrs Sinclair reappeared over the stable door clutching a halter, I had just about enough time to hear her gasp before I heard the scuffling of feet behind me. Quickly, I turned – but I was already too late. Harriet the goat drove into me, knocking me backwards across the stable. I hit the wall with a crash.

'Oh, do be careful!' Mrs Sinclair exclaimed, hands to her mouth, 'She's going for you again! Oh Harriet, stop it!'

Another blow caught me on my hip as Harriet charged

into me again. Not having anywhere to go, I wildly grabbed her head in an attempt to deflect the blow. Undeterred by my efforts, she wriggled free. Pickles idly watched the encounter with practised stoicism.

I was in the corner of the stable as Harriet came at me again. I twisted and looped my arm around the goat, but she tried to shrug me off and drag me round the stable. Releasing my hold, I staggered to the stable door. The wily she-goat readied herself for another run.

'Mrs Sinclair, I'm going to need some help here,' I panted. 'Can you unlock the door so we can get out?'

'Oh, I don't think so!' Mrs Sinclair exclaimed. 'She's very upset . . . I think she needs to stay in there and calm down . . .'

'Mrs Sinclair!' I bellowed as Harriet drove her head into my thigh. I pushed Harriet hard away and moved towards Pickles, who was still totally stationary. If I could keep the donkey between me and the goat, I'd be able to catch my breath.

'Mrs Sinclair,' I huffed, 'you didn't mention Harriet was so protective of Pickles!'

'I didn't want to worry you. I thought you'd be able to see what was wrong from outside the stable.' Mrs Sinclair paused, the stable door still firmly locked between us. 'They both know it isn't twelve o'clock you know. I really don't think it's a good idea.'

'Can you throw me the head collar please?'

I darted around Pickles. Mrs Sinclair made a hopeless throw – and the head collar landed on Pickles' far side. The angry goat was between us. I edged my way past, Harriet watching my every move, scooped up the head collar and, one eye fixed on the overly protective goat, quickly popped it over the immobile donkey's head.

'Okay, Mrs Sinclair,' I said, as she fretted beyond the stable doors. 'I'm going to lead Pickles out, but you're going to have to open that door.'

Mrs Sinclair was frozen in seemingly abject terror. 'What about Harriet?' she exclaimed.

'She needs to stay in here while I check over Pickles,' I replied, earnestly tugging on the halter rope. 'I'm going to be black and blue tomorrow.'

Pickles didn't budge. I lent some weight into him and, begrudgingly, he moved forwards about an inch.

'He just doesn't want to come out – it isn't twelve o'clock yet!' Mrs Sinclair declared.

I manoeuvred into a position from which I could physically edge Pickles out of the stable – but before I had a chance to reply, Harriet charged me again, with what felt like the force of a hundred horses.

Off-guard, I buckled, sinking down on one knee.

'Oh, Harriet, you naughty girl!' Mrs Sinclair said.

As I was struggling to my feet, Harriet barged me again. I was a grown man felled by an angry little goat. Letting go of the rope, I decided enough was enough. I walked round the back of Pickles and put my shoulder under his backside, forcing him forward as best as I could. All the while, I could see Harriet from the corner of my eye, planning her next route of attack.

Pickles may only have weighed one-hundred-and-fifty kilograms, but he would have put a scrum machine to shame. As Mrs Sinclair let out a squeal of consternation, I shunted him towards the stable door. Batting Harriet away, at last I heaved the stubborn donkey through the gap that his owner had finally and very reluctantly, opened up. Once Pickles was through, I quickly followed and Mrs Sinclair swiftly shut the stable door, trapping the vengeful goat on the other side. Recovering my breath, I regarded Pickles closely but he only stood there, totally unimpressed with my efforts.

'They're a couple of characters, aren't they?' I began, catching my breath.

'You did ever so well there,' Mrs Sinclair began. For the first time since I'd arrived, I saw that she was smiling. 'I've never managed to get Pickles out of the stable before noon before.'

'Right,' I said, breath back at last, 'let's check him over. He wasn't eating too well, was he?'

I curled back Pickles' lips to have a look in his mouth. As I gently lifted his head, an almighty crash emanated from the stable.

'It's Harriet!' Mrs Sinclair cried. 'Oh, she's so upset! Listen to her cry!' Mrs Sinclair rushed over to the stable door, cooing words of comfort. 'Oh, she's butting the door!'

As Harriet's bleating intensified, Pickles became animated. Flicking his head upwards, he let out a sudden demonic braying, spraying me with thick globules of spittle. I staggered back, and saw Pickles turn in demented circles. As the two companions called to each other, the noise was deafening.

'I think we'll have to let Harriet out of the stable, Mrs Sinclair!' I shouted, eager to be heard above the beastly din.

'What?'

'Let Harriet out!' I bellowed. 'She'll do herself an injury!'

Mrs Sinclair swung open the door and Harriet bolted straight out of the stable, hurtling to Pickles' side. As if on cue, the head rope was pulled out of my hand and the two of them charged off into the garden.

I turned to look at Mrs Sinclair. Her face was wrenched in a perfect picture of panic. She was frozen that way for a moment, and then every single feature relaxed.

'Oh look!' she cried, pointing. 'Pickles is back to his normal self! He must be feeling better.'

In the garden, Pickles was nibbling at a flower bed, Harriet at his side.

'Oh, it's twelve o'clock!' Mrs Sinclair exclaimed. 'He must have just been feeling sleepy this morning.' She threw her arms around me. 'Oh, thank you Luke,' she gushed. 'You've really put my mind at rest.'

'What about the head collar?' I tried again. 'I haven't really given Pickles a thorough examination.'

'I don't think we need to worry about that now, do we?' she said, marvelling at the two playmates decimating one of her flower beds. 'After all that stress, I think we'd better leave them to it.' She turned to guide me by the arm along the garden path. 'I must say, I do think you were amazing getting Pickles out of the stable,' she went on. 'I've been meaning to teach him some manners and you really took charge of things. I think Pickles responded very well to you.'

I looked back. In Pickles' shadow, Harriet the goat looked up from her nibbling and gave me a look of utter disdain, the like of which I have never seen on human or animal.

'Why don't you come and have a glass of lemonade?' Mrs Sinclair chattered on. 'I have some lovely shortbread treats as well. To be truthful, I make them for Pickles' afternoon snack – but I'm sure he won't mind sharing one with you after all that hard work.'

It was good to be back.

'You're a hero!' Holly told me as she handed Rob and me our list of on-call rota duties for the next three months. 'And we've invited all your favourite clients to the welcome-back-to-normality party!'

'The fact that we've decided to coincide it with an open day at the practice is entirely coincidental,' Rob said, screwing his eyes up as he glanced at the sheet in front of him. 'I'm starting to hate these rotas more than you will ever imagine,' he said to no one in particular.

'You have got to be kidding me,' I replied. 'I just want to be left alone – Italian night classes is one thing but public crucifixion would be preferable to a practice-open-day-welcome-back-party.'

'They equate to pretty much the same thing, these days,' Rob replied. 'Besides, we need to keep a close eye on our very own practice vigilante.'

I looked at Rob and Holly confused. For a moment, I had no idea what Rob meant.

'Oh yes, I can't believe you did that!' Holly shrieked. 'Don't think it went unnoticed, you know. Sheila's friend was watching out of the window . . .'

'Oh, *that*,' I said, rubbing my forehead sheepishly. In the maelstrom of the last few weeks, I'd totally forgotten about that night outside Sheila's flat.

'That Ministry truck was the best part of the job,' I said. 'Am I in trouble?'

'Ask the lady herself.'

No sooner had Rob spoken than Sheila sauntered into the office and eyed us all quizzically.

'Ask me what?' she asked.

'Did Mr Road Rage here solve the delicate parking issues you were having?' Rob began.

Sheila looked at me and smiled. 'He did, actually.' She paused, as if imagining how I might have looked that night. 'I can't believe you did that. You could have caused all sort of trouble – what were you thinking?'

'I sort of wasn't thinking at all,' I began, still uncertain how pleased Sheila actually was. 'But it seemed a good idea at the time.'

'Well, thank you, Luke,' Sheila said, suppressing the smile I could see curling up the corners of her lips. 'I'm pleased to say that my flat hasn't been burnt down and the BMW has been parked neatly at the opposite end of the car park ever since! I wondered what might have happened to change it all so suddenly – but then my neighbour told me all about the antics of some mad man in a big silver truck . . .'

'Just as well he hasn't gone back to his wicked ways – think of the damage you'd do to the practice car!' Holly laughed.

'It's that hot-headed Italian in you,' Rob said with a smirk. 'How was the first class?'

'Sono Luca,' I replied.

'Not bad,' Rob said, nodding sagely. 'I almost forgot we were standing in the practice office rather than on the shores of Lake Garda.'

'Have you found a girlfriend then?' Sheila asked. The joke was clearly hilarious, for Holly laughed almost before the question was finished.

'Is this why you enrolled me for Italian night classes? So I'd meet a girl? You are all touched in the head,' I laughed. 'Anyway, you can't pry about things like that! You lot are as bad as Sam . . .'

Holly gave me a puzzled look, but Sheila quickly intervened. 'Sam's that crazy friend of his he dragged off to Samos, so they could castrate a few hundred dogs,' she said. 'With hobbies like that, it's no wonder you're single, Luke.'

'And you still haven't answered the question,' Holly said, grinning. 'Come on, Luke – we have a vested interest in this – especially Rob.'

I shot them a wide-eyed look. 'What?'

'That isn't the best way of phrasing it,' Rob said, only slightly sheepishly. 'What Holly meant was that we sort of hoped there might be some single ladies there, one of whom you could bring as a partner to the practice-open-day-welcome-back-hero party . . .' He paused, eyes aglow. 'And we may or may not have a sweepstake to that effect.'

I took a moment to consider this new turn of events. 'What exactly were you guys up to when I was off doing my duty?' I asked. 'Plotting my social life for the next fifty years?'

'Rob wins if you have a date for the open day,' Holly said. 'We all want to meet her.'

'Meet who?' I exclaimed. '*I* haven't even met her yet! I've been to one class and all I did was sit at the back trying to pronounce my name.'

'Like being back at University, then,' Rob remarked.

I shuffled to the back of the room. This constant haranguing was too much.

'Hang on . . .' Sheila began. 'He isn't telling us something. Look at his face.'

I paused, aware that I was colouring slightly. The hesitation was all it took for the three of them to close around me, like a horrible Greek chorus.

'Who is it?' Rob needled. 'There is a girl there, isn't there? I knew it!' He almost punched the air with delight. 'I'm still in with a shot at winning this, aren't I?' He put an arm around my shoulder, tried to shepherd me away from the others. 'Look, you bring that girl to the open day, and I'll split the money with you . . .'

'I don't want your money,' I said, shaking off his arm. 'Look, I hardly spoke to her, just a quick hello because we're both, you know, *vets* . . .'

Just saying that word was like waving a red rag at a bull.

'A local vet!' Sheila crowed, her eyes widening. 'Who is she?'

I was backed into a corner, my best friends ranged around me like harpies at a feast. There was no way out.

'She's called Cordelia,' I stuttered. 'She works at Straughton's small animal practice. She qualified from Cambridge, did an extra degree during her training as a vet, in human nutrition.' I stopped, realising I was gabbling. 'Look – I really only said hello.'

'A Cambridge vet – six years of study, two degrees – you're punching way above your weight. I'll be taking bets on how this is going to end,' Rob said with relish.

'Cordelia, lovely name,' Sheila said as Holly clapped in delight. 'I know Jess who works at Straughton's, I may just give her a bell.'

I felt like banging my head against the wall. Cordelia had definitely caught my eye. Arriving a bit late, I had headed for the back of the class and against all odds, found an empty seat that just happened to be next to a pretty blonde in her early twenties. Reasoning that this sort of luck was akin to winning the lottery on six consecutive weeks, I hadn't managed to wipe a smile off my face for the entire class.

Cordelia, possibly thinking I was a little simple because of my idiotic grin, or because I couldn't pronounce a single word of Italian no matter how many times the teacher repeated it for me, sensibly ignored me for most of the class. However, as we started to pack up our gear, I tried my luck with a little light banter and discovered that she was also a vet. Not just any vet either. She was based locally, of a similar age and career stage to me. We also had Cambridge University in common and I'd managed to extend our conversation for a good ten minutes after the class ended. Without a doubt, she was the sole reason I was going to stick with the charade of trying to learn Italian and I just prayed that Sheila and Holly weren't going to stir things up. I didn't even know if she had a boyfriend, all I knew was that I was looking forward to the next night class and hopefully managing to secure the same seat. Shaking my head with a rueful smile on my lips, I headed for the consult room. 'Daisy Patcher please?' I called into the waiting room, as I passed.

A beautiful golden retriever watched me from a sitting position, its owner steadily collecting her things.

'Go on Daisy,' the lady said, jiggling the harness around the dog's chest.

Daisy looked around at her owner and, seeing her starting to rise, stood up attentively.

As Ms Patcher took a step in my general direction, Daisy worked out what was required and, fixing me with her beautiful brown eyes, steadily led Ms Patcher into my consult room.

It was the first time I'd ever had a guide dog come to see me at the surgery and I felt a mild sense of panic. Ms Patcher hovered uncertainly just inside the door and I stood there awkwardly, momentarily unsure what to do.

'There's a chair to your left,' I began. 'If you step forward a bit, mind the door and then – back two paces! – that will be perfect.' I hastily pulled the consult table back out the way and Ms Patcher effortlessly found the seat and sat down. Daisy wagged her tail, immediately sitting just in front of her owner.

'What seems to be the problem?' I asked.

'I need a favour from you before we begin,' Ms Patcher said.

I nodded and waited. Then, suddenly realising that nodding wasn't going to work, I spluttered out 'Of course, no problem!'

Ms Patcher must have sensed my awkwardness because she smiled. 'I need your help with a somewhat delicate matter.' It was Ms Patcher's time to pause, this time, as she worked out how to phrase her request. 'I don't know you, Mr Gamble, and what I am going to ask you may seem a little unprofessional – but please don't take it that way. It's just that this is terribly difficult for me.'

I bent down to stroke Daisy.

'Ask away,' I said. 'And please call me Luke.' Daisy looked up while I was stroking her and panted into my face. 'What's bothering you about Daisy?' I asked. 'I'd be delighted to help such a lovely dog. She really is beautiful – you keep her perfectly.'

'Daisy means so much to me. As I'm sure you can appreciate, the bond between us is very close.' Ms Patcher stopped, her voice on the edge of breaking. 'In fact, to be blunt, she is everything to me and I just couldn't bear . . .'

'Really, she looks amazing,' I said hastily, pushing my stethoscope to Daisy's chest. 'There isn't anything to worry about.' I listened carefully, keen to be right. 'Her heart is strong, her eyes bright, her coat wonderful and you have her weight just-so. I couldn't imagine a more perfect looking Retriever.'

'It's not that,' Ms Patcher said, clutching a handkerchief to her face as she stifled a sob. 'It's . . . it's her ears.'

'Her ears?' I said, lifting up her ears in turn; nothing looked awry from a cursory exam.

'She scratches at night,' Ms Patcher explained. 'Never when she's working – she wouldn't do that – but she just doesn't seem to hear like she used to. Did you notice in the waiting room? She does know her name. She would have normally told me you had called us in but she didn't.'

'Maybe she wasn't sure of me?' I said reassuringly, patting Daisy.

'No.' Ms Patcher was adamant, in spite of what she wanted to believe. 'She knows people, she would have responded.' She paused, frightened of voicing what she really believed. 'She didn't hear you.'

I paused. I didn't know what to say.

'Don't you see, Mr Gamble, the terrible bind we're in? If Daisy can't hear and you put that down in your clinical notes, it gets posted into my dog book and the Association will take her away from me . . .' She paused. 'I just simply couldn't bear it.'

'So . . .'

'Mr Gamble, I'm begging you. What I need from you is your help, to see what you can do for Daisy, but you mustn't write anything down.' She paused. 'Please,' she said, 'please don't tell them. I would rather be deaf and blind myself than lose Daisy.'

Ms Patcher collected herself and, unnervingly, seemed to look right at me.

I was stunned. I knew that clinical notes for guide dogs had to be especially detailed and a record of every visit of a registered guide dog was sent to the Guide Dog for the Blind Association. And surely, if Daisy wasn't fit for work, she was more a danger than a help to her owner.

'I'm sure it wouldn't come to that Ms Patcher,' I said – though, in truth, I didn't know. 'But let's see how bad Daisy's hearing really is.'

I clicked my fingers on each side of Daisy's head to see if

she would be distracted. In response, Daisy just sat there, looking contentedly ahead. I placed a book on the consult table and then suddenly knocked it onto the floor to make a loud bang.

Daisy moved her head slightly. She didn't exactly jump – but it was still a response.

'Did you see that?' I grinned. 'She definitely looked!'

'No,' Ms Patcher smiled, 'I didn't see . . .'

'Sorry,' I stumbled. 'I meant that she did move her head slightly.'

'Daisy's trained not to be distracted when in harness,' Ms Patcher said, leaning forward to tenderly stroke the dog. 'It will be very hard to make her jump when she is on duty. Even if she could hear it, a firecracker suddenly going off wouldn't cause her undue alarm.' Ms Patcher's next words seemed to fill her with emotion again. 'Her focus is on making sure I'm safe,' she whispered.

'I need to see if she genuinely can't hear,' I said. 'Is there a command or something we can give her to see if she responds?'

'We need to take her harness off,' Ms Patcher said, unclipping the first buckle. 'Then you can call her and she should come to you.' First one clip came off, and then a second. All the while, Daisy stood patiently by. 'She won't like being out of harness when we aren't at home so, if you could give her a biscuit and show her you're a friend, that would really help.'

I fetched a liver treat and gave it to Daisy who, free of her harness, stood up and wagged her tail.

'Okay,' I said, 'here goes . . .'

I opened the door and ducked out of the consult room. Out of sight, I waited in the corridor – and then called out for Daisy.

There was nothing. No flash of gold haring around the corner. No eager dog jumping up for another tasty slice of liver.

From the consult room, I could hear Ms Patcher telling Daisy to go to me.

'Daisy!' I called, more loudly this time. 'Daisy, Daisy!'

At that precise moment, Giles appeared and walked past carrying a small Labrador puppy towards the prep room. At the end of the corridor, he stopped, threw me a thoroughly bemused look and, with a slight shake of his head, carried on.

'Give me your answer do, I'm half crazy . . .' he hummed under his breath.

I went back into the consult room to see Daisy facing Ms Patcher, her tail still swinging from side to side as she regarded her owner adoringly.

Ms Patcher was smiling. 'She won't leave me,' she said. 'I don't know if she heard you or not.'

Suddenly, the little Labrador puppy that Giles had been carrying emitted an ear piercing squeak from the prep room along the corridor. I'd left the consult door open and the noise carried into the room quite clearly. Daisy's ears pricked up suddenly, and she turned her head.

'She *can* hear!' I exclaimed. I felt as if an apple had fallen on my head and I'd just discovered gravity. 'Ms Patcher, she turned her head towards the noise of the puppy.'

Ms Patcher could hardly contain herself. She threw her arms around Daisy and hugged.

'It means that, for whatever reason, Daisy's being a bit slow to react . . . but she isn't totally deaf.'

A thought struck me. Perhaps deafness was not Daisy's problem – but we still didn't know what was. I was hit by a strange kind of fear; I didn't want this moment of elation to end, only for us to be brought back to earth by the thought that there was something *seriously* wrong with the beautiful dog.

'Let's have a look down those ears and see if we can see anything obvious . . .' I declared.

Fitting the earpiece onto the end of the otoscope, I bent down to carefully examine Daisy's ear canals. The poor girl stood perfectly still as I carried out the delicate exam.

'Ms Patcher,' I began. 'I think I have the problem!'

She held her hand to her mouth. 'What?'

'Does Daisy like to run in the long grass when she's off duty?' I asked.

'Well, when my sister comes over we do all go out to the fields and down by the river,' Ms Patcher replied. 'She loves to play ball. Of course, I try to join in – but it can be a little hit and miss sometimes . . .'

I grinned. Things were slotting into place.

'That would explain it,' I said. Her ears are full of grass seeds, Ms Patcher! A little sedation and I can get them all out, clean up the ears and she'll be back on track.'

Even though she couldn't see, Ms Patcher seemed to sense that my beaming was getting out of control.

'And we can put this on the notes?' Ms Patcher asked.

'We can shout it from the rooftops!' I said, bending down to give Daisy a rough stroke. 'She's going to be fine,' I said. 'Everything is going to be just fine – you'll see!'

'I think maybe I will Luke,' Ms Patcher said with a big smile on her face. 'I think maybe I will . . .'

Daisy, sensing the change in mood from her beloved owner, beat her tail in feverish agreement.

Six grass seeds later, I waved goodbye to Ms Patcher and

Daisy at the door of the surgery. Though Ms Patcher could not see, Daisy's beating tail must have given her a signal, for she turned around and returned the wave.

Walking back into the office, I must have had an obvious spring in my step. Rob swivelled round in his chair, like some comic book super villain, and fixed me with a curious look.

'You're going to be bouncing higher than that in a minute,' he said.

'Why's that, Rob-a-dob dob?'

'I'll let what you just said pass without comment considering the news I have to tell you,' Rob said arching an eyebrow.

'It's the rota we received this morning,' he continued. 'It's not all that it seems . . .'

We each had an in tray for correspondence, set against the furthest wall, and I went to peruse the memo carefully.

To all staff members,

As of 1st July, our small animal out-of-hours work will be merging with several small animal practices in the area. As a mixed practice, we will provide large animal cover and second on-call services. This marks a significant change in our management, but we feel it will benefit our clients and staff, and are confident that this pooled out-of-hours service will offer a high level of care.

T.G. Spotswode and Partners

I looked up at Rob. He was obviously intrigued by how I was going to react.

'How is this going to work?' I asked, amazed at the memo.

'This is a ticket to freedom,' Rob replied, snatching up the piece of paper and waving it in the air. 'We'll still be on call one night in four – but just as backup! God knows what deal they've all struck to agree to this, but it makes it a billion times easier for us. Those lucky nurses get to duck out altogether.'

'It's called a "working time directive",' a voice boomed from the corridor. Giles appeared in the doorway and, after considering us for a second, fell heavily into one of the chairs. 'Mr Spotswode wanted to call a practice meeting to discuss this but other engagements got in the way. It's been so hard to agree that, once the decision was made, we all had to go for it. New working time directives mean it is much harder for us to staff an on-call small animal hospital. All the other practices in the area are in the same boat, so it made sense for us to link together.'

I shrugged, still pondering the memo, as if there was a hidden secret in there. 'It's going to be strange,' I finally said.

'Strange isn't the word for it – I've been doing on-call for twenty years,' Giles replied. 'Times are a-changing.'

'Where is the on-call going to be run from?' Rob asked.

'It'll rotate amongst the practices, depending who is on duty,' Giles explained.

The three of us sat in silence, trying to make sense of it.

'That's going to be a mission with the phones,' Rob began. 'The clients won't like it.'

'We're rotating to stop them jumping ship and they'll get used to it. Just think what you have to go through to see a doctor out of hours,' Giles replied. 'Anyway, we're going to be backup in case it gets too busy for the duty vet. We still do the same rota on call but we'll have a much easier time of it.'

'That is a cause for celebration in my book!' Rob exclaimed, rising suddenly from his swivel chair. 'And it starts this weekend, which means tonight!' He paused. That first beer, as ever, was tantalisingly close. 'Who's on call this weekend?' he wondered, glancing at the rota again.

'That will be me,' I said, pondering the chart. 'Second on-call – just for those dire emergencies!'

'What happens about home visits – say an old lady wants her pet cat put to sleep?'

'Home visits are discouraged,' Giles said. 'But I have said we'll cover them.'

'Health and safety,' Rob chipped in. 'We can't have a young lady heading into dodgy council estates late at night, so they're sending us farm boys into the mix.'

'Exactly,' Giles replied sadly. 'Times are certainly changing.'

6

JUST CALL ME CLINT

Mr Spotswode quietly regarded me across the desk.

'It's certainly a challenge,' I said. 'I know it's a bit from the hip, but I think I can do it.'

Mr Spotswode tapped his pen on his desk.

'Have you spoken to anyone else about this?' he enquired.

'I have mooted the idea with Rob,' I answered truthfully.

'And?'

'He thought I was crazy,' I replied.

Mr Spotswode smiled. He looked older for some reason and, for the first time since I'd known him, he seemed weary and not quite himself.

'So, you want to set up an independent emergency service, run it from here, employ a team of staff to manage it and get all the practices in the area to subscribe to it? You propose to pay me rent to cover the use of this building at night and you'll assure me that – somehow! – you will also manage your current on-call large animal duties and continue with your day job?'

I winced. Put like that, it did sound ridiculous.

'Let me think about it,' he said, 'and discuss it with the

other partners. I think every practice is recognising that the current on-call arrangement is not working very well.' Mr Spotswode offered me a smile. 'I admire your drive Luke. It does sound a bit ambitious but let's talk about it in a month when I've had time to reflect. I remember I had your fire once . . .' Catching himself, Mr Spotswode stopped short. 'Friday night and, even at my age, we still occasionally celebrate the end of the week. I need to get on. I hope your weekend goes well, Luke.'

I said my thanks and left his office, relieved not to have been shot down for stepping a bit beyond my station. I wondered what could be bothering Mr Spotswode and resolved to mention it to Rob in case he could shed any light on things. Lately, Giles had seemed distant as well, and things seemed not quite right within the practice. It may have had something to do with the recent change in the on-call set up. The out-of-hours system was failing spectacularly. Clients were getting hopelessly confused as to which practice was supposed to be on call on which night, phones were not getting diverted and there was a general sense of pandemonium as to what might happen on any given night or weekend.

The only real winners were the nurses in our practice, who had been taken off the rota completely. While Rob, two other assistants and I covered the large animal side as first on-call, we were also listed as second on-call vets for the small animal side. Part of our duty was also to look after any inpatient checks at our hospital so that our nurses were no longer working nights.

'I miss it,' Sheila said as I collected my things and the on-call phone for the weekend.

'You miss being on call?' I asked, surprised.

'It's when everything exciting happens,' she said. 'You get all the interesting stuff out of hours – critical care, emergencies!' Sheila grinned; she knew how silly it sounded, but she didn't care. 'My days are now routine ops and cleaning kennels.' Then she whispered from the side of her mouth. 'And, you know, I miss the bonus.'

'Don't forget you still have the pleasure of managing us lot,' I quipped.

'Always a pleasure, never a chore,' Sheila laughed. 'I'll have to find other activities to occupy my time – maybe I'll sign up for a language night class, too! How is that going by the way?'

I didn't believe for a second that Sheila was genuinely interested in whether I could say a sentence in Italian.

'You want to know about Cordelia, don't you?' I said, unable to stop a smile spreading across my face. The truth was that I didn't have that much to smile about on the Cordelia front. The last few weeks I'd managed to sit next to her every time but when last week I had finally plucked up courage and asked her out for a drink after class, she'd turned me down.

'Maybe she genuinely had to get back home?' Sheila offered after I'd spilled the beans.

'Maybe,' I said hopefully.

'Never underestimate the complexities of the female psyche! I wouldn't give up just yet, she might just be playing a bit hard to get. Anyway, I have to shoot,' Sheila said, waving me goodbye. 'Have a quiet weekend, Luke!'

I watched Sheila go. 'I'll do my best,' I replied.

'My horse has broken its leg!' the lady sobbed.

I lifted the phone away from my ear and glanced out the window. It was only eight p.m., but already it was black as night. Torrents of rain fell across the hillsides.

'Where are you?' I asked.

'Parlicks Stables,' the voice abruptly stated and hung up.

I rolled my eyes and headed out the door. Parlicks Stables was as rough a stable yard as any I had visited. A motley collection of twenty stables and muddy fields, the people that kept their horses there were tough, rough and rented their individual stables by the week.

Pulling up, I climbed out of the car, cringing into sheets of rain.

'Becca,' a harsh voice called across the yard. 'The cow vet's arrived!'

I grimaced in the direction of the lady who had yelled. She leant against the wall, dragging on a cigarette, sheltered from the rain and staring at me belligerently. She raised a finger and pointed vaguely in the direction of what I assumed was the horse and owner.

Deciding to take a look at the poor animal before I grabbed anything from the car, I set off in what I hoped was the right direction, wondering how a horse in such a desolate flatland could possibly break its leg. Rounding the corner, I observed two figures huddled together in the twilight.

A massive hulking man stood next to an equally hulking woman, holding an umbrella and glowering over a rickety fence into a sea of mud. As I approached, the man looked at me with dead eyes. A spider's web tattoo, fresh on his neck, and arms as thick as my legs, suggested he wasn't someone I wanted to bump into on a dark and rainy night.

'You the vet?' he grunted.

'Yes,' I said simply.

The woman turned towards me. 'He's out there!' she barked. 'Broken his leg . . .'

I peered into the field. 'I can't see anything,' I said.

'He's in the field behind this one, won't come in, just hold-ing his leg up,' the woman said. 'I think it's broken – he won't put it down, must have been kicked by Treena's bloody 'orse. I'll bloody well have her pay for calling you out an' all!'

I looked at her, confused, putting one boot on the fence. 'Isn't anyone out there with him?' I asked.

They shared a bewildered look.

'In this rain?' the woman asked. 'I tried to get 'im in, but the bloody thing wouldn't move so I phoned you. Thought he might follow us but he hasn't.'

'Well, if he's got a broken leg . . .'

'I don't want him shot,' the woman suddenly interjected. 'I've put a lot of effort into him. I want you to fix him up.'

'But he's in the field, by himself, with a probable broken leg?' I asked. I wasn't sure I could quite believe it.

The woman nodded, oblivious to the horror in my voice. 'If you walk over there, you'll see 'im.' I put another foot on the fence and hauled my way over. 'He's a rescue horse, though!' the woman cackled. 'So he can be a bit difficult with blokes. He hates you, doesn't he Jim?'

The man just nodded, still looking at me with a blank expression. I was suddenly glad there was a fence between us.

'Are you coming along?' I asked.

'Just need a fag,' the woman replied, indicating the dead one already in her lips. 'You go and 'ave a look, we'll come over in a minute.'

The mud sloshed over my boots as I trudged across the field, cursing the horse's owner and her knuckle-dragging partner. There was no way the practice was going to get paid for this call-out, I thought, steeling myself to remember to ask for payment before I left.

I wondered what on earth I was going to do with a belligerent horse stuck in the middle of a field with a broken leg. Whether the woman liked or not, if the horse needed to be shot then it needed to be shot.

The horse, a dark bay cob, was holding up its right hind leg and standing isolated in a desolate field. The poor creature looked thoroughly fed up and I uttered some soothing words as I approached. As I reached out to pat it, the horse twisted to try and bite me. I slapped it hard across the nose and it raised its head in annoyance.

'That's no way to treat someone who has come to help you,' I said. The rain had let up slightly, but the sky was still thick grey. 'You need to cut me some slack. I'm all you've got to get you out of this mess.'

The horse looked at me and swished its tail.

I'm clearly going mad, I thought to myself, having a conversation with a horse in the middle of field. As I contemplated my sanity, the horse gave a little whinny.

'Are we going to be okay?' I heard myself say. 'No biting or kicking. It's just you and me, so you need to stand still while I see what's wrong.'

The horse tossed its head.

'Don't move and don't kick me. We need to make a plan and me seeing that leg is the first step,' I said, once again approaching the horse. This time it didn't try to bite me and I ran my hand steadily over its sodden back, tracing the hair down over its right hind leg.

'Well, you haven't got any obvious swelling higher up,' I said, 'that's a good sign. No bones sticking out and it doesn't feel hot . . .' I paused. 'What would in this weather though?' I chortled to the horse.

In reply, the horse just snorted dismissively.

'It's your foot isn't it?' I said, crouching low, still fearful of a sharp kick to the head. I racked my brains. A page of scrawled notes on equine orthopaedics floated in my mind. Only three things cause sudden and total lameness: broken bones, infection of a joint, or pus in the foot. I looked at the leg carefully, the horse shifting uneasily above.

'It doesn't look broken or too swollen around the fetlock so my gut feeling is that you have pus in the foot, my friend. That means an abscess,' I chatted away.

It was good news for the horse, but he still wasn't going to like it. 'I won't have to shoot you,' I said, risking the joke, 'but I am going to have to lance it and get a better look at things . . .'

It meant I was going to have to lift his foot up. I wasn't relishing the job. 'The deal is,' I said, 'if you let me sort this without any fuss, I'll make sure you get into a nice warm stable tonight and out of this god forsaken rain . . .'

I took a deep breath and grabbed the hoof. No kick was forthcoming as I peered at the underside, my face inches from the large metal shoe. The other thing that can cause lameness – the bit I didn't have written down in my equine orthopaedic notes – is a massive sharp stone digging into the soft part of the frog, on the underside of a horse's hoof. I looked up at the horse, and grinned.

'How'd you do that?' I asked, observing the large stone and trying to work out how deeply it had penetrated the sole.

He didn't reply, but I could guess. This field wasn't the most savoury habitat for a horse: threadbare grass on flinty ground and the heavy rain had loosened a lot of the top soil exposing a minefield of sharp stones underneath a thick layer of mud.

The horse suddenly shifted, trying to wrench his leg away.

'Steady on!' I cried. I put out a hand to stop falling, and half-lost it in the slippery muck around our feet.

'I'm going to use my keys to hook this out,' I said, righting myself. 'Haven't got a hoofpick with me, but this will do the job.' Before I began, I paused to turn my head up towards the horse, and whispered. 'Just remember our deal.'

The horse impatiently flicked its ears back and forwards again and taking that as my cue to get on with the job, I hooked the metal end of my car key underneath the stone and eased it out. The stone was a sharp flint and its razor point had driven about 2 cm into the sole. There was no way it would have dislodged itself. Slipping the flint into my pocket, I put the horse's leg down.

The horse immediately walked forwards, testing its back leg. It was totally sound.

'Wait, wait, wait!' I whispered.

Obediently, the horse stopped.

'We struck a deal,' I said, relieved. 'I'm a man of my word. I'll swing things to get you in for the night if you want. Hay, water and a clean dry stable. What do you reckon?'

The horse looked at me as I clasped the lead rope and gave it a pat. At last, as if in agreement, he swished his tail again.

'Right then,' I said, 'let's get out of this mud . . .'

I looked down – and I couldn't see my shoes.

I started to walk forward and the horse dutifully followed. As we stumbled across the field and approached the stable yard, I could see a group of figures clustered together under the shelter of the stable roof, the glow of cigarette ends clearly visible through the gloom.

'Bloody 'ell!' the woman who owned the horse screeched.

'Looks like the cow vet fixed 'im,' the woman who I'd first met agreed.

'Told you it wasn't my 'orse,' another voice chimed in.

'What the bloody 'ell was it then?' the owner shouted.

'Penetrating injury to his frog,' I answered. There was silence. 'Stone embedded in his foot.'

'Is that all it bloody well was? You got it out then, nice one!' She paused, grinning with broken teeth. 'Jim,' she spat, 'I told you to check 'is feet.'

'Couldn't get near 'im,' Jim grunted with a shrug.

The woman took a step toward us, cringing back when the rain doused her cigarette.

'You may as well go and turn 'im back out,' she said. 'He's walking fine now.'

I ran a hand soothingly through the horse's mane. 'Oh no,' I said reasonably. 'We can't do that.'

The women and Jim all looked at me sullenly.

'The flint was razor sharp, it's fifty-fifty that he won't develop a tracking infection into his joint. We'll only know tomorrow.' I was bending the truth, but I didn't care; the horse deserved more than these people were willing to give, and a promise was a promise – even if it was only to a horse. 'To have any chance, he needs to be stabled tonight on a deep bed of clean straw, with some nice hay and water.'

'How's that going to help infection in 'is foot?' one of the women sneered.

'Well,' I said, shifting forward. 'It's a well known fact that horses stabled after an injury stand a much better chance of recovery. We don't want any more mud getting into the wound where the stone was digging in and he'll be able to fight things off if he is feeling happier.' I paused, offering up the halter. 'Jim, could you help me get him into a stable please?'

Without waiting for an answer, I led the horse forwards. Upon seeing Jim, his ears instantly went flat back.

'He hates you, Jim!' the owner laughed. 'I'll do it. You get some hay and water like what the *cow* vet said.'

The owner took the rope off me and led the horse into a stable as Jim shuffled off to attend to his orders, grumbling obscenities under his breath.

I followed the horse to the stable and watched as the owner patted him and gave him a mint from a packet tucked in her pocket. Maybe she wasn't quite as tough as she seemed. I couldn't hear what she said, but as she chatted away to the horse, who crunched on his Polo, he let out a soft whinny.

The owner turned to me with a quizzical expression on her face.

'How'd you know to talk to 'im?' she asked. 'He only lets people who talk to 'im get near 'im – that's why he hates Jim. He won't talk to a 'orse.'

I laughed. 'It seemed the only thing to do,' I replied. 'He was pretty okay after that.'

'Not bad for a cow vet,' she cackled. 'You know how to talk *cow* as well?'

'I'm learning all their languages,' I replied, with a half smile.

The owner stared at me as I hesitated in the doorway, working out how to best phrase my next question. 'I was wondering if we could settle the account?' I said, as boldly as I could manage.

The owner, ignoring me, left the horse's side and pushed past me into the yard. 'Jim,' she shouted. 'Jim!'

I shifted on the spot slightly, uncertain as to how this was going to play out as the hulking figure of Jim loomed round the corner, carrying a bucket of water in one hand and a bale of hay in the other.

'Put 'em in the stable and then pay the vet, he done okay tonight,' she said, much to my relief, before heading back to her friends, readying a cigarette.

I stood motionless as Jim locked me with dead eyes and then with a single nod of his head, went to deposit the hay and water in the stable. When he returned, he reached into his pocket and pulled out a tight bundle of notes, peeled off a few twenties and thrust them into my hand.

'That cover it?' he grunted.

I glanced down at a fist full of notes.

'Thanks very much,' I said.

With another slight nod of his head, Jim shuffled off into the darkness leaving me alone in the yard. I turned my head to look at the horse, which regarded me from behind the stable door.

'Not a bad evening's work,' I heard myself say. 'You mind how you go.'

The horse flicked his ears and as I turned to disappear back into the rain, I heard a soft whinny of response. Maybe I was getting the hang of talking to animals after all!

As I started the drive home, the phone went again. The night was thick above me, and though the rain had let up, occasional gusts still whipped across my windscreen.

'Luke?' a voice began.

I recognised the voice immediately. It was my landlord, who owned the big farmhouse next door to my flat.

'Hello Mr Lock,' I replied, 'is everything alright?'

'I'm sorry to phone you on the practice phone,' he said. 'It's just that my son has returned from University – and . . . er . . . he's brought a puppy with him. A golden Lab.'

'That's nice of him. It'll keep you busy!' I remarked with a smile. Mr Lock's old collie, Bess, had died last year of lepto-spirosis – a disease carried by rats that can infect people as well as dogs. The family had been broken-hearted and I guessed that Matt, Mr Lock's son, had taken it upon himself to cheer everyone up with a new addition for the family.

'Luke, it's just that the puppy hasn't been vaccinated, and I want to get him protected as soon as possible. We're still very raw about poor Bess and, well, I'm sure you understand, we don't want to make the same mistake again.'

'Yes,' I agreed, thinking back to that horrible time. Bess's vaccinations had lapsed and I knew Mr Lock blamed himself for her contracting the disease. The truth was that Bess was eighteen years old, had had a very full life and I doubted the fact that she missed one of her yearly boosters had made that much difference. Vaccinations boost the immune system, they don't prevent infection, and Bess was very fragile with a failing heart and kidneys. It wouldn't have taken much of anything to finish her off.

'I know it's a Friday night, Luke,' Mr Lock said, apologies wavering in his voice, 'but, rather than leave it until next week, I just wondered, on the off-chance, if you had a dog vaccination you might be able to pop into him tomorrow for us, get him covered?'

Something darted across the road in front of me; I slammed hard on the brakes, skidding in the rain – but whatever animal it had been was already long gone.

'Luke?' Mr Lock's voice trembled. 'Luke – are you okay?'

'I'm fine,' I breathed, starting the stalled car up again. 'No problem, Mr Lock. I'll grab a kit, it's no trouble, I'm passing the clinic anyway. I'll come round first thing tomorrow morning.'

'Good lad,' Mr Lock said. 'Thank you, Luke.' He rang off.

I suddenly cursed. I didn't have the practice keys with me; I would have to drive home first, get the keys and then drive back out again to get the vaccine. On a night like this, with the rain returning and the deepening gloom, it was more than I wanted to do. I dropped down a gear to take a sharp corner, and tried to concentrate on the road.

Then, a sudden thought occurred. Tonight's on-call was being done by one of the other practices in town and I could stop by there and grab a vaccine; it would save me about forty minutes of these treacherous roads. Surely, tonight, there wouldn't be any stern disciplinarian, his elbows deep in some poor dog's chest, refusing me a simple thing like that . . .

I hastily dialled the small animal emergency number. The phone rang three times before being answered by a stressed voice.

'Emergency out-of-hours small animal service,' it wavered. 'How can I help?'

'It's Luke here,' I said. 'I'm the large animal vet on duty . . .'

'Yes?' the voice said distractedly, the sound of barking in the background.

'Sounds like you're having a busy one,' I began. 'I wondered if I could swoop by and grab a dog vaccine quickly?'

'Yes, that's fine,' the voice said.

'Which practice are you working out of tonight?'

'Straughton Partners,' the stressed voice snapped back. 'Do you know where we are?'

My stomach gave a butterfly flutter. It was the practice Cordelia worked in but it was quite a large practice, so it was unlikely that she would be there tonight. I tried to push the thought out of my mind.

'I'll be there in the blink of an eye,' I said.

Rain or no rain, I pressed my foot hard to the floor.

I arrived, drenched and shivering with cold. Hurrying from the practice truck to the door, I pressed the buzzer and hopped from foot to foot, just to keep warm. Eventually a harassed looking nurse unlocked the door and I eased my way through.

I couldn't believe how busy it was. A family clustered around a miserable looking cocker spaniel on one side of the room, whilst a red setter stood on the opposite side retching, its stomach bloated, as a worried lady gently stroked its back. A cat sat quietly in a basket balanced on the lap of an elderly man – but, despite a faint trace of blood on its nose, it seemed acutely alert as its green eyes carefully watched the dogs that surrounded it. I walked to the reception desk, just as a tall rangy character came out of the toilet and pushed his way past the family with the cocker spaniel to stand next to me.

Leaning over the empty desk, he shouted, 'You got my cat sorted?'

I looked at him, trying to mask my surprise. His face was screwed up and flushed red.

'I'm sure they'll be with us in a minute,' I began.

'Mind your own sodding business,' he replied, propping himself on the counter.

His eyes seemed to have trouble focusing, his skin was pockmarked and purpling. I guessed he was in his mid-twenties, as I took in his trainers, tracksuit, spiky black hair, two-day stubble, and the couple of earrings in his left ear.

'I'm one of the vets on call,' I said evenly. 'So it is my business.'

He thrust his chin out. 'Well, I want my bastard cat!' he

snarled. 'I don't know what she thinks she's doing in there, but I've been here forever!'

Around me, the people waiting all shrank back in their seats. As if they weren't worried and distressed enough about their pets; an aggressive lout in the waiting room was the last thing they needed.

'Why don't you take a seat and I'll find . . .'

Before I had finished, the door to the consult room opened and Cordelia walked into the waiting room.

'Mr Partridge,' she said calmly, quietly taking in the carnage around her, 'could you come in here a moment please?'

I waved my hand in greeting with a stupid smile on my face, and she gave a quick nod in my direction. The lout gave me a final sneer and pushed his way past. As Cordelia and he disappeared into the consult room, one of the nurses on duty appeared behind the reception desk.

'Hello,' I said, still vaguely looking after Cordelia. 'I'm Luke.'

'Oh yes, Mr Dog Vaccine!' she replied. 'I'm Jess,' she began again, slightly calmer. 'Two seconds and I'll grab it for you, it's manic tonight!'

Jess ducked away to grab the vaccine, but quickly reappeared to call out, 'Mr and Mrs Gilmot, you and Berty will be next,' she said, smiling at the family with the poorly cocker spaniel. 'Mr Gussage, Snowy is doing okay, isn't she? The vet won't be long, Mrs Hoopler, we'll be with you as quick as we can!'

Mr Gussage and Mrs Hoopler offered sympathetic smiles in return.

'Look, do you want me to see someone?' I said quietly. 'I'm supposed to be second on-call anyway . . .'

'Oh, we'll be fine,' Jess said, juggling two bottles of dog vaccine. 'Cordelia has it in hand. She knows Berty well – he's a diabetic, just needs a blood glucose and a slight adjustment of his insulin.'

'How about I see Mr Gussage?' I asked.

Jess was about to make another polite refusal when the phone started ringing, shaking vigorously on the table. She peered up at me, for the first time letting her exasperation show. 'Well,' she said. 'I suppose that *could* be a help . . .'

There came a sudden shout from the consult room. Quickly, I turned around. On the other side of the waiting room, the door flew open and Mr Partridge burst back onto the scene, arms flailing wildly.

'You keep the bastard thing then, kill it or keep it, I don't give a damn! I ain't got time to nurse it.' He turned round, and bawled back through the door in Cordelia's direction, 'Only the girlfriend who likes the thing anyway. I ain't paying that sort of money to fix a *cat*!' He spat the last word like it was the worst word in the English language.

Something fell from Mr Partridge's tracksuit pocket as he flung his arms in the air. It had hardly hit the floor before he stopped his swearing and quickly scrabbled to pick it up. He wasn't quite quick enough though because I, Cordelia, and every client in the waiting room had clearly seen what he'd dropped. There was a momentary pause. No one really knew what to say. Mr Partridge had dropped a used syringe and needle but he didn't seem in the least embarrassed.

'You're a useless vet anyway; I'll sign the God damn paper!'

Cordelia's face was one of cold, composed fury. Five feet five inches tall, blonde, and beautiful, she was not intimidated in the slightest by the oaf lumbering in front of her. Her eyes blazed. In perfect silence, she handed a pen and the form, upon which he scrawled his name. Taking the form back, she looked Mr Partridge square in the eye and pointed to the exit. Looking about him, Partridge decided enough was enough and, with a final barrage of expletives, stormed off into the night.

Silence settled across the waiting room. Behind the reception desk, Jess nervously apologised to whichever poor client was on the other end of the line.

I threw Cordelia another little wave, but she didn't seem to notice. At the front of the room, she cleared her throat. 'Mr and Mrs Gilmot, let's have a look at Berty, shall we?'

An elderly couple nodded gratefully and rose from their seats. Within seconds, a soft chatter had risen again. Normal service had resumed. This woman was awesome, I thought to myself. What she had done was incredible, way beyond anything Sam or Rob and I might have managed. She had confronted a drugged-up lout almost twice her size, kicked him out of the surgery – and was now unflappably dealing with an overwhelming string of emergencies.

As Berty went into the consult room, I turned to look at Jess, that stupid smile back on my face. She looked at me quizzically.

'Impressive, wasn't it?' I said, flushing a bit.

'His girlfriend's cat has been run over,' Jess explained. 'We think he did it, but he swore it was his neighbour. He wanted us to put it down, say it had died on arrival so he could take it back to her.' Jess paused. 'He's trouble through and through, he came in here last month with a dog that had been stabbed. We reported him to the police and thought that was the last we'd see of him . . . until tonight.'

'So what happened tonight?'

'Cordelia wouldn't lie,' Jess shrugged. 'She didn't want to put the cat down, so she got him to sign a form to hand it over to us.'

'He didn't like it much, did he?'

'She got the signature and that's all that matters,' Jess replied. She looked eager to establish that my offer of help hadn't suddenly been taken back. 'Do you want to see Snowy, then?'

'Bring it on,' I answered.

Quickly slipping on a lab coat, I smiled at Mr Gussage and invited him and Snowy into the consult room. Snowy had been in a fight with the cat next door and had a small bite wound on her face. Like many wounds, it looked worse than it actually was – and, once she was cleaned up and the blood had been washed away, you could hardly see the puncture wounds.

'I was worried it had scratched her eyes,' Mr Gussage said.

I had a sudden flashback: my first night on-call with Mr Spotswode's practice, taking a scalpel and lifting Mrs Beasley's cat's eye out of its socket.

'If it's any consolation,' I said, 'the other cat probably came off worse. The cats that have wounds on their faces are normally the victors. It's the ones with wounds on their tails you have to worry about.'

'But surely face wounds are more serious?' Mr Gussage asked.

'Well, the ones with tail wounds are generally the losers and get bitten around the tailbase as they turn to run – they are much more likely to be attacked again. No one messes with the boss cat,' I said. 'Snowy clearly stands up for herself. Whoever was fighting with her will know that now!'

'My wife will be delighted to hear it!' Mr Gussage exclaimed as I handed him a course of antibiotic tablets. 'Although I think Snowy will be under lock and key for a few days now, no matter what I report back.'

As I took Mr Gussage back to the waiting room and bade him goodbye, Jess caught my eye from the reception desk and urged me over. The collection of people still waiting for help with their sick animals had finally diminished and I hurried over.

'Cordelia is just seeing Mr and Mrs Hoopler,' she said, 'but we have a bit of a problem . . .'

'What's that? There's no one else to see is there?' I asked.

'Mr Partridge is back,' Jess replied, her tone hushed. 'He's in the car park . . .'

I crossed the room and, putting two fingers between the slats of the blind, peered out of the window. Sure enough, at the other end of the car park, the silhouetted figure of Mr Partridge was lurking in the shadows.

'Do you think I should phone the police?' Jess said.

'He doesn't seem to be doing anything in particular,' I said. 'He's just standing there, watching the building.'

Before Jess could reply, Mr and Mrs Hoopler came out the consult room, worry etched on their faces. Cordelia walked with them to the doors.

At the door, Mrs Hoopler turned, ashen-faced, to Cordelia, her husband's arm around her shoulder.

'Please call us as soon as you've done the surgery on Florence,' Mrs Hoopler said.

'Of course,' replied Cordelia. 'I'll be in touch in a few hours.'

Once the Hooplers had gone off into the car park where Mr Partridge still lurked in the undergrowth, Cordelia turned, threw a grave look at Jess, and marched back toward the consult room. As she went, I took a step in her direction.

'Hi Cordelia . . .'

She squinted vaguely in my direction and gave me a little smile. 'Hi,' she replied, before turning back to Jess. 'Florence has a twisted stomach,' she said. 'We have an operation on our hands.'

'Oh no,' Jess replied. 'I'll go and set up theatre.'

A sudden loud slam at the front door made all of us freeze.

'What is that?' I demanded, peering out into the dark.

Mr Partridge materialised from the gloom. He rained heavy fists at the door, shouting out another string of obscenities. Behind the reception desk, Jess let out a little scream of terror.

'He can't get in,' Cordelia said calmly. 'Not if we don't buzz him.'

'But what about clients who want to come down to the surgery?' I asked.

'All in good time,' Cordelia replied. 'Let's go and set up for Florence.'

The fists rained down again. I hurried back to the window, peering out between the blinds. Mr Partridge disappeared for a moment, and I contemplated whether I should do anything about him. I didn't really fancy heading back out into the sheeting rain to face down a psycho dog-and-cat-killer.

'I'll stick around,' I mumbled. 'Extra pair of hands if you need them . . .'

Cordelia nodded and I followed her and Jess through to the prep and operating theatre.

The layout was fairly standard for a small animal practice and, as Jess efficiently started laying out all the materials required for the operation, Cordelia flicked on a small monitor on a shelf.

'We can keep an eye on our special friend,' she said as the CCTV screen flickered into life.

A grainy black-and-white image showed Mr Partridge still loitering in the car park, swigging from a can of drink.

'Drink and drugs, just what the doctor ordered,' Jess commented, glancing at the picture. 'Are you sure we shouldn't call the police?'

'Let's focus on Florence. With any luck, he'll get bored and will have gone home by the time we've finished,' Cordelia replied.

Just as she finished speaking, Jess let out a gasp. We turned and looked at the monitor.

'He's gone round the back,' she said. 'Luke, he's urinating on your car!'

Sure enough, Mr Partridge was relieving himself on the Car of Power.

'I know it needs a wash,' I said, 'but that's a bit extreme.'

'I think it's time to call the police,' Cordelia sighed as Mr Partridge moved to another car in the car park – a pale blue Mazda.

'Oh, Cordelia, that's yours!' Jess exclaimed.

We watched as Mr Partridge once again took position and readied his aim.

'Oh, I *love* that car,' Cordelia breathed.

I glanced at Cordelia and willed her to keep her chin up. Just as I did so, Mr Partridge looked straight into the camera and gave us a one-fingered salute.

'I'll sort this clown out,' I heard myself say. 'Be back in a minute . . .'

Cordelia didn't appear to hear me, transfixed by what was about to happen to her car.

I bolted out of the operating theatre, hurtled through the waiting room and, fumbling with the latches, bustled back into the rain. Haring around the side of the surgery, I saw

Partridge turn away from the CCTV camera and adjust himself at the hood of Cordelia's car.

'You!' I bellowed, through a sudden gust of wind. 'What do you think you're doing?'

Partridge turned round with what only can be described as a demonic grin.

'I am having,' he declared, 'a piss on this car!'

I took a stride toward him. Then, knowing I was now in the range of the cameras, I took another. 'No you're not,' I said.

'Just what are you going to do about it?' he snarled back, reeling from side to side.

I hesitated. I had no plan. I had charged out of the surgery, almost as crazed as Partridge, and – I had to admit it – half of me had done it just to see what Cordelia would think of me. I thought to myself: what would Clint Eastwood do if someone was having a wee on a car belonging to a girl he fancied?

'Hey, pack it in!' I said lamely, not having a .44 Magnum to hand and not really sure what else to do.

From the corner of my eye, I saw Cordelia and Jess appear in the doorway of the practice. They looked ghostly through a thin sheet of rain. In front of me, Partridge span around and marched forward, pushing his face into mine. This is not cool, I thought. I wondered if Jess and Cordelia had called the police . . .

'I said,' Partridge shouted, showering me with thick warm spittle that I could feel, even through the rain, 'what are you going to do about it?'

The rush of blood came faster than I anticipated. This lout was traumatising Cordelia and Jess and, while I didn't care too much about my car, I cared about Cordelia's.

I shoved Partridge hard in the chest and he shot backwards, flailing drunkenly and landing in a heap on the ground.

I looked round at Cordelia and, sheepishly, shrugged. I hadn't meant to push him so hard. Suddenly, Jess cried out. By the time I understood and turned back, Partridge was already on his feet. He took stock, and then ran at me snarling, 'I'm going to smash your face in.'

I managed to dodge his wild swing and then he crashed into me. Neither of us could get in any clean blows as we were too close, hugging each other in some disgusting embrace. My hand shot upwards but, instead of punching him, I grabbed him by the throat and propelled him to the wall by the entrance to the practice. Beside me, I heard Jess and Cordelia shouting – but there was no escape from the situation now.

Partridge's head smacked hard into the brick and he rebounded, falling forwards and staggering into me. It was my turn to trip now, and together we plunged to the rain-sodden concrete. With his face and cheap lager breath pressed against mine, I rolled him over and, finally – still sprayed with spittle and swearing – I straddled him.

As the fight went out of Partridge, I wondered what on earth to do now. I looked back to Cordelia and Jess for a clue. Suddenly, Partridge grabbed my shirt and pulled it up under my armpits. I must have looked ridiculous, my belly out, straddling some drunk scrapper in the car park. I was acutely aware of Cordelia's presence. This definitely wouldn't have happened to Clint Eastwood.

I had to finish things. The only way to get Partridge to release his grip would be to land fifteen stone on his groin with my knee, or hit him hard in the face, but Cordelia and

Jess were watching and I didn't really want things to escalate into a full-on brawl.

'Let go of my shirt!' I hissed.

Partridge didn't breathe a word, still dazed from hitting the wall.

'Let go of my shirt!' I hissed. 'I look ridiculous!'

'Let him go!' Cordelia cried out.

Was she saying that to me or to Partridge? I tried to twist my head round, but it was no good; my shirt rode up higher and I turned back. At University I'd done five years of combat karate, I even had a black belt – why couldn't I deal with a single, almost comatose man? I imagined Sensei Lewis and Sensei Mulholland turning their backs on me, Sensei Lewis shaking his head in despair and uttering the word, 'Muppet'.

'Honestly, let go of my shirt,' I tried.

Partridge and I locked eyes.

'Please let go of the damn shirt,' I said again.

I realised I was on the point of begging. Perhaps he was shocked into action by my desperation, because suddenly, he let go. Standing up quickly, I pulled my shirt down, resisting the urge to kick Partridge hard.

'All okay,' I said, backing away and raising my hands. 'Nothing to see,' I said, throwing a look at the two shocked faces in the doorway. 'All over!'

Partridge scrambled to his feet, dusting down his own ruined top. He took a step back, fixed me with a look half-way between righteous anger and bewilderment. 'You're mental!' he hissed, and scrambled away.

I stood and watched him go. When I turned around, I caught sight of myself in the windscreen of a neighbouring car. I was drenched from head to foot, my shirt smeared against me like a great streak of filth. Perhaps I looked as wild as Partridge had.

I turned back. Cordelia was peering at me oddly through the rain.

'He had a big bladder didn't he?' I said. If it was meant to be a joke, neither of them laughed. 'I don't think he'll be back,' I said confidently. Inwardly, I cringed as the words escaped my lips. 'No sir,' I rambled on, desperate for a way out. 'He'll have to find other cars to wee on,' I finished.

There was a long, lingering silence. Perhaps it was just wishful thinking, but I fancied I could see Cordelia's lips turn up at the corners, the merest hint of a smile.

'Inside, Clint,' she said. 'Now the serious work has to begin.'

'Right you are,' I said, grateful for the lifeline she'd thrown me. We all trooped back into the practice building.

'Luke, I need you over here. I need to get a catheter in Florence, get her sedated and pass this stomach tube.'

I obediently held Florence steady as Cordelia skilfully slipped in the catheter.

'I haven't done this operation before,' she said. 'I'm going to need some help.'

I was amazed. Cordelia seemed so in control, I just assumed she had everything in hand. A twisted stomach or Gastric Dilatation Volvulus (GDV) was notoriously one of the most difficult of all the small animal emergencies that could come into a practice. Not particularly common, they occur when the stomach has flipped around in the abdomen, leading to gas build-up and the cutting off of the vital blood supply to essential organs. To fix it, the stomach had to be deflated, twisted back into position and stitched to the body wall. Survival rates were about fifty-fifty and time was of the essence.

'No problem,' I mumbled, flashing back to my first New Year's Eve on duty. 'Just one other item we're going to need . . .'

Jess and Cordelia looked at me expectantly.

'A surgery book?' I said with a smile.

We swiftly prepped Florence, and Cordelia eased the stomach tube down her oesophagus towards the stomach. As she did so, she cast me a worried look.

'It won't go all the way in,' Cordelia said. 'The twist is blocking it . . .'

It was time to roll our sleeves up.

'Okay,' I said, 'let's get in there and I'll untwist it.'

I cut down into Florence's abdomen. Very gently manipulating the stomach, I untwisted it by just a couple of degrees. The tube slid forward and gas shot out.

'Fantastic!' Cordelia said with a big smile.

'Fantastico,' I repeated. I saw Jess smirk as she noted down Florence's heartbeat on her anaesthetic monitoring sheet, and instantly I felt stupid.

Cordelia quickly scrubbed up and prepared to join me in the surgery. With the book open, we rotated the stomach anti-clockwise and prepared to suture it to the right hand side of the body wall.

'How are we going to do this?' Cordelia asked.

I didn't know. I pedalled back frantically through all the books I had read. I was months and months into this job now, but there were still a billion things I didn't know, including but not confined to, how to impress girls with car park fighting and dodgy Italian.

'I think belt loop gastropexy is the key,' I blurted out.

'You just read that, didn't you?' Cordelia asked me, smiling.

I shrugged, desperate for something to cling on to. 'It's the only technique that has pictures in the book,' I said.

Cordelia laughed – and, instantly, I felt a hundred times stronger. At last, I was even a tiny bit funny . . .

I peered into Florence's abdomen; the spleen was engorged and had a bluish tinge.

'That spleen doesn't look good,' I commented.

'I think we should take it out,' Cordelia said and looked at me questioningly.

'Controversial,' I replied. 'A lot of people say leave them in . . .'

'If it's damaged, it'll release micro-thrombi into the blood-stream and Florence could die,' Cordelia said. She was obviously better at memorising textbooks than me.

I peered hard at the spleen. It did indeed look much bigger than it should have done and had a swollen, unhealthy look to it.

'Have you ever taken a spleen out before?' Cordelia asked.

'Hundreds,' I replied earnestly. 'Dogs, cats, cows, the odd human being . . .'

'Well, do it now,' she said evenly.

I stepped back, only a fraction.

'It's a big job,' I mumbled.

'Then we'd better get on with it,' Cordelia quipped, a half smile playing on her lips.

'I don't want to fight about this,' I said.

'Good, or you'll lose more than just your shirt,' Cordelia said. This time she didn't seem to be joking – but, behind her, Jess still laughed.

I felt the colour rush to my cheeks.

Without further ado, we quickly set about performing a splenectomy. Working together, we carefully dissected around the blood vessels, tying off the ones we had to cut through and, with the spleen out, inserting the belt loop went smoothly. In silence we stitched up Florence and, feeling suddenly exhausted, we carried her to her kennel. Behind us, Jess started the clean-up procedure. Like washing up after a big dinner, it was the worst part of the operation.

'Quite a night,' Cordelia said as we laid Florence down.

'*Sì*,' I replied.

Cordelia bent and stroked the unconscious dog's head.

'You are rubbish at Italian,' she commented, without looking up.

I bent down to give Florence a gentle pat and check her drip.

'*E vero*,' I said.

I paused, glancing at the long line of stitches along Florence's abdomen.

'Sorry about the little scrap with Mr Partridge,' I began. I didn't mean to say it, but the words just tumbled out.

Cordelia laughed. 'You stopped him weeing on my car,' she said.

'There was a lot of wee going on there. I wonder how many cans he'd knocked back?'

'It was . . .' She fumbled for the word. '*Almost* chivalrous.'

'Will you have that drink with me sometime?' I blurted.

Cordelia looked at me. 'Will you promise not to get in any fights and not to take your shirt off on the high street?' she asked, unsmiling.

'The high street is safe, I promise.'

'*Suppongo di sì*,' she said. Then quickly, she turned on her heel and marched off to help Jess.

Giving Florence a final pat, I got my things together and readied to leave the practice.

It was almost dawn, I was exhausted, dirty and unkempt, and I had to get home. I wanted a shower, I wanted some food, I wanted some sleep. But – more than anything else – I wanted my Italian dictionary.

I had no idea what Cordelia had just said.

7

A GOOD START

'How are you finding it?' Holly asked me.

I looked at her with rings under my eyes, my hair standing on end and a small smear of toothpaste dried on the corner of my mouth.

'Moderately tiring,' I replied.

'When are you going to sleep?' she pressed me.

I crouched to squint at the duck in front of me. 'I will sleep when I'm dead . . .' I half-grinned.

The duck opened its beak as if to comment but thought better of it and blinked back at me. I stroked its head gently, waiting for the anaesthetic to take effect.

'No, my friend,' I reassured my trusting patient, 'you are going to sleep much sooner than that and you're not going to quack it . . .'

Holly put her hand to her mouth, starting to shake. Whether it was the state of me, the fact I was talking to a duck, or the terrible joke, I wasn't sure – but it wouldn't be a normal morning without Holly losing control.

'How about you?' I asked, raising my eyebrows conspiratorially. 'I hear you've taken on some really hardcore night work?'

That did it, she was off. It had been pretty good going, though. We'd almost had a straight minute's worth of conversation without Holly bursting into hysterics.

'Very funny,' she said, reining herself back. 'I'm loving it, but it's . . . sometimes a bit tougher than I thought it would be.'

'How so?' I asked. On the table, the duck's head started to weave from side to side.

'I had to attend an old man who had had a stroke this weekend,' she replied, placing a hand on the duck's back to steady it. 'It was my second night on call and it was really sad to see him like that, his independence suddenly wiped out in minutes.'

Free of her night duties at the practice, Holly had signed up to a voluntary group called First Responders. It was incredible that this bubbly, giggly girl would now be the front line for 999 emergencies in the rural area where she lived – but it was also hard to imagine anyone better to have on your side to keep your spirits up until the ambulance arrived.

The duck's head finally started to drop as Holly readied the anaesthetic machine.

'How does First Responders actually work?' I asked.

'When someone phones 999 from our area, we get bleeped and then we cover until the ambulance crew can get there,' Holly replied, placing an oxygen mask over the duck's beak as it lay down.

'You literally just drive round there?' I asked, somewhat incredulously. I was positive I wouldn't have a clue where to start if it were me.

'We go in pairs,' Holly replied. 'So I'm doing it with my dad at the moment.' She paused; this time she managed to strangle her laugh. 'He had his pyjamas on under his trousers last night, they were poking out the top!'

Holly's dad ran a local garage and I'd met him briefly when Holly's family came round to look at the practice one day. They all seemed like lovely people and it was easy to work out why Holly was always so cheerful. Her dad came across as a very practical, friendly man and I was vaguely aware that Holly had told me he and her brother also helped to run the local fire brigade for their village. I shook my head as I thought about it; the family clearly put others first and yet still had so much time for each other.

'So by day you book in ducks for me to operate on and by night you save lives?' I remarked. Holly was never to be underestimated, I thought to myself.

'You save lives every night, too – I only do it one in three!' Holly laughed.

I had just worked eleven nights straight as well as the weekdays at the practice. Mr Spotswode had finally given the go-ahead for me to trial the setting-up of a dedicated emergency service. It was exciting times – exhausting, but a brilliant opportunity for me. Buoyed by the successful outcome of Florence's operation, I was relishing the challenge of running the out-of-hours service. It was early days and I had yet to recruit other vets, but with everyone so utterly fed up with the on-call moving between different practices, I had to seize the day before someone else did. The deal was that I kept the money from clients seen out-of-hours but had to pay staff costs as well as rent. Furthermore, while I got it going, a percentage of everything I did went to the practice for drugs and medicines I used and, in return, they would provide me with back-up if I got really stuck.

I doubted my efforts at running the fledgling emergency service could even come close to Holly's heroics as a First Responder. For a start, I was grafting to get on in the world, while she was doing it as an altruistic calling. I also suspected I'd be a liability with a defibrillator, whereas Holly was now authorised to drive around with one in the back seat of her car.

'You know, I once helped make sure all the old ladies gave twenty pence to enter the cake sale at the local church. That's a ticket to heaven right there – I think you've got a raw deal trying to earn yours with all this First Responder business . . . You should have spoken to me, I could have saved you a heap of graft. They have regular cake sales!'

'If I wasn't a vet nurse, I think I would have become a paramedic,' Holly mused. 'Look, he's totally asleep now,' she went on, gently stroking the top of the duck's head. 'We'd better begin.'

I closed my eyes for a moment as a wave of nauseous fatigue washed over me.

'Are you feeling okay?' a voice said loudly, by my left ear.

I jumped. Over my shoulder, Rob loomed, his eyes fixed on the duck.

'What have you got on here, then?' he boomed.

'We have a delicate operation that Holly has kindly booked in for me,' I said, evasively. 'This is Fred. He's a ten-year-old drake and I'm going to sort him out . . .'

Rob took a step back, considering the way I was hunched and the way poor Fred was prepped.

'You have got to be kidding me?' he began. 'It's an eye, isn't it? You're going to remove another eye!'

I paused while readying a tray of instruments for the operation and took a deep breath.

'Look – do you want to do it?' I protested.

'You know what? You inspire me to learn more about eyes – like how to fix them. You are taking the ethos of being at the cutting edge of veterinary medicine a little too literally – curing animals doesn't revolve around chopping things out all the time!'

'It's *her* fault,' I said, pointing at Holly who was now starting to shake again.

'It's not normal for a vet to do this so often, you know. Just wait until your new girlfriend hears all about your worrying habits!'

I unwrapped a scalpel blade and dropped it with a clatter to the surface of the tray. Fred must have sensed it in his dreams, for momentarily he twitched.

Holly clapped her hands. 'Oh yes!' she shrieked. 'How's it going with Cordelia? Didn't you go on a date?'

'*One* date,' I said, shaking my head wearily. 'One date – we're not exactly an item, yet. I'm desperate for more, but I've just done a solid block of on-call and I'm on holiday next week. Not good . . .'

'He brings it on himself,' said Rob, circling the table and the unconscious drake. Holly nodded in agreement. 'How he thinks he can work two full-time jobs and still romance Cordelia is beyond me.'

'He's giving it a good try,' interjected Holly.

'What idiot agreed to cover for you at your new fancy emergency service whilst you're off on holiday, swanning around getting sunburnt? How do you think my personal life is going to fare?' Rob asked.

I threw him a dirty look and, sighing, he helped Holly carry Fred through to the operating theatre by ensuring the mask over his beak remained securely attached.

'Not a problem,' I said. 'I've got a locum vet all lined up to cover it, you've just got to do one night and manage it in case things go wrong . . .' I was lying, but Rob didn't need to know it. I needed that holiday, but all of my time had been taken up and I hadn't had a chance to figure out who would cover the emergency service yet. I made a mental note to get cover sorted after I had finished operating on Fred. 'All the ladies in the local area can breathe a big sigh of relief that you'll still be around most of the time,' I added.

'You need someone to help you run this service, Luke,' Rob said, sincere at last. 'You're going to kill yourself. Look, you know I'll help you if you get really stuck, but we have a large-animal rota as well, and you already owe me two nights for that.'

Rob was right; I had had to swap out of two nights on call for the large animal stuff because I didn't have cover for the small animal side of things. I wondered, once again, if I had taken on too much. Perhaps Mr Spotswode's scepticism had been well founded.

'Are you sure you don't want to come in with me?' I asked, perhaps more plaintive than I meant to be.

'If I did that, I'd run the risk of being as sad and lonely as you,' Rob replied, flashing a grin at Holly. 'Besides, you need me fresh to run the show whilst you're doing your zombie impression during your day job.'

'I am totally focused on my day job,' I replied, slipping my surgical gloves onto the wrong hands.

Rob was about to leap on me for my mistake when, suddenly, Mr Spotswode appeared in the operating theatre, Sheila at his side. The three of us looked up, hunched around the little drake. I frantically flipped the gloves round.

'Luke, I'll make this brief, as I can see you are about to operate,' Mr Spotswode began. Then, suddenly, he paused, looking at Fred's prostrate form. 'Luke,' he went on, 'are you cutting *another* eye out?'

Rob sniggered. 'It's good to have a specialty,' he whispered.

I looked at Mr Spotswode. 'It's ulcerated and there is a huge abscess in it,' I replied earnestly, desperately hoping my boss hadn't noticed the glove fiasco. 'It's causing him a lot of pain . . .'

'You've done a lot of these since you've been here, haven't you?'

Rob kicked Holly to stop her from laughing.

'A few,' I replied.

Mr Spotswode's eyes rolled, but he said nothing more.

'You all need to hear this before the gossip begins,' Mr Spotswode stated. 'Sheila here has just resigned from the practice.'

The silence was deafening. Rob and I stared hard at each other, and then at Sheila.

'Sheila,' I began, 'you can't be . . .'

'I'll let Sheila explain the detail,' Mr Spotswode said, 'but, put simply, she is coming to work with you, Luke. Sheila is going to be your Head Nurse at the emergency service.'

I elbowed Rob.

'Well, that's great for Luke,' he said, 'but who's going to be our Head Nurse?'

'It has yet to be decided,' Mr Spotswode replied. 'That drake looks like he might be coming out of that anaesthetic, Luke. Hadn't you better get a move on?'

Mr Spotswode turned on his heel and left us all standing there, mouths agape.

Sheila grinned and came forward to help us with the drake.

'It's just what I need, Luke,' she said, filling the hole left by our continuing silence. 'I've been needing a change for a long time, something to challenge me. I miss the emergencies more than I ever thought. My mother is a night shift worker – it's in my blood.'

'But you're going to have to work with Luke!' Rob exclaimed. 'All the time!'

'Well, not quite,' I chipped in with a huge grin on my face – it was the best news possible as far as I was concerned and Sheila grinned back at me. 'She's going to be working with you while I'm on holiday . . .'

I took up my scalpel and started my incision to remove poor Fred's eye.

The drizzle was getting worse as flickering rays of sun battled through heavy morning clouds. I squinted at the road ahead and flicked on the windscreen wipers. They twitched forward a few inches, only to stop, leaving the rain to thicken on the windscreen. I sighed and heard Sam softly chuckle beside me.

'I just can't believe you somehow talked me into this,' he said, shaking his head.

'You wanted somewhere exotic!' I replied.

'But not another flipping animal mission! Are you now an official crazy?'

We hit another pothole in the road, which sent us bouncing sideways.

'It's really hardcore, this one,' I replied.

'Just because you almost have a girlfriend you think you can do this sort of thing – some of us are playing the field and you are seriously hampering my credibility! Only saints or mentals pile off on crazy animal missions – and, let's be honest, Luke, neither you nor I are ever going to be taken for saints.'

'Speak for yourself. I'm spiritually pure,' I replied, swerving to one side in an effort to avoid a massive truck charging down the wrong side of the road towards us.

'Pure as an oil slick!' Sam yelled. 'Can this thing go any faster?'

'This jeep is a masterclass in roadworthiness,' I said. 'No door handles, the fan belt screams in pain with every gear change, no handbrake, no biting point on the clutch . . .' I turned to him and beamed. 'You want me to go faster?'

Sam huffed and stared out the window into the drizzle.

'What about the indicators?' he asked after a moment's pause.

I raised my hands off the steering wheel for a second and grinned.

'Your guess is as good as mine!'

Suddenly, we rounded a corner to face the oncoming glare of two sets of dazzling headlights about a hundred metres ahead.

'Luke!' Sam exclaimed. 'Luke, eyes on the road!'

Up ahead, two buses were running parallel towards us and the gap between them seemed to be about half the width of our vehicle. I banked to the left, but there was no room to squeeze through; I banked to the right, and the story was the same. Time was quickly running out, the two huge buses bearing down upon us. With a sudden intake of breath, I pushed the rickety old truck back into the middle of the road, leant hard on the horn and, half closing my eyes, aimed for the diminishing gap in the middle of the road ahead.

'Hang on!' I shouted, through gritted teeth.

The shrill blast of three horns stung through the air, but their piercing drill was smothered by the sound of Sam's manic laughter. Somehow, by a cat's whisker, we had passed between the two coaches and come out the other side.

'I think I've wet myself,' Sam gasped, still laughing and gripping his knees with both hands.

I have no idea how we made it but, pulling off at the next stop to check the guys who rode with us in the back of the truck were okay, it seemed that, as far as life-threatening episodes on Indian roads go, it was a minor one. The guys seemed to have hardly batted an eyelid as we skimmed between the buses and they cheerfully informed us that, to come through unscathed on this notoriously dangerous road between Coimbatore and Mavanella in southern India, was a minor miracle.

Sevar, a forest Tribal who was hanging onto the back of the jeep with one hand and balancing fifteen boxes and my pack on the roof with the other, giggled as he informed me in his broken English that we still had the hill section to come, with thirty-six hairpin bends in a two-mile stretch of downhill road. It was definitely the wrong time of day to be drenched in a cold nervous sweat.

'Where are we going again?' Sam said.

'To a place near Ooty, an old colonial town,' I replied, not wishing to confuse things by explaining we were actually going to a small village several miles away.

'I was supposed to pick this holiday,' Sam whined. 'After that Samos joke it was my turn – you must have got me at a moment of weakness.'

'Look,' I said. 'I promise this will beat the week you planned in Ibiza. You said you wanted exotic women? Well, India is exotic – you're halfway there!'

'India isn't a woman I can seduce with cheap beer!' Sam protested. 'Honestly, I am seriously re-thinking our relation-ship. It's getting ridiculous.' We settled back into the car, coaxed her into life and set off again. 'Remind me of this mission, Luke? I think I need to hear it one more time. You know, so that I'm spiritually fulfilled before we plunge off a mountain.'

I sighed and started the story again. A small network of animal charities had started emailing me for advice after word had spread about the Samos mission. Joeri, being a part of this group, had told everyone about our previous trip and, over the last few months, I had been collecting short-dated medicines, which I then sent out to places where they could do some good.

Quite out of the blue, I had been emailed by a group of American tourists who had been on holiday in India. Somehow they had found this charity network on the internet and appealed for help. A group of feral dogs had badly savaged a respected doctor in a remote part of India. The doctor was very influential in her local community; she and her husband owned the local hospital in which she was hospitalised for four weeks after the attack. The local township decided that action was needed and set aside some funds to pay per head for each dog killed and collected. Local groups of men had been unleashed on a brutal mission, armed with large wooden sticks and a bundle of intra-thoracic injections of magnesium sulphate to kill as many dogs as possible. They were little more than bounty hunters. One of the big problems with this was that the men were piling the bodies of the dead dogs by the side of the road and the rich American tourists who had been staying at the five star hotel in town, to visit the tigers in the local nature reserve, were understandably horrified. The tourists didn't get anywhere with their appeals to the local authorities and hotel management, but having contacted a small animal charity on the outskirts of the town called IPAN (India Project for Animals and Nature), they had started an international campaign to raise funding and volunteers which they planned to channel through IPAN in an effort to prevent the culling. It was this campaign that had somehow found its way to my inbox.

After replying to the email asking for more details, I had shown the story to Mr Spotswode who had approved it as a worthy mission and given me a few days' extra holiday and a large donation of medicines to take. I then received some donations from the American tourists to help fund the trip and, combined with a legacy from my grandmother – who had recently passed away and left me almost the exact sum of money required for a flight to India – I decided fate had a hand in things and phoned Sam.

'And you convinced me to cancel a week of sun, beer and skinny-dipping to head to an Indian slum with you!' he reminded me. 'This is honestly the last time, the absolute last time I am doing one of these trips with you. You need to be sectioned!'

'Look,' I replied, 'this is the ultimate holiday, no one does this sort of thing . . .'

'For good reason,' Sam replied. 'We're risking life and limb just driving, let alone grappling rabid dogs!'

'Your mum will be so proud of you,' I said.

'Keep my mother out of this.'

'I can't help it if your mum has a soft spot for me.' I grinned as Sam rolled his eyes.

'My mother thinks you and I are idiots. The only reason I'm here is because you promised to buy all my beer on this trip – and I'm holding you to that.'

'Consider yourself swimming in beer – after we've saved the dogs.'

I turned my attention to the road as we started our descent and the first hairpin bend approached.

'I'm closing my eyes for this next stretch,' Sam said, not rising to the bait.

'Me too,' I replied.

As we finally arrived at the shelter, I was pondering Nigel Otter, the man who ran the local charity IPAN and who was coordinating the mission on the ground. It was Nigel, an Anglo-Indian, fluent in Hindi, Tamil and English and raised in the Nilgiris, who had liaised with the American tourists and who had got us permission to come and work under the wing of his charity. Situated just outside the town, his shelter was in the foothills of the stunning Nilgiris mountains and bordered the national park, offering a sanctuary for all species of animals.

We'd met him at the airport in the early hours of the morning and he'd subsequently asked us to follow him on this little journey back to his shelter. Apparently his 'boys' didn't like driving and so I had been shown the driving seat. During our brief introduction it became clear that Nigel didn't do problems. He joked that I would be fine; he'd taught himself to drive on the Indian roads, after all, and it was easy compared to the UK.

Within about ten minutes, Nigel, knowing that sink-or-swim was the only way to learn to drive in India, had very wisely disappeared ahead of us and my directions had been shouted to me through the window from the boys in the back of the truck. Fighting waves of fatigue from the long night flight had been easy as adrenaline coursed through me at every bend, turn and junction. The little drive sounded such a simple request, but I may as well have been plunged into a bear pit for the good it was doing my nerves. I suspected it was just a taste of the challenges to come.

The schedule for the week promised to be fairly unforgiving, with the main focus on the dog neutering in the slum but the plan also included treating some of the villagers' sick animals first while we got to know everyone. Apparently, our trip to the town was destined to be a high profile mission as local TV and newspapers were poised to chart our every move. Nigel wanted to initiate us into the IPAN style of MASH clinics before we started.

It was now about 10 a.m. and we'd had about two hours' sleep in the last twenty-eight hours. We dropped our packs at the shelter and Nigel suggested a cup of tea to revitalise us whilst he outlined the plan for the day.

'There is just one thing,' he said, 'before we go round the shelter . . .'

Sam and I waited expectantly.

'There's a dog that has just come in,' he said, nervously. 'Can you look at it?'

'No problem,' I replied, standing up.

Beside me, Sam also dragged himself upright with a mumble.

'Here we go again,' he said under his breath.

The dog was a massive German shepherd, a breed we were both well used to treating. The big difference was that this particular dog had already lost the lower part of one of its back legs from a gangrenous snake bite, and the huge rotting stump had been smeared with a liberal helping of Tumeric to mask the smell. The poor dog was in agony and snapping at anyone that went near its leg.

'This is quite possibly the most horrible thing I have ever seen,' Sam commented as he bent down to look at the leg, the dog emitting a low growl through a tight piece of cloth wrapped around its muzzle.

My eyes watering with the overpowering smell of Tumeric and rotting leg, I murmured my agreement as Nigel came and stood beside me.

'Luke,' he said.

I turned around, grateful for a gulp of clean air.

'There's a cow that has a problem,' he said. 'Do you think you could look at it?'

Sam turned towards us.

'Good idea,' he said sarcastically. 'You head off to look at a nice little cow, I'll stay here and sort out the rotting stump of a killer German shepherd. In fact, you should both go, I don't need any help with this.'

Nigel nodded, happily. 'That's good,' he said. 'You stay here with Sevar and Luke can come with me to look at the cow.'

Sam's face took on a look of incredulous disbelief. Did Nigel not understand sarcasm? Flashing Sam a smile, I followed Nigel out of the door as Sam's mouth started to work like a fish.

Nigel gestured for me to get in the jeep and we drove out of the shelter, turned left and, two hundred metres further on, pulled up by the side of the road.

'The cow is just here. I know the family well,' Nigel said, as he pointed towards a small shack set in about twenty square metres of hard-packed dirt.

I got out of the car and peered towards the shack, just as an entire family filed out of the house and lined up outside the front door.

'Come, meet them,' Nigel said, leading the way and chatting a greeting to the family in Tamil.

The head of the household was a small tough man with greying black hair and sharp brown eyes, who stood barefoot as he discussed the cow's plight, his head bobbing from side to side.

Nigel seemed to be explaining who I was and, simultaneously, the whole family offered a greeting and beamed in my direction. I beamed back as Nigel pointed to the side of the house. Together, we set off.

I didn't need to take a detailed history to work out what was wrong. The collapsed cow had apparently slipped in a water trough and now couldn't get up – in large part, I deduced, because its leg was sticking out ninety degrees from where it should have been.

The family had worked this out for themselves and they clustered around the cow, which was chewing on long pieces of cut grass piled in front of it, pointing at its leg and its abdomen, talking at me in Tamil.

'Nigel, can you help me with what they are saying?' I asked, turning to see Nigel with his mobile phone pressed to his ear.

Nigel nodded at me and smiled as he continued his phone conversation.

I had no idea what I was supposed to do. There was no way this cow was going to stand. I was uncertain what Nigel might have told them about this strange English vet who had wandered into their midst. Back in England, there would have been only one thing to do with this cow. What on earth did everyone expect from me?

I patted the cow and examined its head to bide some time whilst Nigel finished his call. Two of Nigel's boys, friends of Sevar, headed over to Nigel as he rang off.

'They say they love the cow,' he said with an encouraging smile. 'It's sacred to them, you see, part of the family. Also, Luke – it's pregnant.' He paused, clicking his heels together. 'Luke,' he went on, 'I have to go – there's a problem I need to attend to. I'll leave you with two of my boys, I'll only be half an hour.' He knelt down and patted me on the back. 'Do what you can,' he said and with a final, flourishing wave, he turned and marched back to the jeep.

It was my turn for my mouth to work like a fish. The two

boys Nigel had assigned to me beamed big smiles – and then a panicky thought dawned in my mind.

'Does anyone speak English?' I asked.

A bank of smiling faces looked back and then they all started replying in fluent Tamil.

As a bucket of water and a bar of soap was brought to me, I resolved to work out exactly how pregnant the cow was. A half-baked plan started to formulate in my head; the family regarded this cow as one of the family, and so I needed to treat it as such.

I rolled up my sleeve, soaked my arm in the water and lathered up with soap. To the amazement of all the spectators, I then proceeded to determine how far in calf the cow was. The children giggled, the men looked agog and the women beamed with amusement. My arm came out a sticky brown and two more buckets of water rapidly appeared from nowhere. Excited chattering filled my ears, but at least I now knew the cow was at term and due to calve any day. If we could somehow support her, induce the calf, then maybe, just maybe, we could splint the leg so it could heal. I had antibiotics and pain relief in my bag – I'd never tried to fix a cow's broken leg before and the logistics of attempting something like this on a big animal made it more difficult, but as long as she was out of pain, I was happy to give it a go.

I smiled at my audience and then tried to describe what I wanted us to do. I pointed at the leg and mimicked bandaging it. Then, I held my leg out straight as if rigidly fixed and hobbled about with a straight leg. If there had been any confusion to my sanity to start with, the matter was no longer one for debate. Everyone started laughing, the children copying me in my ridiculous hobbling action. Even Nigel's boys were maniacally grinning. Too late, I realised that I too was laughing as I danced crazily around the yard. Only the cow seemed unimpressed, chewing on her cud and looking at me as if I were the village idiot.

As the laughter continued, items started appearing – someone brought another pile of grass for the cow, one of Nigel's boys materialised with a bag full of cotton wool and bandages, sticks started to pile up, and I picked the axe up to attempt to cut down some bamboo from a cluster of small trees across the road.

My cunning plan was to rig up a splint of bamboo, bandage the cow, get it up and hope it would be able to support its own weight. Enthusiastically wielding the axe, I started to hack at the bamboo. Quickly proving to be as adept at this as a one-armed monkey, one of Nigel's boys very politely stepped forward and, gently placing his hand on the axe, removed all sharp implements out of my reach. Two seconds later, a fifteen-foot section of six inch thick bamboo was placed at my feet.

Splicing it up accordingly – or, rather, indicating how I wanted the bamboo to be spliced up accordingly – we eventually rigged up a two-sided splint with bamboo. Grappling things into position with the father of the family, we managed to strap it either side of the leg and pad it out with wads of cotton wool.

Excitement mounted as Nigel returned to observe my handy work, a big grin on his face. In front of the shack the cow was still nonchalantly chewing on its cud with a huge splinted bright green dressing around its leg.

'You've been busy,' Nigel said, smiling as the family chatted away.

I stood up, dusting down my hands. 'If we can induce it to calve, it'll be lighter and might just be able to stand,' I replied, wiping a sheen of sweat from my forehead.

'They told me you examined the cow quite thoroughly!' Nigel laughed.

'Well, it was a bit tricky to ask how far in calf it is,' I said, a touch defensively. 'My Tamil needs a bit of work.'

'It's a good thing,' Nigel said reassuringly. 'They are all very impressed.'

'Sorry,' I said to Nigel apologetically, 'just hoping this is going to work!'

'Time to stand her up?'

I nodded and Nigel directed his boys to come and give us a hand. Half the family stepped forward to assist. Together, ten of us put our arms under the cow. As we carefully lifted her to her feet, she didn't bat an eyelid, lowing only when she could no longer reach the mound of cud.

So far, so good I thought. The splint looked to be supporting the leg and the cow seemed comfortable. If only she would stand by herself . . .

'Luke, I think you should come and see this,' Nigel said.

He was standing on the opposite side of the cow to me. Someone stepped forward to take my place and, as I walked around to Nigel, my heart sank.

'This leg is also not good Luke.'

I felt ridiculous. I hadn't even thought to check the other back leg, which had been tucked under the cow. It was hanging limp. I felt for the break and, sure enough, it too was broken.

'No one mentioned this leg was also damaged,' I said to no one in particular, vaguely trying to justify my stupidity in not having done a thorough examination.

I took a deep breath. Everyone looked at me and I got the feeling that they were feeling almost as sorry for me as they did for the cow.

'I'm sorry,' I said to Nigel. 'Please tell everyone to gently put the cow back on the ground. I should have checked this other leg before we started the splint.' I paused. Sometimes I really hated this job. 'It won't manage with two broken back-legs.'

Nigel nodded and translated. A chorus of murmurs rose in the background as I racked my brains as to what we could do. I remembered bitterly the puppies on Samos, the hundreds and hundreds of cows and sheep we had slaughtered when Foot and Mouth raged across the countryside. I braced myself for what had to be done.

'Nigel,' I said. 'There is nothing I can do for this cow. One broken leg, and perhaps we could have . . . come to an arrangement. Two, and . . .'

Nigel shook his head sadly. 'I understand, Luke. They understand as well. They'll feed and water it here, very sad . . .' He paused, listened to the Tamil chattering, then turned to me once more. 'They say when it fell in the water trough, its back legs went apart and broke. They know it will die, Luke, but it is sacred, so they cannot kill it.'

I looked back at the unfortunate beast. Oddly, it still looked content. 'But it won't be able to calve like this,' I protested. 'Soon enough, it's going to get pressure sores, the legs will ache and the cow will be in terrible pain. We can't just leave her lying there like that.'

Nigel looked at me sympathetically. 'No one wants to see it suffer, Luke, but they cannot kill it.'

It was a terrible dilemma. Although the cow looked comfortable enough right now, not being able to turn itself, she would be lying in her own muck before the day was out, her legs swollen and painful, infection beginning to set in.

The family stood around the cow, murmuring to each

other and gently patting it in turn. It was clearly a much-loved pet as much as an economic mainstay. It suddenly struck me that the farmers back home got upset if one cow died – and they had herds of over two hundred animals; this family had three cows and this was the only one in calf – this was a catastrophe for them on a massive scale. Without it, they would have no milk to sell or drink and no calf to rear up to expand their small herd.

With an arm around Nigel, I quickly escorted him away from the cow.

'Nigel, I want to buy the cow off them,' I blurted out. I didn't know why I was whispering; nobody could understand a word I said.

Nigel looked at me calmly. 'Why would you do that?' he asked.

Perhaps it didn't make sense but I knew, with a sudden adamancy, it was what I was going to do.

'If I buy it, it helps them out, right? And, Nigel . . . if I buy it, I can kill it, and they won't have to have done anything wrong.'

'Yes, but Luke . . .'

'I spare it a slow death,' I said. 'And, well . . .' It was here that I came unstuck. I paused momentarily, gathering my whirlwind of thoughts. 'Look,' I tentatively began. 'The calf is almost to term, right?'

'Right.'

'So I might be able to cut it out,' I said, my mind racing with the probabilities. They weren't great, but I figured that it was worth a go; we had nothing to lose.

'Cut it out?' Nigel asked. 'Once you've shot its mother?'

'There's no religious problem with them selling me the cow is there?' I asked.

Nigel smiled.

I thrust my hand into my pocket for some rupees. 'How much is a cow?'

Nigel didn't say anything but examined the rupees I clutched. Taking a thousand rupee note, he nodded to me and turned back towards the family, beckoning the father to walk with him a little way.

Everyone must have realised what was happening because, suddenly, beaming smiles fixed on me from all angles. I was drowning under those grins when Nigel returned with the father of the family. With gestures, they took me to one side.

'You now own this cow,' Nigel said. 'The family would like to thank you.'

I nodded at the father who clasped my hand. Embarrassed, I smiled my thanks to him.

I was the proud owner of my first ever cow – and it even had two broken legs!

'You've bought a cow?' Sam exclaimed.

'Yes,' I replied. He had spent three hours operating to remove the rotten stump of the snakebitten German shepherd – and, to be frank, it was showing. His face glistened with sweat and his eyes were drawn. I bet he was dreaming of being in Ibiza . . .

'So whilst I have been battling against the odds to try to remove the most infected, disgusting rotten stump of a back leg I have ever seen, you've been buying livestock? Dare I ask why?'

'You've done an amazing job on it,' I said. A beautifully neat wound was stitched over where the horrible stump had been removed.

'Never mind the leg!' Sam sighed. 'That's sorted . . .' He

paused. 'Not, of course, that I could have done with a hand or anything. I mean – key thing to nip out and go shopping during times of animal emergency. Just out of curiosity, how did you pay for the cow?'

'Oh, I didn't use the money for the dogs, I used . . .'

'You used our money that we changed at the airport, didn't you? You spent our beer money on an Indian cow!'

'Not *all* our beer money.'

Sam raised an eyebrow.

'I used some of our souvenir money too.'

Sam was aghast. 'Some people buy puppies to take home to their family, you buy an Indian cow! This better be a special cow!'

'It is special,' I said. 'It cost a thousand rupees.' I rattled through the next words. 'Oh, and it has two broken back legs.'

Sam's eyes widened.

'A thousand rupees?' he repeated.

'Yes, a thousand rupees,' I replied.

'A thousand rupees, £12, $17 – doesn't matter how you look at it, that's about ten beers over here! I suppose the broken legs were a unique feature you just couldn't resist?'

'Something like that,' I replied. 'You see, Sam, we're . . . How do I say this?' I stopped, seeing Sam's ire rise. 'We're going to shoot it and cut an almost to term calf out of its uterus,' I concluded.

Sam's jaw dropped.

'I need you to help me. Nigel has an old captive bolt here for emergency euthanasia and I'm going to give it a quick clean and service. Then we can sedate the cow and move it down here.'

'To shoot it and cut it open?'

Sam looked at me through a haze of fatigue and disbelief. Then – just as I'd known he would – he started nodding in weary acceptance and patting the German Shepherd. It was just about waking from its anaesthetic, and its tongue lolled out sadly.

'About rounds off the day,' he murmured and followed me out of the door.

Nigel was waiting by the side of a large pick-up truck when we got back to the cow. The family, incredibly pleased to see I had brought a friend, couldn't do enough to help us. As the sedative kicked in, they helped us load her into the pick-up and, lost in a hundred different farewells, we set off on the short journey back to the shelter.

'Have you done this before?' Nigel asked me.

'Shooting, yes,' I replied candidly. 'Caesareans, yes . . .'

'Just never at the same time,' shrugged Sam.

Nigel was quiet a moment.

'You will need to be fast,' he said.

'Yes,' I said.

'Is this calf going to survive?' Sam enquired. 'Bit of a brutal entry into the world isn't it?'

Both Nigel and I turned to look at Sam, who raised his hands in resignation.

'I think it's a brilliant idea,' he said. 'Forgive me for asking stupid questions.'

I suddenly grinned at Sam. The rings under his eyes, the fact he had worked tirelessly to help the dog, the very fact that he had trekked out to help me in India after the time we had spent in Samos . . . I felt a sudden warmth towards my best friend. He would always see me right if I was in a fix.

'Don't get any weirder on me,' Sam said, returning my

grin. 'You are already beyond the realms of normal weirdness and now you have a demonic grin on your face.'

Back at the shelter, we worked to lift the prostrate cow out of the truck. I could tell that the sedatives were beginning to wear off, but she wouldn't have to suffer any longer. I drained a tin cup full of water and looked around.

In moments, Sevar, Nigel and the boys standing around us were all laughing. I wasn't quite sure who was laughing at whom, or if we were all simply laughing at the ridiculous situation we were in, but it helped immeasurably. I knew, then, without a doubt, that we were doing the right thing.

As the laughter subsided, I took up our gun, slipped a cartridge into the captive bolt and took aim at the poor cow's head.

She had a glazed expression in her eye. She lay in the yard on a layer of straw, exactly the best place for her. It was the last thing she ever knew. Without words, I squeezed off the shot – for a second I hated myself for having such well-practised ease – and then, dropping the gun, I raced to her left side, lifted my knife, and sliced deep into her flank.

There was no hesitation as I cut into her abdomen. The cow had died instantly, her eyes fixed and dilated as I tore into her uterus and grabbed one of the calf's hind legs. Pulling hard, I lifted the entire calf out in a swift movement, a surge of power coursing through me as I wrapped both arms under the small form and lowered it to the straw.

The calf was wet and warm. I cleared mucus from its mouth and felt for a heartbeat. It was there. Clasping a piece of straw, I gently introduced it into its nostril.

'It's alive!' Sam exclaimed.

Sure enough, the calf sneezed and a new life had entered the world.

Nigel stepped back. The first darkness of dusk was just descending, and a cool breeze blew across the scrub.

'Good start,' Nigel said softly, 'good start.'

8

ELEPHANT KISSES

The night passed fitfully, a few hours seemed like minutes. After shooting the cow, Sam and I had retreated to our allocated room with a new addition to our little gang. We had taken the orphaned calf with us.

Now we were once again all awake, and dawn was breaking. Sam looked at me from his bed, bleary eyed with a blank expression. His face was lined, pale as a ghost.

'It's still alive,' he breathed, as the sound of the calf's incessant bleating echoed around the room.

'Definitely alive and definitely hungry,' I replied, casting a look at the pile of straw at the foot of my bed. The calf's little head swivelled, looked straight at Sam and bleated in agreement.

'Your turn,' I said, pushing my head back onto the hard pillow.

Before turning in that night we had stripped as much colostrum as we'd been able from the dead cow's udder, and supplemented it with normal cow's milk. It was the most nutritious thing the calf could be drinking, and would give it the best possible start but we had to be awake to feed it every two hours throughout its first night. Keeping the calf warm, fed and close at hand meant we could give it a fighting chance. It was the least she deserved after such an abrupt entry into the world.

Sam grunted, heaved himself off his bed and shuffled across the room. The calf nudged him as he approached.

'Woah, steady girl,' Sam said as he adjusted the teat end on the bottle before the calf started to greedily suck it down. 'Give me a second!'

A knock sounded at the door.

'Luke, Sam, are you ready?' Nigel's voice politely asked.

'Almost,' I replied.

'Good,' Nigel replied from the other side. 'We'll leave in about ten minutes, okay?'

'No problem,' I said as Nigel's footsteps receded from the doorway.

'Nice shower by the way – definitely going to wake you up . . .' Sam commented as the calf finished the bottle.

Hauling myself out of bed, I padded through the open archway to find the shower. A bucket of cold water was balanced next to the toilet.

'Time to wake up,' I said with false conviction. Promptly, I tipped the bucket over my head in one swift motion. I couldn't help the practically sub-human cry that erupted from my lips and which must have been heard as far away as Pakistan.

I heard Sam laughing in the room next door.

'When did you shower this morning?' I asked.

'You already know the answer to that one,' Sam chuckled.

'No wonder you don't have a girlfriend.'

'No wonder you're destined for a mental institution by the time you're thirty-five,' Sam replied.

We gave the calf a helping hand to stand up and the three of us shuffled into the morning light, ready as we would ever be to face our second day in this strange land.

The Doctor stood on a chair, leaning over the anaesthetised dog, and peered into the wound.

'Look, you push the other testicle up from the scrotum towards the incision,' Sam said, more than a little exasperated by his protégé. 'No, don't wipe it, you dab the swab! If you wipe the blood you dislodge any clots forming and it will keep bleeding! I've told you this about twenty times!'

We were on our second day of operations and word had spread like fever throughout the local community. A television crew had fleetingly stopped by to film us hard at work, several newspaper journalists had interviewed Nigel about our rabies prevention programme and the crowd, which had grown steadily since our arrival, formed a near perfect semicircle as we cracked on with an endless stream of bitch spays and dog castrations.

Sam's assigned task was to train up an Indian vet known only as 'the Doctor'. Technically, his presence allowed us to work legally – we needed to be under the supervision of an Indian vet in order to satisfy Government officials – but, while he was theoretically in charge, he had only just qualified and needed a crash course in how to operate. Having been impressed by Sam's surgery the previous evening, Nigel had asked Sam to tutor him.

The Doctor, who was about five feet tall, had to stand on a chair to see what he was doing. With a smile big enough to split his face, he beamed at his tutor. With each command he had to repeat, Sam's voice climbed higher and higher in pitch but the Doctor, infuriating Sam, only beamed some more.

My job, meanwhile, was to power through the basic surgeries, neutering animal after animal, working with Sevar as my assistant. Sevar spoke fairly good English and he chuckled and laughed throughout the day, about what I had no idea but as long as I was keeping him happy, I didn't mind. A team of twelve boys, all under Nigel's tutelage, scurried about preparing dogs for surgery. Sevar and I leapt from one to the next like men possessed, in an eternal crusade of castration and vaccination.

'Where are all the boys from?' I asked Sevar as he unpacked the next bitch spay kit.

'We are all from the forest,' Sevar replied casually. 'We live near the shelter, we stay or go depending on what needs to be done.'

'How many people does Nigel employ?'

'As many as we need,' Sevar said, pausing for a moment as he carefully phrased his next sentence. 'He is a very good boss, like family. If we are sick, he helps us, looks after our families. Always looks out for us. He is a very good boss.'

Although we'd been there only a short time, it was very clear that the 'boys' were utterly loyal to Nigel. They were all in their late twenties or early thirties, a tough bunch of capable characters. They didn't seem to mix with the crowds that gathered to watch us, and if anything, were given space as they passed through them. I had a sketchy understanding of their background – being Tribals meant they were outside the caste system. They were an indigenous people who kept themselves to themselves and lived in the forests and mountains of the Nilgiris, and were regarded as outsiders by the townsfolk.

I was about to make an incision when Sam's voice once again rang out around the operating area.

'No, I said don't wipe it! You dab – see, dab, dab, dab!' Sam exclaimed, prodding the Doctor with his finger.

The Doctor, with skin thicker than an elephant's, nodded and beamed irrepressibly.

'Dab, like this, dab dab, dab,' Sam continued.

'The Doctor, he likes Sam very much I think,' Sevar said, chortling away as he watched Sam take the Doctor's hand and mimic the dabbing action.

'I think the Doctor is going to have to get the hang of dabbing if their relationship is going to continue,' I said.

'Oh yes, he understands now,' Sevar said approvingly as Sam's voice once again echoed out.

'Thank God. You've got it. Dabbing. Finally!'

I turned back to the bitch lying in front of me.

'How many have we done?' I asked.

'About seventy, I think,' Sevar replied, bobbing his head cheerfully from side to side. 'But we have plenty more yet . . .'

Behind us, another batch of dogs arrived in the back of the jeep.

'They seem very calm,' I remarked. The dogs waited patiently in the back of the jeep, a piece of cloth tied firmly around each of their muzzles.

Nigel materialised from the surrounding chaos to lean over the operating table.

'They are calm when they are caught – not before! They are very good with each other, they are social animals, all from the same pack,' he said, watching me tie off the cervix of the bitch I was operating on and then start to close her back up.

'You should go with them to catch some dogs,' Sevar chipped in. 'It is quite an experience.'

I had had experience catching wild dogs before, but somehow, the thought of traipsing up a hill with a bitch-in-heat, followed by these particular wild dogs did not fill me with pleasure.

'Why don't you go with Nagresh to catch the next batch?' Nigel asked.

I finished stitching up the dog and, glancing across at Sam, still trying to show the Doctor the basics of neutering, I stifled a laugh. The Doctor had placed a headlamp on his head, which kept slipping down to his nose and Sam was trying to adjust it without much success.

'Sam is a bit busy at the moment,' I said, 'but I think he'd like to go too.'

'Haha! I think Sam has indeed got his hands full.'

I looked back. From out of nowhere, another dog was scrabbling at the Doctor's behind. Sam flung his instruments to his table and harried the dog away.

'Okay,' I said, peeling off my gloves. 'Where do we start?'

I followed Nigel across the compound. Around us, his boys were bundling the newest arrivals into their enclosures. The dogs seemed to obey them instinctively and seemed at ease being carried about.

'They're very good with the animals,' I said as we hurried to the keep.

'They are natural,' Nigel replied, weaving his head from side to side as he explained. 'These people, you cannot find others like them with this work. In the forest they can track anything; they climb trees like you wouldn't believe – no ropes, just bare feet. They are unique. Nagresh, he is very good. You will learn lots from this.' Nigel stopped. 'These boys don't speak English,' he went on. 'You would do well to watch for the directions. It can be a bit dangerous and . . .' He paused, looking for the word. 'Quite dirty.'

I didn't have a chance to ask Nigel exactly what he meant by dangerous and dirty because the next moment, we were standing in front of Nagresh. The short man smiled up at me warmly and, without words, firmly directed me to climb into the back of the jeep. Three other boys hopped in after me, one carrying a long pole and the others holding what looked like wire leads.

'You use wire leads?' I asked, eager for something to say.

Nagresh looked back from the front seat and simply smiled again. Around me, the boys started to laugh.

As we pulled out of the compound, I gave Sam a cheery wave. To the great amusement of the boys sitting with me, he looked back with an expression of mock despair.

We started down the hill away from the compound and the crush of traffic was terrifying. Taking evasive action to swerve around a large cow calmly chewing cud in the middle of the road, Nagresh steered us directly across the oncoming traffic. Horns blared out on all sides and, without batting an eyelid, he pulled up. We had parked beside a bridge spanning the muddy river that flowed into the heart of town.

As we dismounted from the jeep, Nagresh gave directions to his team. He was clearly going to go first; I was then to be flanked by two of the other boys, whilst the third remained with the vehicle. I looked about, bewildered. I couldn't see how street dogs would be anywhere near such a busy road. Then, Nagresh edged between two stalls on the side of the street and we started to drop down steep steps, under the bridge and away from the incessant bleating of horns.

The smell hit me about halfway down and, for the first

time, I could see the sprawl of shacks and the full extent of the slum lining the riverbank, stretching out of sight towards the heart of the town. It was the area that everyone tried to avoid and, as such, it was a dominion of its own. Hands appeared, groping out from each side, and suddenly Nigel's boys crowded close, barking out commands I couldn't understand. Oblivious to their own safety, they balanced on the edge of each chipped and broken concrete slab, determined to make sure I didn't trip or fall.

Feeling like a total hindrance to my companions, some sort of giant baby that couldn't be trusted to take a single step without help, I finally reached the bottom. Around us, the slum was a patchwork quilt of corrugated crooked roofs. The shacks were held together with tin, plastic, cardboard and whatever other materials the occupants had managed to scavenge and ingeniously weave into their walls. People clustered around open cooking pots and a well trodden path snaked from the bottom of the steps into the depths of beyond.

Purposefully, we followed Nagresh towards the river. Soft sibilant sounds emanated out to us from the surrounding shacks. For a moment I could barely believe we were in the same town, only metres below the living breathing city. Down here, the makeshift streets were teeming and, as we walked among the dilapidated homes, there was a definite sense of cohesion in this community that had slipped through the cracks. Faces peered at us as we walked around but Nagresh and his boys were clearly approved visitors. Residents called out and directed us with helpful gestures to tell us where the dogs were located. Children dressed in scraps of rag skipped behind us and wide eyes watched me lumber amongst the homes, totally disorientated.

Slum dogs were supposed to be the most dangerous dogs to approach – packs of animals that scavenged on the waste of these dwellings. They served a useful purpose in hunting vermin and warning slum dwellers if strangers were in their midst, but they had a reputation for ferociousness and, after dark, they effectively sealed off the boundaries of the slum. It was these dogs that were truly feared by the people of the town above and, although the men working for the local government had been able to catch and kill some of the friendly stray dogs that lived about town, they had never dared to risk catching any of the slum animals.

Nigel had told me that a small minority of slum residents wouldn't approve of any sort of neutering because they needed the dogs to breed so they could take away their puppies and sell them, but they were few in number and no one seemed to object as we went deep into the heart of the shacks.

At last, we reached the banks of the thick brown river. The smell was stinging my eyes as Nagresh held up his hand. Wrapping a thin wire loop around his waist, he made two flicking motions with his hand. My companions promptly disappeared. Alone, I stood only ten feet behind him, unsure of what to do next.

It was then I saw his target. A large black-and-tan dog, stocky and scarred, stood frozen at the edge of the river-bank. Clearly sensing something was amiss, it darted quick looks at Nagresh as it moved its head around, weighing up which direction to run. With the wire lead still held round his waist, Nagresh moved forward. Instantly, the dog turned as if to flee – only to find one of the boys blocking its retreat. Quickly, it turned again to run in the only remaining direction available. Somehow, the other boy had got there first.

Realising it was trapped, the dog growled, its hackles rising. There was only one option left. It sprang forward and hurtled straight toward Nagresh.

Moving with a feline agility, Nagresh twisted sideways to allow the dog the option of running by him and directly towards me. The dog, recognising a soft target when he saw one, didn't hesitate and took his chance. It was my turn to freeze. The dog was bearing down, I was suddenly the last line of defence against a large feral slum dog, and I had no idea what the boys expected of me. Was I simply to offer my arm as bait and try to wrestle the dog to the ground as it clamped on?

As the dog darted through the gap, Nagresh's hand suddenly let fly the thin wire lead that had been looped round his waist. It whipped out as a lasso, skilfully wrapping itself around the dog's back leg.

The dog snarled and reared back with snapping teeth but before it could lunge, another wire was around it. Suddenly, the catching pole appeared from nowhere and fell around its neck. The dog thrashed, momentarily throwing the two boys off balance but, quick as lightning, Nagresh hurled himself onto its back and wrapped a strap of cloth around its muzzle. It had taken about twenty seconds and the dog, knowing it was well and truly trussed, finally gave up. Wild eyed, it lay there, eyes fixed on me as if to accuse me of something terrible.

Nagresh flashed me a brilliant white smile.

Releasing his wire loop, he indicated for one of the boys to carry the dog up to the truck and then we were off again to catch another. Within the hour, eight dogs were in the back of the vehicle. I could only stand and watch, marvelling at the technique. Nagresh and his boys were like a pack of prehistoric hunters, or wolves taking down a bison; an expert squad of dog catchers, the like of which I'd never seen.

When we returned to the neutering camp, carrying the spoils of our expedition, Sam was busy operating and the Doctor was having a go at his first solo castration.

'Did you have a nice trip?' Sam asked as I tumbled out of the jeep.

'You have to see these guys in action,' I replied. 'It's incredible.'

'No,' said Sam. 'What's really incredible is that the Doctor knows how to dab.'

Hearing the comment, the Doctor looked up and beamed that face-splitting smile at me.

'You're imparting some advanced surgical techniques,' I grinned.

'I'm imparting quality hard-earned holiday time to work in an Indian slum whilst you jolly about buying cows and sightseeing,' Sam replied.

Giving Sam a cheerful thumbs-up, I found Nigel on the phone, pacing up and down the side of the compound, an excited gleam in his eye. He caught sight of me and gave a big smile. Hanging up his phone he turned to talk to me.

'Luke, they have stopped the culling policy!' he exclaimed.

'Already?'

He practically danced around.

'Isn't it wonderful?' he began. 'The papers wrote about our work, the television crew showed us on the local news, and they have agreed that vaccination and neutering is a better way to do this! They will not pay for any more culled dogs.'

'That *is* wonderful!' I said.

Nigel shook his head from side to side as he spoke, clearly

delighted with the call. 'This is everything we hoped for. I have another meeting with the authorities this afternoon, but we will set up a programme here and help manage all the dogs. Over seventy dogs in two days – a very good start!'

Nagresh and Sevar came over to stand with us and Nigel told them the good news. With a big whoop, Nagresh called out the information to the rest of the boys.

Lost in the cheering, Nigel put an arm around me and took me to one side.

'Luke,' he began. 'There is one more thing – can you come to the meeting with me? It would be very helpful in writing the declaration and I can introduce you to the local Government officials.'

I threw a look back at Sam. I didn't have to think too hard to know what expression would be on his face if he caught me driving off again. I shrugged and looked back at Nigel. 'Let's roll,' I said.

'I took the liberty of grabbing some medicines from your supplies, I hope you don't mind.'

I paused. I wondered what sort of offices we were going to be visiting where we needed a load of medical supplies.

'Come on,' Nigel said. 'Before it gets too late.'

We hurried past Nagresh, the dogs and the boys, cleverly circumventing Sam and the Doctor who was gearing up for another spay operation, and climbed back into the jeep. As we pulled away, the traffic was as bad as ever. Nigel carved through the oncoming vehicles and forced his way into a lane.

'The calf is doing very well,' Nigel said, slamming the jeep into a gap between two oncoming cars. 'We will give her back to the family if you agree?'

'Sounds an excellent plan,' I replied. 'Although,

technically I should sell her back to them. I think two-thousand rupees, don't you?'

Nigel looked at me, his eyes furrowing. It took a moment of horrible silence until he realised I was joking.

'A good return on your investment!' he laughed. 'They will be overjoyed to have the calf healthy, you have really helped that family – they are very deserving people I think.'

'How is the dog doing?' I asked.

Nigel shook his head sadly.

'The dog is not so good,' he admitted. 'Luke, she passed away in the night. There was no pain but the poison was in her blood and it was left a very long time. It is a great shame.'

I was silent.

'I thought the surgery was perfect,' Nigel commented.

'Sam will be crushed,' I said.

Suddenly, we veered off the road. Only a moment later a temple loomed in front of us; it certainly didn't look like the sort of office any Government officials would reside in.

'Where are we going?' I asked. Nigel hit the brake and guided the jeep between two small, stubby trees to rest outside the temple. 'I thought we were going to some offices.'

'All in good time,' Nigel replied. 'Just this one stop first, we take a look and see what we can do.'

Climbing out of the jeep, I looked up at the huge Hindu temple and wondered what on earth we could be doing here. Guessing that the temple must have had some dogs that needed treatment, I grabbed the box of medicines Nigel had packed and quickly followed him across the hard-packed earth.

'You see,' Nigel began as we walked down the side of the main temple towards the outbuilding behind, 'the elephant is most sacred.'

I stopped but Nigel carried on walking, and I hurried to catch up.

'Elephants?' I said. 'I've never . . .'

'You can treat a cow, you can treat an elephant.'

I was still lagging some way behind and scurried to keep up.

'That's not exactly true,' I said.

'They represent Lord Ganesh,' Nigel explained. 'One of the Hindu faith's most important gods. They are often hired by smaller temples on festival days but bigger temples, such as this, have their own elephants.'

A small shot of adrenaline coursed into my veins. I had come here to treat street dogs, not to lay hands upon an elephant.

'You see,' Nigel went on, 'I feel very sorry for temple elephants. They are no better than captive elephants and they are all sentient, social animals. The mahout will establish their control of the animal with systematic beating when the elephants are young. The elephants, they learn their place and the mahouts then control them. It really is very hard.'

'I thought they were all well looked after?' I asked.

Nigel looked over his shoulder with an expression of anguish.

'They are never truly domesticated,' he said. 'How could they be? The mahout, he must be with the elephant all the time. These temple elephants, they stand on hot tarmac all day, they do not hear the call of their brothers. It is a very bad life. They have no stimulation and are chained, surrounded by noise, pollution and crowds. The mahout has no veterinary training to attend to them so they suffer very badly. The mahouts can be good or bad people but they are always just making money out of the animal.'

I was surprised by Nigel's damning viewpoint. Perhaps it was my own naivety, but I had always assumed that temple elephants would get the best of everything.

'The mahout will typically take half the money the elephant makes from the blessings it gives, the other half goes to the temple. It is a terrible business for the elephants. Often captive elephants crippled in logging camps will be sold for this purpose. Very stressful life for beautiful animals, it makes my heart cry, truly.'

We rounded the back of the temple. All around us was silence; I couldn't believe we were only a few hundred yards from the chaos of traffic and screaming cars.

'This animal here is suffering and they phoned me to come and look at it. I have been before to try to help it and it is very sad. It is a difficult thing, Luke, but we need to keep these people on side. Were it up to me, they would not have elephants like this but they are very important in the community so we will do what we can for the elephant and we cannot lecture them too much.'

At last, we came to the enclosure at the rear of the temple. The elephant stood with its mahout on a concrete pad with loosely scattered straw around its feet. Tentatively, we approached. The elephant had big sad eyes, but he didn't once look at either of us as we approached.

Nigel introduced me to the mahout and his assistant, who grinned and indicated the elephant in front of them, as if I might have missed the three-tonne beast.

I flashed a look at Nigel. I had rarely seen elephants, let alone been up close to them.

As I walked forwards, the mahout barked a command and a large grey trunk swung up and touched me on the top of my head, then on the face before being lowered again. I froze, unsure what to do or say. Although Indian elephants are much smaller than their African cousins, it was still a huge animal that dwarfed me and one I didn't know how to read at all.

'You have just been blessed,' Nigel said.

'A big wet elephant kiss,' I smiled apprehensively, 'I feel special.'

'That is how they spread tuberculosis,' Nigel commented as an afterthought. 'It is a big problem in India.'

'Nice to know,' I replied with a slight shake of my head. 'You rarely get a kiss for free.'

Nigel smiled. 'People pay a lot for those blessings, it is an honour.'

'Well, consider me honoured.' I pressed forward, my entire vision blocked by a big wall of wrinkly grey. 'What am I supposed to be looking at exactly?' I asked.

'Firstly, he wants to know if she is pregnant,' Nigel said.

I looked at Nigel and the mahout, who both returned my gaze expectantly. I had not the faintest idea how to tell if the elephant was pregnant. A cow I could rectal, but I would need a stepladder and a six-foot arm to do that to an elephant. I also thought the elephant might somehow object. Waiting for inspiration to strike, I looked at the rounded body and peered between its back legs.

'Luke, what are you doing?' he asked quietly.

'Just looking for the teats,' I said. 'Maybe she's bagged up.'

Nigel leaned in. 'The teats are between the front legs.'

'Ah, yes, I was just checking things, you know,' I said, acutely embarrassed. Things were not going well; I didn't even know where the mammary glands of an elephant were and had just assumed that, like a cow, the udder would be between the back legs.

Nigel smiled. 'You haven't done much with elephants have you, Luke?'

'No, Nigel, I come from the south of England. We don't have many elephants in Dorset.'

'Sam told me you were an exotic vet.'

I looked at Nigel and saw a big grin on his face. Naturally, Sam had put him up to this! The penny dropped. This was my punishment for keeping him away from a week of sun and sand in Ibiza yet again. I had been stitched up.

As Nigel realised I had worked out what was going on, his face creased into laughter.

'Very good,' I said quietly, determined not to let Nigel and Sam get the better of me. 'Tell him I think it is pregnant.'

I stood up and looked at the mahout as Nigel translated. Pleased, the mahout nodded vigorously in agreement.

'He thinks so too, he just wanted to make sure,' Nigel said, the grin still on his face.

'No doubt about it,' I said with as much conviction as I could muster. 'Can we go now?'

Nigel paused.

'I am afraid not, Luke. On the other side there is a wound and the elephant has a problem with its front foot.'

Moving right up to the gentle giant, I ran my hand from the elephant's trunk over its shoulder and then walked slowly around. A thick metal chain was looped around one of its back legs and bolted to the concrete stand. It was the trademark sign of a captive animal.

The elephant stood stoically as I switched sides and it took me seconds to see the problem. A large open wound was dripping pus down the animal's flank.

'I need to start by cleaning this out,' I said. 'Can you ask the mahout to bring me some water please? I have some chlorhexidine here to wash it with. Tell him this will need to be done twice a day.'

I quickly forgot my nervousness of the big animal as I cleaned and scrubbed the wound, spraying with antibiotic afterwards. Pressing the can into the mahout's hand, I showed him what he would have to do.

'Now what about the foot?' I asked.

With a quick command from the mahout, the elephant lifted its leg and I peered at the damaged and ulcerated sole beneath.

'This must be agony,' I breathed, swooping the can of spray back off the mahout and applying it liberally to the affected area.

As the elephant put its foot down, I turned to the mahout and stamped my foot.

'This concrete is hard,' I snapped. The elephant had not been harmed in an accident or attack; this was simple thoughtless, bad husbandry. It didn't need an elephant expert to see that these injuries were wholly preventable. 'The straw is not enough, and the elephant cannot lay down on anything but concrete! These sores are from the pressure.'

Nigel repeated what I was saying.

'I'll get you some antibiotics and pain killers to give the elephant,' I went on, 'but you must make a mattress for the animal to lay on or it will only get worse.'

Seizing the idea, Nigel discussed at length how best to make a giant straw mattress for the elephant and the mahout nodded enthusiastically.

'He has never been shown anything like this, he says. He has been with this elephant for ten years and it has always had sore feet.' Nigel shook his head sadly. 'They just do not think about it.'

I didn't breathe a word. Even if I had wanted to berate him some more, I couldn't have done it. I was transfixed by the elephant. I found myself resting a hand on its head, the rough grey skin firm against my palm as it looked right into my eyes. Its steady gaze was slightly unnerving. When I first arrived it had seemed to have a dull expression, but now it looked alive. I was almost overwhelmed with an incredible sense of empathy for this wonderful, trapped animal. I wanted to cut her chains and set her free.

'They look into your soul,' Nigel said softly, standing beside me.

'Yes, they do,' I replied as the spell was broken.

The mahout issued another command and the trunk once again rose in blessing. I watched the elephant's eye as it tiredly waved its trunk about my head; the dull bored look was back. Somehow it didn't feel so special this time.

'Well, how did you enjoy it?' I asked as Sam and I adjusted position in our luxury economy seats.

Sam observed me for a moment with bags under his eyes, his face etched with exhaustion. 'You mean the ten days in Ibiza, drinking beer, chasing women and generally recharging batteries?'

'Yes, the exotic adventure, once in a lifetime experience?' I said, trying to figure out how I could squeeze my legs into the constrained space. The seat in front of me was already in full recline and we'd been on the plane about ten minutes.

'I don't know yet,' Sam replied with a crooked smile before turning his head to look at me whilst wiggling his feet. 'I'm thinking about it. Certainly more than you're going to enjoy this ten-hour jaunt back to London!'

'Rather be cramped for ten hours than a dwarf for life,' I retorted, flinging my leg into the aisle.

We waited in silence as the engines started to rumble and we taxied to the runway. In front of us, somebody was chuntering about their holiday, the beautiful things they had seen, but all I could think of was the street dogs in the slums by the river, the pus leaking out of the temple elephant.

'Come on Luke,' Sam began. 'Are you going to share? You've obviously got something on your mind.'

I knew what Sam was thinking. I only grinned.

'You looking to buy more cows with broken legs, is that it? Looking for a chance to peer between the back legs of some more elephants?'

'Only how to save the world, Sam.'

'Save the world? I bet Mr Spotswode will have something to say about that.'

Sam was joking, but he was right. I remembered feeling the same way on the day we had left Samos – that there had to be a way vets like us could help out in the world, and not just with the pets and farm animals back in England. Surely it was these sorts of missions that being a vet was all about.

We had done good work in Samos, but perhaps we had done better work here. The change would be lasting. The local government had stopped the culling of the dogs; the local community was really supportive of the project. Nigel was going to run follow-up teams and had already asked me if I could find any volunteers to do the trip again. The cow episode had been so rewarding and made the farm routines back home, the ones I had found so exciting only months ago, seem mundane in comparison.

'You can't think like that, Luke. There's people who need you at home. What about your new Italian fixation?'

I lifted a finger to my lips, and Sam groaned.

'You're never going to tell me all the details about her, are you?'

The plane roared as it began its run to take off.

'Great we found that little dog,' I remarked, to change the subject.

Sam nodded in agreement. 'Hopefully the prolapse will stay in. It looked quite fresh didn't it?'

'Yes, I think it will be fine.'

We had seen the little dog in town, and its prolapsed anus had been obvious from a distance. Using one of Sevar's sandwiches, we had managed to tempt the dog right up to the truck and, after it had eaten, we simply picked it up, popped it in the truck and got it back to the camp to sort her out. Everyone had fallen in love with her and I had overheard Nigel saying he wanted to take her to join the shelter's very own pack.

'What if there was a vet charity?' I began. 'Something that gave free veterinary resources to animal charities and sanctuaries, just like we've been doing, all over the world.'

Sam closed his eyes. He had always been a nervous flier, but this time it wasn't the take-off he was groaning at.

'All over the world?' he asked. 'Luke, one day we *are* going to Ibiza.'

'Ibiza can wait,' I grinned. 'You can go to Ibiza when you're retired.'

'I'm going to have to retire if you keep dragging me round on this little crusade of yours.'

The plane wobbled as we took to the skies.

'I'm serious,' I said. 'It wouldn't have to just be us. There could be other vets, other resources – where they're needed, all over the world.'

'That's nice – do you get to wear a cape as well?'

Ignoring Sam, I continued. 'Vets could volunteer to help charities like Nigel's, we could formally collect short-dated medicines and get them out to places where they can do some real good and not go to waste.'

'How about pants outside your trousers? Do you get to choose your own colour?' Sam drawled.

'I've got to think of a name though,' I said, thinking aloud.

'How-to-ruin-my-friend's-chances-of-getting-a-girl-at-every-given-holiday-opportunity charity?' Sam chipped in, his eyes barely open.

'Worldwide Veterinary Service,' I mused. 'What do you think?'

I looked across at Sam, and got the only reply I could have expected. Gently, he was starting to snore.

9

LEUWEN

The practice had been unusually quiet and before dusk we all traipsed out to a pub, where the landlord's loyal dog trotted over to give a welcome to his team of favourite veterinarians. He was an elderly collie and for some reason always seemed pleased to see us despite taking numerous trips to the surgery, for vaccinations, a check-up or worse.

Sam and I had been back from India for two nights. I had been thinking solidly of the next mission I might go on, and how to coax other people to join me, but I imagined Sam somewhere, savouring the beer I had promised him all that time ago and poring over his holiday brochures. I suppose he had a point – all work and no play wasn't good for anyone, but there was no way I wasn't going to do my utmost to twist his arm into taking him along wherever I went next.

'An animal charity?' Rob asked. The barmaid brought over our plates whilst Holly and Sheila leaned into the table to listen as I sketched out my plan. It wasn't much more than a vague collection of ideas, yet, but I was certain it made sense.

'Don't let Mr Spotswode know,' Holly giggled. 'There aren't enough hours in the day . . .'

'Sounds exciting,' Sheila said. 'But how do you go about setting up a charity?'

I'd looked it up on the internet and it seemed doable. There would be some paperwork, I'd need some money to show the organisation had momentum, but a few memorandums and articles of association and I'd be away.

'How do you intend to manage that whilst working at the practice, doing your one in four nights large animal cover and running the emergency service?' Rob asked with a raised eyebrow.

'And dating Cordelia?' Sheila chipped in with a wry smile.

I'd asked Cordelia on a proper date and couldn't wait for the relationship to progress.

'Next Wednesday is the night,' I said as Rob fixed me with a beady eye. 'Restaurant booked, all set – the place has great reviews.'

'You'll just be writing your "articles of association" during the *hors d'oeuvres* . . .' Rob said, flashing Sheila a look.

Ignoring him, I carried on. 'Look, I can type out the documents during the quiet nights at the emergency service – it really isn't a massive deal, I just need trustees.'

I looked directly at Rob.

Rob reeled back. He skewered a piece of scampi with a fork and pointed it accusingly at me.

'No way,' he said. 'Absolutely no way. I know what you do to people, your friend Sam is a living example of someone who gets suckered into your plans. By all accounts, he's still recuperating from your last "holiday".'

'I think you'd be excellent Rob, you should definitely do it,' Sheila said.

'Who asked you? Why don't you do it?' Rob said defensively.

'I need a vet,' I shrugged.

'Cordelia!' Rob protested. 'She's your wannabe girlfriend, she should do it!'

'It has to be a man,' Holly said, with an almost completely straight face.

'It does not have to be a man,' Rob said indignantly, not sure what to make of Holly's apparent seriousness.

'Are you saying you aren't man enough for it?' Sheila chipped in, as Holly started to laugh.

I was enjoying this. Quietly, I sipped my pint.

'Look, this is crazy, trustees have responsibility, we would have to make sure this lunatic doesn't go bankrupt.' He gestured vitriolically with his scampi-skewered fork, but the nugget just dropped off the end and skittered away over the floor.

'Anyway, how will you raise the money to get your charity idea off the ground?' he finished.

Holly started to giggle, clearly something was on her mind.

'What are you thinking, Holly?' Sheila asked.

'That will be the first time today,' Rob commented drily.

'That's not nice,' Sheila said, slapping Rob on the arm.

'Neither is putting my brand new paediatric stethoscope in the washing machine. It was supposed to be red and now it's pink!' Rob exclaimed. Beside him, Holly almost fell off her chair, shaking.

'I was just thinking . . .' Holly said, in between fits of laughter, 'Luke and Rob could do a . . . *balloon* dance. You know, really cause a stir, really make some money.'

'They'd only need tiny balloons,' Sheila said, winking back at Holly.

'I am honestly going home if this conversation doesn't improve!' Rob declared.

We sat, silently eating and drinking for a moment, sharing looks across the table. Whenever I caught Holly's eye, she had to look away. Whenever I caught Sheila's eye, she just shrugged.

'No,' I said, downing my knife and fork. 'I've been thinking about this a lot. I'm going to do some sort of event to raise money that is really good, show something really impressive.'

'Well, that rules out a balloon dance,' Sheila said, setting Holly off again.

'He'll rope us all into a Full Monty,' Rob muttered. He was sounding more and more like Sam every day. 'Just you watch, he'll have us plastered all over the newspapers.' He paused. 'Or die trying,' he added.

'I'll come up with something, just you wait and see,' I promised, flashing the three of them a big grin.

'Well, you could start by coming up with another round of drinks and progress from there,' Rob declared, grounding his empty glass onto the table top with hearty laugh.

Coming off a night shift with a heavy headache, I hurried through the practice, readying myself for the day ahead. In the waiting rooms, the day's first patients were busy sniffing at each other and yapping out their discontent. Sheila waved to me from the reception desk as she finished off the filing from the previous night's duty before she headed home, and I scurried between two over-zealous mastiffs to reach her. She already had a pot of coffee on the go.

'You look exhausted.'

I shrugged. 'You say it how you see it, Sheila.'

The work at the emergency service had been relentless. For the last week I had been struggling with cover and, on the nights I was off, I was catching up on the night cover I owed Rob for the large animal work in my day job. I was living on a diet of coffee and adrenaline now, determined not to let Mr Spotswode know how weary I was feeling. As I took my first slurp, he sidled through, tipped us both a hello and disappeared into his office.

'I don't think he noticed,' Sheila began.

'Noticed what?'

'The bags under your eyes. It's like you're carrying a tonne of bricks.'

'It's . . . complicated,' I said.

'Complicated isn't the word. Last night you did an entire consult asleep!'

I scratched my head, racking my brains. 'What do you mean? We saw the choking dog at nine and the cat at about midnight and . . . that was it, wasn't it?'

'Do you remember a large Labrador with diarrhoea belonging to a certain Mr Pipe that came in about three this morning?'

'You're winding me up,' I insisted.

'Not in the slightest! You were asleep.'

I had once been a bit of a sleepwalker, but this was another sphere altogether.

'You got up, saw the dog, mumbled to Mr Pipe, asked all the relevant questions, injected it and went back to bed,' Sheila said laughing.

For the first time, I was worried. I paused before taking another sip. Perhaps running on coffee was not an entirely good idea. 'You're joking, surely?' I replied. I had absolutely no memory of seeing the dog.

'I came in the consult room to make sure you were okay, but you treated it fine and then just left the room and went back to your bed. Mr Pipe thought you were a bit odd, but he seemed perfectly happy. I priced it up and sent him away again.'

I stumbled to the sink, drained the coffee away, and splashed some cold water on my face.

'You haven't told anyone, have you?' I asked.

'I think everyone knows you're burning the candle at both ends, Luke.' Sheila paused. 'Just so long as you aren't going to attempt any splenectomies or leg amputations whilst you're asleep. Look, are you going to have a good night's kip tonight?'

I hesitated. It hadn't been part of my plans.

'Wednesday night, remember – I'm taking Cordelia out for dinner,' I said. 'We're going to that nice country restaurant I talked about. I've a table booked by the fire, we're all set.' I paused. 'That locum has said he'll pitch up okay for his night shift of power, hasn't he?' I asked.

I could detect a hint of hesitancy in Sheila's voice. 'You mean Aldolpho? Well, yes, he's promised to be here,' she said. 'I'm sure he'll be fine . . .'

'What's the matter?' I asked.

'Well, he's just not, you know, very natural,' Sheila replied. 'But I'm sure once I get to know him and he's relaxed, he'll be fine. Is he experienced?'

I hadn't met Aldolpho. He was a locum I'd tracked down, had been working emergency shifts at a clinic in Leeds – but, if ever I was going to have a successful date with Cordelia, he had to be solid. I could live without being dragged away from that first kiss to bury my hands in a truculent guinea pig, or diagnose a dog with a common cold.

'Look,' Sheila said, 'it won't be a problem. You have a nice meal tonight and I'll take care of Aldolpho.'

A bell rang in reception and Holly stuck her head around the door.

'Luke,' she said. 'First patient. It's Mr Baffer, with another frog.'

I shared a look with Sheila. 'Never a dull moment!' I grinned, and turned to face the day.

That night, the restaurant was perfect. Cordelia and I sat round a snug corner table, the fire crackling beside us and the plates of delicious food just kept on coming.

'This is lovely,' I commented, tucking into the juicy steak in front of me.

'It's great,' Cordelia said with a smile. 'Thank you for asking me.'

'Bit different food than I ate in India!' I replied, sinking my teeth into a particularly tender piece of steak.

'I would love to go to India,' Cordelia said wistfully, 'it sounds amazing. How are your plans coming along to set up your charity?'

'I need something big to be taken seriously,' I replied.

Cordelia arched an eyebrow. 'Always helps,' she said with a half smile playing on her lips as I flushed slightly, and gave a nervous laugh.

'I mean, do some sort of event to get the charity really noticed,' I explained.

'Jess's friend did a race across the Sahara desert,' Cordelia said. She put her knife and fork down and eagle-eyed me across the table. 'One hundred and fifty-two miles of desert. That was impressive, but maybe that's taking things to the extreme.'

'I don't mind extreme. I handled Partridge, didn't I?' I said, laughing.

'The *Marathon des Sables*,' Cordelia said seriously, 'is

billed as the toughest footrace on earth.' This, she seemed to be saying, was a challenge.

'I could do that,' I heard myself say brazenly.

'It really is very tough,' Cordelia soberly explained. Was I wrong, or was she withdrawing the challenge? I couldn't let her do that. 'Jess's friend is an amazing runner, he runs every day, marathons all the time – he's virtually a professional and even he found it hard. People have died on it.' She paused. 'It was just an idea, that's all . . .'

'Knocks Holly's balloon dance idea into a cocked hat though, doesn't it!' I declared, taking a swig of wine for courage. 'That's what I'll do, the *Marathon des Sables*. Decided.'

'Balloon dance?'

'Really doesn't matter,' I hastily replied, 'this is the ticket, you've come up with a winner!' I beamed.

'Have you ever run a marathon?' Cordelia asked.

'Anyone can be a runner,' I replied evasively. Possibly, the challenge was going to my head. 'I might not have the build of a runner, but I can run . . . admittedly a bit like a duck but even ducks can run.'

'Ducks waddle,' Cordelia said, and smiled.

'I can do that too,' I laughed.

'But how are you going to manage doing a marathon every day for a week – across the desert?'

'I'm a natural athlete, honestly,' I said with a grin.

Cordelia politely set down her knife and fork and, crossing her hands, looked at me across the table.

'I think setting up the charity is a fantastic idea and you do need to do something to get it off the ground.' She paused. 'Luke, I feel bad about suggesting the *Marathon des Sables* – it's a bit crazy . . .'

She took a long sip of red wine. This was my chance. If I

wanted out, she was giving me an out. But I wasn't about to let it go that easily.

'I think it's a great idea,' I said with as much conviction as I could muster. 'I mean, it's got to be something tough hasn't it and I love crazy!'

'It would be really impressive, Luke, but no one would blame you for deciding against it,' Cordelia said.

I looked at Cordelia; little did she realise she had just said the words that sealed the deal. My heart lurched. That was it! I couldn't wriggle out of it now, no matter what.

'I'm all set for it, really, I'm all geared up,' I said.

'Okay,' she said after a pause, 'but how are you going to find time for a social life with your desert run and all your on-call?'

Too late, I realised that the piece of steak in my mouth was far too big. I seemed to be chewing it endlessly. It might have been wishful thinking but I sensed the question was loaded. Cordelia was right, though. How was I to keep everything going *and* try to have a girlfriend all at the same time? Grinding down on the meat, I had far too much time to ponder.

'It's all going to settle down,' I replied, still forcing the steak down my throat. 'I'm getting really good vets in now to run the emergency clinic and the on-call for the farm is very quiet. I was hoping we could make these dinners a regular thing, go out a bit more?'

'That would be nice!' Cordelia beamed. 'But I'm glad you are doing the on-call – gets me out of it!'

'The lengths I go to, in order to impress.'

I was about to put another huge chunk of steak into my mouth, but suddenly thought better of it. 'I know I've been a bit busy,' I continued, 'but I think Mr Spotswode is probably the most supportive boss ever – he pretty much gave me Sheila to help run it. The locum vets are a bit of an unknown quantity but I'm recruiting for permanent ones and I think I have two poised to get on board. I'm getting my life back with immediate effect!'

It was tempting fate and I should have known better. Before I had even finished speaking, the phone started to buzz in my pocket.

I looked apologetically at Cordelia and glanced down at the display screen.

'It's Sheila,' I mumbled, 'from the emergency service.'

Momentarily, I closed my eyes, praying that there wasn't some dramatic emergency.

'I'm sorry,' I said, beginning to stand.

Cordelia gave me a half smile and nodded in understanding.

Excusing myself from the table, I hurried out of the pub and answered the phone.

'I'm so sorry Luke, I really am,' Sheila began, clearly distressed. 'But we have a big problem here. Aldolpho is with a client and he's refusing to do a caesarean on the bitch. The dog is a Ridgeback that's been whelping since lunchtime and she's really in trouble. He says that all his cases resolve medically. I don't know what to do.'

I paced the parking space, feeling angry. The stars were out in full, there was a waxing moon; it was the perfect night for a romantic encounter.

'What's his problem?' I snapped. Immediately, I felt a chill of guilt; it wasn't fair to be so short with Sheila. 'Aldolpho, I mean.'

'I don't know, Luke.' There was a hint of desperation in her voice. 'The bitch needs a caesarean, he's already given four injections of oxytocin and she's in trouble. She's flat and painful.' Sheila stopped.

'What is it, Sheila?'

'I think she'll die without proper help. Aldolpho doesn't know what he's doing.'

I looked through the pub window. Cordelia sat there at the table, her eyes sparkling. Out here, I could have howled into the night. I wrenched my eyes away.

'I'll be there as soon as I can,' I said. 'And Sheila, I'm sorry, I'm just . . .'

'I know, I know. Thank you, Luke.'

I walked back into the pub. At the table, Cordelia was waiting expectantly. It wasn't until I looked down that I saw she'd already paid the bill.

'I'm so sorry,' I began. 'It's a caesarean . . . the locum . . .'

Cordelia smiled in sympathy as I tailed off helplessly. 'It's okay – I understand.'

There was nothing more I could say. In that moment I vowed to myself that I'd get proper help at the clinic, get my nights back and nail this marathon – and then I'd win Cordelia. After that, I got myself back to the practice. I was not in the best of moods.

'This dog needs a caesarean,' I said in no uncertain terms. On the other side of the consult table, Aldolpho stood gawping.

Bramble, the poor dog in question, looked at me with dull eyes. A friendly Ridgeback weighing over forty kilograms, her distended abdomen was painful to touch and it occurred to me that I'd never seen a pregnant dog in so much discomfort.

'I have never had to do the surgery, they always produce the puppies in the end,' he said defensively, his thick black eyebrows meeting above a protruding bony ridge.

'You've been qualified three years and have spent the last

six months in an emergency clinic!' I railed. 'Surely you've had to do caesareans!' I rounded the table, brushing Aldolpho aside. 'This dog is in pain,' I said. 'There's a puppy stuck! Didn't you wonder why your first injection of oxytocin had absolutely no effect? How many have you given her?'

Aldolpho shrugged. 'Four,' he conceded.

'Four? You've given four repeat injections to make her uterus spasm – she's exhausted and painful. She needs an operation!'

'I never needed to do one,' he repeated. 'They always eventually come with the oxytocin.'

I was exasperated. Across the room, Sheila's eyes begged me to be quiet.

'Just look at her!' I said. 'This dog is going to die.' Aldolpho balked, outrage flashing across his face. 'This dog has been trying to give birth for nearly twelve hours and not produced a single pup. She is utterly exhausted, she needs fluids.' I lost it. I'd had enough. 'She needs a proper vet!'

'You are rude,' Aldolpho replied.

'You are incompetent,' I shot back.

Afraid that I was going to tear chunks out of Aldolpho, Sheila scuttled forward. 'Luke,' she began, 'the client is still here, he really wants a word with you.'

I took a moment, breathed deeply, and turned away from the locum vet. I couldn't stand to look at him.

'Sheila,' I began. 'Would you mind getting a catheter into Bramble whilst I see the client to try to put right this mess he's created?'

Behind me, Aldolpho paused, thinking about what I'd just said. 'I go home now,' he began.

'I think that's a good idea, Aldolpho,' Sheila interjected. 'You need to rest. Luke and I will take care of things from here.'

I bit back the words that were coming to my lips and

nodded wearily. Aldolpho was booked in to do the next three nights on-call – clearly that wasn't going to happen.

'This isn't going to work out, Aldolpho,' I said, taking a deep breath and calming myself down.

Aldolpho appeared to consider my comment before stiffly replying. 'I will send you my invoice for tonight,' he said before turning on his heel and walking off, slamming the door behind him.

'Fantastic,' I said, looking across at Sheila. 'No vet down here again for another three nights and I'm on large-animal call for two of them!'

The only thing that stopped me from beating down the walls was the look poor Bramble gave me from the consult table, her eyes wide with a sudden flash of hope. I knelt down and ran my hands over her. I could tell from a thin scar in her belly that she had had a caesarean before. Perhaps she knew what was coming. The gears were working in her mind, and she had a terrible apprehension about what was to happen.

'Let's worry about that later, shall we?' Sheila replied firmly, focusing me on the task at hand. 'I'll get Bramble ready for surgery. You need to see the client.'

I paused. Sheila was right. I crouched low to Bramble, teasing her ears, and whispering that I would do everything that I could.

'How is the client?' I asked, picking up on a slight hesitation in her voice.

'Not angry as such,' she said, 'but it's . . . tricky. The client, Mr Lurger, has brought a friend with him, his brother-in-law apparently. Luke, you should know he's been a bit difficult.'

I watched Aldolpho through the window as he trudged to his car.

'I don't think this night can get much more difficult, Sheila,' I said, bracing myself for a tricky conversation as I turned to head into the consult room.

Mr Tubbie fixed me with a hateful look as I walked through the door. His companion, a thin mousey man with sunken eyes and a pointed face looked at me accusingly.

'Hello Mr Tubbie,' I said with a sense of heavy trepidation washing over me. He looked much the same as the last time we had met: that same rotund belly, that same sense of smug self-satisfaction.

'This is my brother-in-law,' Mr Tubbie coldly replied. 'Your "associate" has kept us waiting here for three hours watching the dog deteriorate. You may as well put it down now and we can agree a figure for the puppies you have killed. Your vet should have operated as soon as we arrived. I'm holding you to account.' When he was finished, he stabbed a fat finger in my direction to emphasise his point.

Ignoring Mr Tubbie, I looked at his brother-in-law. 'Mr Lurger, my name is Luke Gamble,' I began.

Too late, I realised immediately that Mr Lurger knew exactly who I was; his lips turned upward in an untoward grin.

'I'll be taking care of things from here on. As you'll be aware, Aldolpho has tried to medically induce Bramble, but she is still not contracting so I'm afraid surgery is our only option.'

Mr Lurger sneered and gave a sidelong glance to Mr Tubbie.

'We know she isn't contracting,' Mr Tubbie butted in. 'She's been whelping for nearly twelve hours, he should have done surgery straight away rather than waste time with these injections. He's the one who's caused this problem. The pups are probably all dead! It'll ruin her as a breeding bitch.' He stopped, stepped forward with clasped hands. 'So you should put her down,' he said, 'admit your mistake and compensate us accordingly.'

I took a deep breath. In the room behind me, I could hear Sheila whispering soft consolation to the poor bitch.

'I'm guessing you have this all worked out, don't you, Mr Tubbie?' I said evenly.

'How do you mean?' he asked, suddenly taken aback.

I didn't want this. I could tell I was spoiling for another fight with Tubbie, and I tried to rein myself in. It had already been a long night, and I didn't need to make it any worse.

'I saw the scar on Bramble's abdomen, Mr Tubbie. She's already had one caesarean in her life – which means your brother-in-law was almost certainly advised not to mate her again.' I paused. I could tell how this was going to work. You didn't need to be Columbo to work it out. 'Mr Lurger here, who seems to be incapable of speaking, breeds Bramble to sell her puppies, so he got her in pup again knowing she would be high risk. You left it eight hours before bringing her to the emergency service and now you are going to try to put this on me for the fact that she needs an emergency caesarean.'

'Correction!' Tubbie's brother-in-law spoke for the first time, his voice a nasally whine. 'She *did* need a caesarean. Your vet's dithering has put paid to her chances. If he had done a caesarean straight away then I would happily have paid the bill. But now you may as well put the bitch down and pay me her worth for future litters.'

'We've been here before, haven't we Luke?' Tubbie interjected, delighted with himself. 'Only, this time, it's me saying put the animal down . . . and, this time, you know I'm right!'

I looked back. I paused. Damn them, but Tubbie and Lurger might have a point. The bitch was flat, she was high risk, and the surgery would be a nightmare with so much scar tissue from the previous operation. No matter how I argued it, Aldolpho should have done a caesarean straight away and everybody in the room knew it.

'I'm not prepared to give up and put her down without trying,' I began, knowing that neither were at all interested in that argument.

'Are you willing to put her through all that unnecessary suffering only to put her down later?' Mr Tubbie haughtily asked. I burned red that the odious little man was questioning *my* animal ethics, after all I had seen and done at his farm. 'I'm not paying for the operation. I want you to put her down and compensate me.'

'What if I operate and save her and some of the puppies?' I asked. I was on the back-foot, and it did not feel good.

Lurger looked pointedly at the clock hanging on the surgery wall. 'You'll have killed some of the puppies by now so you already owe us for them,' he sneered.

'We all know that the likelihood is that there is scar tissue in her uterus from her previous operation. There was probably a dead puppy in there before you brought her down here. You'll have a hard job proving otherwise.' I looked Lurger square in the eyes.

'Either way, you know our feelings about it. If that dog suffers needlessly then I'll have you for that as well,' Tubbie insisted.

'Each puppy is worth about £800,' Lurger nodded. 'There would have been nine or ten, I'm sure, and then the cost of a pedigree breeding bitch – you'll owe me about £12,000 by the end of the night.'

The way he looked at me sealed everything I thought about them. I just wished I were still in that restaurant with Cordelia.

'I'm not going to put her down and write you a cheque,' I said. 'You came here for us to help Bramble didn't you?'

Mr Tubbie just grinned at me wickedly. 'Of course we did,' he said.

'Then you'll have to go home and get out of my way,' I replied.

Back in the operating room, Sheila had prepared Bramble as best as she could.

'She's really gone down in the last fifteen minutes, Luke,' she began as I hurried to start scrubbing up.

'I'll tell you who I want to put down,' I hissed, 'and it isn't Bramble.'

'You know the clients?'

'I know the short fat one. He's the farmer I had the trouble with over that cow, when I first arrived.'

Sheila looked at me blankly.

'Put it this way,' I said, drying my hands and arms. 'We have a history.'

I hurried over to check Bramble's colour.

'She's becoming toxic,' Sheila said.

Sheila was right. Bramble was in a bad way. I hoped, above everything else, that I could get her through this, prove Tubbie and Lurger wrong. The only thing to do was to get ready with the scalpel immediately, get those puppies out and hope for the best.

'No pre-med,' I replied, 'we'll go straight off with propofol.'

It took about ten minutes to get Bramble ready for theatre, Sheila hastily clipping and scrubbing her abdomen. I was about to perform an operation on a dog for which I had no consent form signed, and which the owners had specifically requested I euthanise. I didn't know where I stood, legally. I had a nagging feeling that if the owners wanted you to put down their animal, you were supposed to do it or get them to sign it over to you. Ninety-nine per cent of people would sign an animal over to a vet rather than have it euthanised needlessly but ultimately it was down to them. I could probably be strung up for this but I didn't care.

'Tubbie and Lurger want me to euthanise Bramble, admit full responsibility for the complication and pay compensation,' I suddenly blurted out. If only, I thought, Bramble could understand what her *loving* owners had in mind for her.

'Do you remember those cats that Giles was asked to put down?' Sheila said, weighing up the options as she adjusted the fluid rate on Bramble's drip.

'The ones that belonged to dear old Mrs Finch?' I asked.

Mrs Finch had been in her nineties and loved her cats. When she passed away, her nephew had brought the cats to the surgery to be put down. Apparently it was what Mrs Finch wanted when she died; she couldn't bear the thought of them being without her and thought it was the kindest thing.

'How did he get out of that?' I asked.

'He didn't,' Sheila replied. 'Mr Spotswode talked to the nephew and managed to convince him that wasn't what Mrs Finch had meant, but it was touch and go. Giles was really torn up about it. When he phoned the council for advice, he was told he should do it.'

I knew how much Giles would have been torn. It was a difficult thing to go back against a protocol order like that, and I didn't know if I'd have the stomach for it.

'What do you think about Bramble here? Am I doing the right thing?'

'The right thing by poor Bramble at least!' she said, smiling encouragingly.

I grinned back. 'No Mr Spotswode here to bail me out tonight,' I said.

Sheila smiled at me. 'You know he'll back you up when the chips are down. Besides, look at it this way – have you got £12,000?'

I considered it for only a second. 'I haven't got £120.'

'Well then, you had better be on top form for the next hour!'

With that, I made my first incision.

The scar tissue made the wound bleed more than usual as I sliced into Bramble's abdomen. The uterus bulged and strained as I entered the cavity and, immediately, I could see why the poor dog was in so much pain.

'The uterus is torn,' I said to Sheila who was monitoring the anaesthetic with hawk eyes. 'She's been straining so hard against a stuck pup.'

It was a serious business; the uterus tearing would result in leakage of the fluid into the abdomen, causing a nasty peritonitis that would undoubtedly kill poor Bramble.

With great care I examined the tear. It wasn't full thickness and hadn't gone all the way through the lining of the organ. Perhaps we had caught it just in time. Gently incising over the fine tissue, I began to extract the puppies, rapidly clamping off each umbilicus, clearing airways before handing them to Sheila. Working deftly, she tried to revitalise each limp form.

'Let's inject Dopram straight into the umbilicus,' Sheila said.

I looked at her, dumbfounded.

'I know it isn't by the book,' she said, 'but Giles does it every time and it works wonders, I promise. I have it ready here in an insulin syringe, just a tiny bit.'

The puppies weren't responding. Only one had rallied but

three others were very slow and only just on the edge of pulling through.

'We don't have enough hands, Sheila. I have to get the rest of these out and get this uterus stitched,' I said helplessly.

I delved into Bramble to ease another pup out but retracted my hands quickly. A loud bang, as of a slamming door, echoed through the practice. I darted a look at Sheila.

'I locked up,' she said. 'I promise . . .'

Before she could finish, the door to the op theatre swung open and Holly appeared.

'You started without me!' she exclaimed.

I looked at Sheila, who simply shrugged.

'Sorry it took me a while to get here,' Holly went on, quickly wriggling out of her coat and scrubbing up. 'I just got your message, was out seeing an old lady who had fallen down some stairs and broke her leg.'

'As you do,' I said, with a feeling of immense gratitude.

Sheila beamed at her friend.

'I tried to get Holly before I bothered you Luke, I thought the two of us could have handled Aldopho.' Suddenly, Sheila was bundling two puppies into Holly's arms, and the two of them were launching into work.

Holly laughed. 'I wouldn't miss a caesarean for the world!'

With Holly rubbing each pup vigorously, Sheila injecting Dopram and monitoring the anaesthetic, at last the tide turned. Seven puppies later, we stood back to admire our night's work, all in great spirits.

Only one of the pups had died. It was the puppy who had jammed sideways just in front of the cervix, blocking the passage for all the others behind it. He lay sadly on one side, while his brothers and sisters mewled around each other.

I flushed the uterus and checked my line of sutures. Part of me was desperate to spay poor Bramble so that Lurger couldn't do it again but I managed to restrain myself; if I did that I really would have been in breach of my legal standing.

As I finished the last stitch in Bramble's skin, I looked at Sheila and Holly. There was no better team of nurses to have in an emergency.

'She's got great colour Luke, she's going to be okay!' Sheila beamed.

'Hardcore healing!' Holly exclaimed.

I smiled back, rising to wash my hands. I was going to pick up the phone and tell Tubbie and Lurger everything that had happened, that Bramble had survived and so had her puppies, that there was not going to be any ridiculous compensation claim against Mr Spotswode and his practice.

I was going to love every minute of it.

My first night off in what felt like an aeon, and I fell into my armchair at home like a warrior returning from a particularly vicious Crusade. Everything ached. I picked up the phone to call Cordelia, thought better of it, and put it down again. I'd seen her twice since abandoning her between the main course and dessert, but I wasn't yet convinced I was clawing my way back into her affections. I tried to call Sam instead, but there was only a message on the other end of the line. Sam, it seemed, had finally taken himself off to Ibiza for a week of sand and surf. I was beginning to think that was the best idea for me as well.

I must have nodded off, because the next thing I knew, the doorbell was ringing. Weary, and quite possibly still asleep, I floundered to the door and opened it. Cordelia was standing on the doorstep, a heavy bundle in her arms with a blanket draped over it. I caught a fleeting reflection of myself in the window glass: bedraggled, hair everywhere, with a soup stain on my front and still in weeks-old pyjama bottoms.

'Cordelia!' I exclaimed. 'I . . .'

'Nice to see you keeping up appearances,' Cordelia smiled.

I invited her in, scrambled off to make tea, and when I returned she was sitting on the sofa, the large bundle in her lap seemingly wriggling.

'You need encouragement to get out and run,' Cordelia began, the blanket slipping slightly as whatever small form huddled in her arms gave a little yelp.

'What's under the blanket, Cords?' I asked.

She shifted just a little, and suddenly something reared out of the blanket. From Cordelia's lap, a little puppy looked up at me with big brown eyes.

'What the . . .' I said, completely shocked.

The puppy was none other than a Ridgeback.

'It's not . . .' I began.

'No, it's not,' Cordelia said. 'Give me that coffee and I'll tell you all about your new training companion.'

Open-mouthed, I handed Cordelia the coffee. The puppy promptly leapt from her lap and gambolled into the kitchen where he did a wee on the floor.

'You'll need to get used to that,' Cordelia said, as she smiled.

The puppy sat down and watched me. It was irresistible and I couldn't help giving it a stroke.

'Luke, meet Leuwen,' Cordelia began. 'After you told me about poor Bramble, I spoke to my boss who *accidentally* left a telephone number on my desk for Ridgeback Rhodesian Rescue.'

I raised my eyebrows as Cordelia paused for effect.

'Did it occur to you to wonder why Bramble was so lovely and yet her owners were so horrible?' she asked.

'Tubbie,' I replied, wondering where this was going.

'The reason Bramble is such a nice dog, is that she's from the Rhodesian Ridgeback Rescue Society. It turns out that Lurger was allowed to take Bramble on the pretence that she was going to live on a farm with his sister. Part of what he promised was that, once Bramble was settled, he would get her spayed and she would be a much loved family dog.' Cordelia shook her head sadly and, as if in response, Leuwen idled over to her and cocked his head. 'He lied through his teeth and instead took Bramble back to his house in the town. He's been using her for breeding ever since, mating her with a Ridgeback belonging to one of Tubbie's friends. You've no idea how much he's made . . .'

Pedigree dogs like Bramble could make people a lot of money. She was being farmed, and I had no doubt that she was being farmed just as brutally as Tubbie farmed his cattle.

'I spoke at length to the secretary of the society, a nice lady called Hilary. It became pretty evident that you'd have to be very brave indeed to risk crossing Hilary when it comes to Ridgeback welfare.' Cordelia paused. She took a sip of coffee - but it was evidently not to her taste, for she quickly set it aside. 'So, I . . .'

'You told them about Lurger!' I exclaimed.

Leuwen yapped.

Cordelia nodded. 'Hilary was horrified,' she began. 'Apparently, the whole re-homing had been quite controversial in the society but all Lurger's references had checked out.

They'd even done a follow-up home visit to make sure it was all in order.'

'Let me guess,' I said. 'A delightful tour round Homestead Farm?'

'Exactly,' Cordelia said. Lurger had used Tubbie as a front to get the dog, all so he could pump out puppies and turn a profit.

'So what happens now?' I asked.

'Now,' said Cordelia, 'Team Hilary moves in.'

By the time Rhodesian Ridgeback Rescue had got to Lurger, all the puppies but one had been sold. There were teams trying to track them now, making sure none of them had gone to some unscrupulous owner, somebody as dastardly as Lurger and Tubbie themselves. Meanwhile, the team had confronted Lurger himself in his house at the end of a terraced block of drab gray buildings. In the doorway behind him as Lurger had opened the door, Bramble – recuperated at last from her epic ordeal – had been found guarding the last remaining pup.

'The society are considering legal action!' Cordelia said, delighted. 'Men like Lurger crumble pretty quickly. Hilary just marched in and took Bramble away. She's going to look after Bramble herself, make sure she gets the life she deserves.'

I grinned. 'That really is the best news I could have had today, but it doesn't quite explain this little guy,' I said, as the puppy attacked my sleeve. I wrestled him off and he nipped playfully at my finger.

'Ah, well, Hilary might have heard, *somehow*, about this charity and challenge of yours. Her friend Janet breeds Ridgebacks and had just had a litter and we *might* have been talking about, well, you know, how useless you are at running, and how *perhaps* you might need something to encourage you on those training runs . . .'

As if in agreement, Leuwen squeaked out a little yap.

'How am I going to look after a puppy?' I protested.

'You spend enough time with the dog from next door,' Cordelia grinned. 'So now you have your own. And, anyway, I can't have dogs where I live. And he's so sweet.'

I looked up.

'You're joking, I can't take a puppy running – it can't run far yet, it's bad for its hips! It's too young. It'll have to come to work with me. What do I feed it? I'm totally unsuitable to have a dog.'

Cordelia shrugged. 'You can't run far yet either, you can get better at that together. Stop being such a big girl, you'll be fine,' she said, beaming. 'Look, I need to leave you two to get acquainted.'

'Leave me? But . . .'

'You look after dogs every day, Luke. Don't tell me you don't know what they eat . . .'

I gave up. Cordelia had won again. I couldn't back down, and she knew it.

'Leuwen, you say?' I asked, trying the name out for size.

'It's a bit different,' she replied, sidling to the door, 'but somehow it suits him. I'll see you later – you're on farm call tomorrow, aren't you?'

I nodded mutely.

'So now you have some company!' Cordelia gave a wave as she shut the door on her way out.

After I had watched her disappear, I looked back at the little form in front of me.

'Leuwen, is it?' I asked.

The puppy looked right back at me and promptly did another wee on the floor.

* * *

'You're an hour late,' Rob muttered as I tumbled into the practice, soaked to the skin.

'It's a long run to work,' I answered, shaking off my coat like a dog would its fur.

'It would be a lot more sensible to drive,' Rob replied.

We'd been having the same conversation every day for what felt like months. With Leuwen on board, I'd had an excuse to ramp up my training. I still ran like a fifteen-and-a-half stone duck, but now I ran like a slightly faster fifteen-and-a-half stone duck. Except for my nights on call, I'd been running to and from work every day, and slowly it was getting a little easier.

'The quest of love!' Rob declared looking at my bedraggled form.

'It's a quest of trying to get to work on time.' I replied wearily.

'I've been thinking,' Rob continued. 'If you do actually manage to survive this race, I might actually manage to be a trustee. You're making me feel bad with all this effort.'

'Will you sponsor me?' I asked, holding out my hand to seal the deal.

'Of course I will. Don't push your luck, though' Rob said, shaking my hand warmly. 'You have some serious catching up to do around here if you are even going to reach the start line.'

'I'm sorry about this morning, I had some trouble,' I replied, tugging the lead attached to my wrist.

'He still hates the rain, then?' Rob asked. He started to smile as I tugged Leuwen towards a kennel and endeavoured to get myself into the consult room so I could deal with the backlog of patients queuing up.

'He *hates* it,' I said, exasperated. 'Every single bush, every bus stop, every bit of cover he can get to – he dives under it and I have to literally drag him along.'

'Shame it's winter in England,' Rob said pointedly. 'My advice is set your alarm clock a bit earlier.' He paused, tousling Leuwen's fur. 'I've seen a couple of your appointments, but Mr Spotswode knows you're late again. He isn't impressed by this training regime of yours – especially as he seems to be paying for it.'

I breathed deeply.

'I did my best to cover,' Rob went on, 'but this is the third time you've been late this fortnight.'

There was no denying it. Rob was right. 'I know. I'm sorry. Thanks, mate,' I said.

Grabbing Leuwen a quick bowl of food, I hurtled off to attend to the morning's dramas. First up was another of my old friends.

'I've been waiting for twenty minutes!' Mrs Beasley declared.

'I know, I'm sorry Mrs Beasley,' I began, still out of breath. 'How is Thomas?'

'I am not here to see you about Thomas,' Mrs Beasley said.

I could detect some uncertainty in her frosty exterior and, intrigued, I nodded encouragingly.

'Can you check this kitten over for me?' Mrs Beasley asked. Slowly, she lifted a cat box onto the consult table. A small flea-ridden white kitten mewed pathetically inside.

'Goodness, this is a little one, how did you come by him, Mrs Beasley?'

Gingerly, I examined the miserable little kitten. I had only rarely seen a more dejected looking animal.

'I found him on my doorstep,' Mrs Beasley began. 'He has

fleas and probably worms, I just want you to make sure there is nothing else.'

'Well, he definitely needs treating as you suggest,' I began, lifting up the encrusted kitten. 'Lots of TLC and I think he'll come good.' I paused, listened to his breathing. 'His heart is strong and he's hydrated. Do you want me to take him in and get him to the Cats' Protection League?'

Mrs Beasley looked suddenly furious. Instantly, I knew I was wrong; Mrs Beasley wasn't the sort to come in and abandon a stray kitten with us, no matter how politely and privately I'd thought she was framing the request.

'Good gracious, no!' she haughtily explained, a look of disdain on her face. 'Thomas and I are more than capable of taking care of this little kitten.'

I paused. I was still dripping wet and cold to the bone, and I suspected that anything I might have said now would only provoke Mrs Beasley more.

'Well, I'll put some kitten wormer and flea treatments up for you,' I said, the only thing I could possibly say. 'You'll need to worm it again next month as well though - one treatment probably won't crack it.' I hesitated to put the kitten back into the box, but finally I popped her inside and handed it back. 'Nice to see you,' I said.

Baffled, I walked toward the consult door to open it for Mrs Beasley. By the time I had got there, I realised that she wasn't following. I looked back. Mrs Beasley was still standing at the consult table, the box in her arms.

Suddenly, her voice cracked slightly. 'It's my sister!' she cried out, as if it caused her actual pain. 'I need you to go and visit her. She has some pets at her home that need attention – one in particular.'

'Mrs Beasley,' I began. 'What's happened?'

Normally, Mr Spotswode would have done the home visits. I tried to drag some more information out of her, but every time she stammered through the words.

She finally said, composing herself, 'I'd cover all the costs of the visit to see her, but something needs to be done.' She paused. If she could have done, she might have put her hands together in entreaty; it already sounded as if she was begging. 'And please, Luke, I need you to treat this confidentially among the other staff at the practice.'

I was gobsmacked. Mrs Beasley was actually asking me for a favour.

'You mean, you don't want anyone here to know I am going on a house visit to see your sister?' I tailed off as Mrs Beasley's face screwed up.

She reached into her coat pocket and handed me a neatly-folded piece of paper.

'Also, don't let her know I'm covering the costs for this, you can tell her I sent you, but not that I'm paying,' she said. 'That would be a breach of our *friendship*, wouldn't it, Luke? And you vets have a code of honour, don't you?'

She walked past me, turned on her heel and nodded. 'Thank you, Luke.'

The paper in my hand, I watched Mrs Beasley, astonished. She might be interfering in her sister's affairs, but for whatever reason, she clearly wanted to help her. She'd also actually said thank you. I couldn't help giving my reflection a giant grin in the screen of the nearby computer.

The address took me to the outskirts of town and one of the grottiest estates I had ever attended. Wheelie bins were strewn in the middle of the road, graffiti dotted every panel of fence and the whole place had an air of neglect.

Weaving the Car of Power around a discarded gate, I found Flat 22b and surveyed my surroundings. Never in a million years did I expect any relative of Mrs Beasley's to live in a place like this. No wonder she wanted the mission done in secret and hadn't gone straight to Mr Spotswode. Mrs Beasley would surely regard it as unthinkable to be associated with someone living in a place like this.

I turned in my seat to look at Leuwen who was fast asleep in the back. I shook my head; he was the most laid back dog on earth. He could sleep through the end of the world itself.

'Well, keep an eye on the car,' I said to Leuwen, reaching out to give him a farewell pat.

Naturally, he didn't stir.

'Don't worry about it, you take it easy,' I said to the sleeping form. 'A million other dogs, they'd want to get out the car and have an adventure, they'd actually be disappointed to be shut in, but you're *special*,' I murmured to the immobile dog. 'You stay here and get your strength up. We're running tomorrow morning – rain or shine – and we aren't going to be late!'

Leuwen opened one eye heavily before closing it again.

I shook my head – some training partner! – and jumped out of the car.

Lugging my box of medicines, I walked along the broken concrete path towards the iron stairwell that would take me to the entrance of Flat 22b.

'What do you want?' screeched a voice as I hovered outside the dirty blue door, paint flaking and the number hanging crooked.

'Mrs Smith?' I yelled, bending down towards the letterbox. 'I'm the vet, your sister asked me to stop by.'

'Bloody interfering woman, thinks she's doing her good

turn!' the voice slurred to the sound of several deadbolts being drawn back.

As the door swung open, the stench of dirty cat litter and general waste cut through a thick haze of smoke. Mrs Smith peered at me from the doorway. She had the same beaked nose as Mrs Beasley and a similar haughty expression, but there the similarities ended. Whereas Mrs Beasley was always immaculately dressed, Mrs Smith was in a ragged grey cardigan, a large hole on the left elbow, mismatched socks and a pair of oversized brown slippers. Mrs Beasley had jet black, carefully groomed hair and her complexion was dark; Mrs Smith, meanwhile, had straggly grey hair to offset a sallow face and bright red cheeks, marred with thick purple veins.

'Who'd you say you were?' Mrs Smith demanded, screwing her eyes up at me.

I peered into the gloom. There was stale alcohol on Mrs Smith's breath and I tried not to gag. 'I'm Luke,' I repeated. 'I'm a vet. Your sister asked me to stop by.'

Mrs Smith looked dubious but, at last, she stepped back.

'Well, come and take a look then, it's probably about Jeremiah – he hasn't been eating well.'

I carefully entered the flat, poised to take my shoes off. Quickly, I changed my mind. They were much cleaner than the floor I was walking on.

The flat was in such a state of disrepair that I had seen better-looking bomb sites on the news. The TV was blaring in the background, there were piles of plates and magazines stacked everywhere, cats draped themselves on the furniture and I saw a large white cat, remarkably glossy and well conditioned, sprawled out on the sofa.

'Oh, that's Queenie! Queenie, Queenie, Queenie!' Mrs Smith crooned, hurrying over to claw her prized possession.

Queenie purred and regarded me with opal eyes.

'She had a litter. But my *precious* sister has taken them all away,' Mrs Smith said sadly. 'All of them,' she seethed. 'But I've still got Queenie, haven't I love?'

I suddenly felt very sorry for Mrs Smith. It dawned on me that her pets were everything to her and living in this horrible estate as a chronic alcoholic couldn't be easy. Queenie at least explained the presence of the white kitten that Mrs Beasley had brought to the surgery for me to examine.

I cast about for somewhere to put my box of medicines. I bent down to stroke Queenie and then jumped backwards. I hadn't noticed the large tank on the floor by the sofa, tucked behind the coffee table. Unbelievably, a large bullfrog looked back at me.

'You've got an African bullfrog!' I exclaimed, unable to hide my surprise.

'Oh yes, you know your frogs, do you?'

'I've had my encounters,' I replied.

'Big Ben I call him, he's very well. It's not him I'm worried about.' Mrs Smith smiled. 'No, come over here.'

I shook my head in amazement and followed Mrs Smith to the far corner of the room, tripping up as I did so. As I cast my eyes downwards, a familiar name caught my eye. *How to Look After your Bullfrog* by Mr Rodney Baffer was on top of a big pile of books.

'This is Jeremiah,' Mrs Smith said, spinning around suddenly, a large object clutched in her hands.

I flinched, then recovered myself and studied the animal being held out to me. I gently put my hands around the large tortoise and walked over to the window.

'Jeremiah has a very overgrown beak,' I said, vaguely wondering if now was a good time to discuss the appropriate husbandry of tortoises.

'He's very particular with that beak of his.'

I took hold of Jeremiah and studied him keenly.

'Jeremiah needs a vivarium, UVB light, a balanced diet,' I began. When there was no answer, I looked up; Mrs Smith was off talking to Queenie and seemed to have momentarily forgotten my presence.

Jeremiah seemed bright enough. He waved his legs strongly in the air and wiggled his head about, not at all intimidated by me examining him. He had a single horny claw at the tip of his tail and I vaguely remembered that this identified him as a Hermann's Tortoise – one of the most commonly imported species into the UK.

'You know Jeremiah is a CITES Appendix 1 protected species, don't you Mrs Smith?' I asked.

'Queenie knows all about that,' Mrs Smith replied, oblivious.

'Where does he live?' I enquired, fearing the answer.

'Oh, he has a room in the kitchen but I bring him in here during the day to keep me company,' Mrs Smith replied, reaching for a tall glass full of clear liquid. 'Would you like a drink?'

I thought better of it. Besides, vodka wasn't really my tipple.

'Very kind, but I'll just trim Jeremiah's beak and that way he should be much happier,' I replied. 'Can I see the kitchen?'

'Oh yes, you go through.'

Holding Jeremiah carefully, I gingerly stepped over more piles of books and magazines and headed towards a dirty white door. Gently opening it, I peered inside the room.

Mrs Smith had converted her kitchen into a series of vivariums; the glow of UV lights bathed the room in eerie light. Windowless, it was nevertheless a complete hub of glass tanks and heat lamps, and I guessed that thousands of pounds had been spent on decking the place out with special-ist reptile and amphibian equipment. It went some way to explaining why Jeremiah was in such a good condition aside from his beak, and the fact that Big Ben had looked like a cover model for Rodney Baffer's book.

Mrs Smith appeared at my side with a lopsided grin, sipping from her glass.

'Very impressive,' I said.

'Not bad is it? Queenie doesn't like it in there, though!' she cackled.

With a pair of clippers, I neatly trimmed Jeremiah's beak, jamming his mouth open with a needle cap. When I handed him back to Mrs Smith, she beamed.

'At least my sister is good to *you*, Jeremiah,' she whispered to the tortoise.

'How much do I owe you?' she slurred, turning to me.

'Oh, it's a free visit, we do them every now and again – community service,' I mumbled.

I touched my finger to Jeremiah's shell to say goodbye but before I could say the same to Mrs Smith, I heard a sudden commotion outside. I scrambled back, crashing into a tall vivarium as I came, and pulled back the curtains. Behind me, Mrs Smith seemed not to have noticed. She simply stood there, ogling Jeremiah with genuine affec-tion, the top-up effects of whatever was in her tall glass clearly hitting home.

There came another sound – a shattering of glass, and then a car alarm blaring. I scanned the vehicles below, a horrible foreboding in my gut. Somewhere, a dog howled fiercely. Its barking rose, wildly, into the night.

I turned. For the first time since she'd started on what I

presumed was the vodka, Mrs Smith fixed me with a look. 'Tell my sister I said *thank you*,' she ventured.

I nodded, snatched up my kit, and started to run.

On the stairwell, I almost lost my footing. I careered around the landing, crashed out the front door. The car alarms were still blaring, and the sound seemed to be spreading, the call taken up by other cars up and down the block.

In between the alarms, the dog still barked.

I hurtled along the road, dropping my kit as I went. Up ahead, the window of the practice car lay smashed in pieces across the ground. I hurried forward, ducked my head in where the window used to be – and the back seat was empty. Leuwen was gone.

I didn't know what to think. I pictured going to Cordelia, telling her what had happened, promising her I would get him back. I pictured my morning runs, without having to drag the obstinate pup out of the shelter of some hedgerow. I pictured my empty house – no mess on the floor, no dog hair on the seats.

Out there, in the din of alarms, the dog barked again. I must have heard it about two or three times before it pulled me from my thoughts. Quickly, I slipped into the driver's seat, fumbled with car keys, killed the alarms and listened. With a twist of the keys, I turned on the headlights and there, trapped in the beams, I saw it . . .

Against one of the garages on the other side of the block, two youths stood, petrified, one of them scrambling to see if he could haul himself onto the roof. In front of them, there was the shape of a small brown dog. The scene looked comical but the little dog was clearly ferocious. Snarling, its hackles were raised, its head ducked down as if itching to attack – it was utterly fearless.

'Leuwen!' I cried.

I leapt out of the car and hurried across the street. Halfway there, I stalled.

'Leuwen?'

Leuwen didn't move, his eyes transfixed on the two youths in front of him.

The tallest of the boys clocked me. In the darkness, his eyes seemed to be pleading with me.

'Call him off, Mister,' he stuttered. 'We're sorry, we didn't know, it was an accident.'

I inched forward, laid a hand on Leuwen's back. Only when I was touching him did his barking begin to cease. I whispered to him, and for the first time he took his eyes off the youths, flicking me a look.

'You're not going to dob us in, are you, Mister?'

'You should always let sleeping dogs lie,' I replied, patting Leuwen, immensely proud.

The youths turned to look at one another. I thought they were about to embrace, grateful to still be alive but then, quick as a flash, they took off, feet flailing behind them as they disappeared into the night.

'Good boy,' I said, 'I knew you had a bit of life in you.'

Leuwen almost ruined it by wagging his tail.

10

Sand, Sand and More Sand

The Berber tent flapped in the wind as sand sliced through numerous rents in the worn fabric. There was no way it would protect us from the force-five gale raging around the camp.

They'd warned me about this but, naturally, I hadn't listened. Even Cordelia had given me a way out but, naturally, I hadn't taken it. There wouldn't be a wind howling like this over the fields of the West Country back home but this was the choice I had made, and there was no backing out now.

I glanced around the tent's grainy interior. Eight dishevelled figures, covered by a thin film of Saharan grit, huddled together in silence as the storm ravaged the bivouac. The wind had been unrelenting for five hours and the initial thrill of being in a desert sandstorm had been rapidly dispelled as we'd battled to keep the tent upright. Not all our fellow competitors had been so lucky, much to my guilty amusement; groups of competitors lay practically smothered under flattened tents, their bags submerged by the hot sand.

I lay down and stared outside the tent. The scorched world

still seemed incredibly surreal. Just two days before I had arrived in Morocco, I had been on a calving at Hightown Farm after seeing a seamlessly endless stream of small animal consults. Now, I was in a different world. For ever and ever, there was only the desert – and the only animal in sight was my fellow man. I wished that Leuwen were here; there was certainly no rain for him to be bothered about and I could do with the company. More than that, I wished Cordelia were here. I pictured her greeting me with open arms upon my frankly-ridiculous-but-still-victorious return. It was the one thing that would keep me going.

The last few months had gone with a blur. Squeezing as many training runs as possible in between nights and week-ends on call had exhausted me. The only respite had been successive dates with Cordelia and I'd found myself literally running towards them as time ticked by. She'd watched my pitiful attempt to become an ultra endurance athlete with wry amusement but had always been poised with a ready word of encouragement about the charity and end goal. Somehow I'd even managed an eighteen mile training run the week before I was due to start the race. It signalled a milestone – and although not quite a full marathon, I felt I was on track.

'Everyone says if you can run a straight 18 miles, you can do a marathon. You're going to do this,' Cordelia had said with a smile, pushing an A4 file into my hands.

I glanced down at the homemade book and flicked open the cover. 'What's this?' I enquired.

'It's just a few guidelines you may find handy. Jess's friend told her that most people suffer from poor nutrition, electro-lyte imbalances, that sort of thing. It caused the majority to drop out the year he did it.' Cordelia paused, 'I just jotted down a few pointers you may find useful – how to manage your salt balance and some ration formulations that may help you. Do you like crushed pot noodles and pepperoni sausages?'

I laughed, remembering Cords had done an extra degree in human nutrition at Cambridge, and clutched the book tightly, the thoughtfulness of it touched me to the core. No way I could let her down – it was no longer just about me; my friends, family and my girlfriend had all put lots into getting me through the race with unfailing support – and Leuwen had suffered no end of wet morning runs!

I cringed from a sudden flurry of sand and inched back into the tent. Around me, there came a muted titter from my newfound companions. The people I had met so far had been frankly, fairly intimidating. I realised, for the first time, how much I was missing normality. I pictured Mr Tubbie out here and, for a moment, that brought cheer to my heart.

'So what's the hardest thing you've ever done before?' one of them asked. To his credit, he was trying to get the conversation flowing but I don't think any of us were in the mood for chit-chat.

I didn't think taking Leuwen for a walk in the rain would crack it and wondered what on earth I was going to say as each of the others started to answer in turn.

'Florida Ironman,' one of them replied. 'It was a total epic – I really struggled on the marathon stage.'

I looked across at him. Ripped with muscle, he looked every inch the ultra athlete.

'I didn't find Florida Ironman too bad – Lanzarote was a tough one,' another voice said.

I inwardly groaned. Ironman was a 2.4 mile swim and 112 mile cycle ride, all polished off with a full marathon.

Everybody I was with was a total nutter – and I was completely out of my league.

There was a momentary pause and I realised it was my turn.

'I once picked up this flat-packed lawnmower,' I said. 'The box had stated a self-assembly time of thirty minutes. It took me forty just to get the thing open, unpack the bits and spread them on the lawn. In fact, the whole thing took me all afternoon, hellish job – definitely right up there . . .'

There was a lingering pause.

'Yeah,' said a deep voice. 'They can be right bastards those self-assembly kits, can't they?'

I looked over at who had spoken and sharp eyes glinted back at me in amusement. Everyone laughed. I breathed a sigh of relief; perhaps this wasn't going to be so bad. For the first time in three weeks, I felt a glimmer of positivity about being stuck in the middle of the Sahara desert. The only ways out were running across it or being airlifted out as a medical casualty – and there was only one of them that was going to win me Cordelia's undying love and the future I wanted.

After landing in Ouarzazate, I had wandered aimlessly about the hotel where all the competitors were told to gather for pre-race briefings. Something in me really wanted Sam to be here but there was no way I was going to lure him into this escapade the same way I had lured him to Samos and India. We were allocated a roommate at random for the first night, before being bussed out to the desert the following day. I scanned the list of competitors to see where I was staying and who I'd be sharing with.

Nick was the first person I spoke to. He was waiting in the

room as I dragged my bag through the doorway. An RAF navigator, Nick was in his early forties and super-psyched for the race. He looked me up and down, and I had the ominous feeling that he was judging my chances – not just of reaching the finishing line, but of survival itself.

'You endured anything like this before?'

I shrugged. 'I was a student for years,' I said. 'I've endured a lot.'

Everything about Nick's gear was perfect. He had planned for every contingency, every possible thing that might go wrong or right. He spent the night ogling his pristine back-pack and weighing the sachets of sun cream he had set aside for each day.

'What factor are you using?'

I produced my bottle of supermarket own-brand and tried not to register the flickering look of disquiet in Nick's eyes.

As Nick gloried over his prize rucksack, I looked at my own ragged pack. I had discovered a large tear in its bottom just after I had got back from the calving at Hightown Farm. A single glance at the three-inch line of crude nylon stitches with which I had repaired it said it all to Nick. Fatherly, he sat me down and didn't waste a second in putting me straight about a few things concerning the ideal preparation for a race of the magnitude of the *Marathon des Sables*. I listened as attentively as I was able but my head was spinning with thoughts of back home, and long minutes later I came to from my daydream to realise I hadn't heard a word poor Nick had said.

'Are you okay?' he kindly asked.

'Just pre-race nerves,' I said.

'You should settle yourself down.'

'Maybe a beer would do the trick?' I ventured.

Nick's rolling eyes said more than words ever could.

'I'll join you,' he said, 'for an *orange juice*.'

Wolfishly, I grinned. 'No problem, one beer and one orange juice!' I declared.

The next day, we woke before dawn and boarded the coaches that would drive us out to the bivouac and awaiting sandstorm. As we rattled along, it naturally transpired that Nick was also something of disaster guru.

'See, when a plane goes down, the key thing is to get out of it as quickly as possible. It's the fumes that kill everyone,' he said earnestly.

'I thought it was the 30,000 foot drop?' I replied.

'That as well, but if you do get to the ground, you need to be right out that door. I can't stand it when they put fat people in the emergency exit seats! Key positions like that, you need someone who can leap up and get that door open and get everyone out.'

I nodded in silence, gazing out at the dry brown desert beyond the windows.

'I'm reading this book, *Great Escapes in Military History*, fantastic stuff. Now, if this bus crashes . . .'

It was too late, I had already tuned out. The race would be nerve-racking enough, and now I was worried about the bus ride and the plane journey home as well.

As we disembarked from the coach in order to climb into the back of army trucks which were destined to transport us further into the desert, I unfortunately lost Nick in the crowd. Momentarily I felt a terrible guilt for abandoning my new best buddy so quickly, but it didn't last long – Nick was so organised he would have a contingency plan for getting to his tent without a hapless sidekick in tow.

Covered in dust from the bumpy ride, I dragged my bags towards the ring of makeshift camps, wondering where on earth the British contingent were supposed to be located.

'Do you want to come in here?' an amused voice piped up from somewhere on my left. 'You look like you're struggling a bit.'

I turned to see a small man looking at me, wearing a pair of mirrored sunglasses and a big grin. He seemed as out-of-place as me, his chubby face topped with a mop of spiky brown hair. It occurred to me, suddenly, that if he'd possessed two large middle incisors he would have resembled a large beaver.

Naturally, I liked him immediately.

'If you've got room, I'd love a spot,' I replied.

'It's a free-for-all!' he said, laughing. 'Eight to a tent, find your home for the next week! We've two spaces left in here and you're welcome.' He paused, head bobbing up and down. 'My name is Chris by the way.'

He eagerly shook my hand and gestured towards the tent opening. As I walked forwards I glanced in the reflection of his sunglasses and realised why he had been wearing such a hearty grin. I had been standing at the back of the army truck and, as a result, was coated in the filth and dirt from the last leg of the journey. Sweat had left streaks down my face and my long blond hair was sticking out at all angles. I looked like I had already run for a week, and the race had not even begun.

'Worzel Gummidge would be proud,' I said.

Ducking inside the entrance, a sign pinned to the outside caught my eye – the number 98 read large and proud.

'Home sweet home!' the voice said behind me. 'Even to scarecrows! Welcome to Tent 98 . . .'

The sandstorm whipped in suddenly only an hour after we arrived and lasted most of the afternoon.

'We've got two days of kit checks and pre-race preparation and then it's the big off,' said Chris, after we'd done all the introductions.

'Perfectly logical,' said one of the Ironmen, introducing himself as Omar.

I liked Omar; he had an easygoing nature and, of course, a glass eye that rattled in its orbit. The result of a drunken bar fight in Spain over a beautiful señorita, the unnerving stare it radiated gave him a rugged edge – although watching him pop it out of the socket and give it a quick wipe was a surprise. I had already taken a lot of eyes out of animals in my time at Mr Spotswode's practice - but this was particularly gruesome.

'Got to keep the sand out of it,' he said apologetically to the big man sitting on his left, giving it a wipe.

The big man, John, winced. 'That might be one of the most horrible things I've ever seen . . . and I'm a fireman,' he said.

'You should have seen the mess after the guy smashed a bottle in his face!' Migs, Omar's friend and fellow Ironman, chipped in.

'Was she beautiful?' John asked.

'Very beautiful,' Omar replied with a shrug.

'Did you marry her?'

'I never saw her again,' Omar said candidly.

'Still – what memories, and he's great at dressing up as a pirate for a fancy dress party!' Migs laughed, slapping his friend on the shoulder.

Having only met Nick, a handful of paratroopers and army instructors at the hotel, it was refreshing to find myself in a tent along with a policeman, a fireman, two lawyers, two IT guys and a stockbroker. Despite the fact that one of them had almost joined the territorial SAS, collectively they seemed the most ordinary people of everyone I had met on this godforsaken race.

I felt I'd landed on my feet and the next day flew by. Spot checks were made of our packs to make sure that we all had essential first aid equipment along with rations for the week, a snake venom kit, a torch and a route map, medical card and emergency flare.

'Bit drastic isn't it?' Dylan began as we filed back into the tent, turning over the flare in his hands.

Dylan was the youngest of our little group. Wiry and lean of frame, he had a barely suppressed boundless energy and exuberant attitude to life.

'It's as much for someone else as yourself,' Lee, a policeman, chipped in.

'You mean if you find some poor sod collapsed and they've wasted their own flare?' John, the colossal fireman asked.

'Especially on the night stage,' Lee replied with a twinkle in his eye. 'This is billed as the most hellish footrace on earth for a reason you know. I hear that these flares go off all over the place once the race starts . . .'

'Like your backside during the night, you mean?' Rupert chipped in. A senior partner in a top law firm, he had marked himself out as the intellectual superior of the group, chatting away in fluent French to the local Moroccans who passed the tent.

Lee looked at him, and a horrible silence quickly descended. Around me, the guys quickly averted their eyes, like men in a saloon desperate to get out of the way of the coming gunfight.

Then, just as quickly as the atmosphere had soured, Lee

grinned. Stepping forward, he put a finger in Rupert's chest and prodded him backwards.

'You leave my backside out of this!' he said.

We all slept fitfully that night. By the time morning came, I was the first awake. I stood in the eerie pre-dawn light in the sand outside the tent, watching the camp stir. When the men behind me rose, and the banter started again, the queasy feeling in my gut gently subsided but it wasn't going to stay away for long. The race was about to begin and suddenly my legs felt hollow.

'My pack is too heavy,' came a grunt from behind me.

I twisted round. We were coming up to the first check-point; amazingly I had already managed about seven miles and despite pre-race nerves, I actually felt okay – almost enjoying it. Omar slung his pack down beside mine and looked at it.

'Your pack is about twice as big as the allowed limit, isn't it?' I commented.

'Yes, I think so,' Omar replied. God knows how he managed to get it through the pre-race checks and past the scales.

'What have you got in there?'

'Spare shoes, I like to wear slippers in the evening,' he said evenly, taking a sip of tepid water.

My expression said it all. I just couldn't believe the utterly ridiculous situation we were in. I was standing next to a ripped Ironman who was lugging a pair of slippers across the Sahara for foot comfort in the evenings.

Omar contemplated his pack for a moment and then bent down, flinging things out in a pile. It took him moments and then he stood up, readjusted a few straps and flashed me a grin.

'Perfectly logical to cut this down, that's much better,' he said.

'The slippers?' I asked, looking at the pile of items: tracksuit bottoms, extra ration packs and a spare metal water canister.

'The slippers stay,' he said, laughing, and with that we turned to trot off over the dunes. I considered the warm sun, the soft sand, the light banter – maybe it was a holiday after all.

Omar and I had arrived at the first night camp as dusk was setting over the Saharan grit that circled around us. I was exhausted. My back ached, my feet were sore and I had only managed the first day. Berber tents had been erected by the nomads employed to transport the camp from night stop to night stop and were arranged in a circle. Finding the one with a large '98' flapping outside the door, I pretty much collapsed inside and fell asleep in a matter of minutes.

'How you managing your water?' Dylan asked as I shuffled alongside him. It was the second day of the race and . . . well, I was still alive, so that was something.

'So, so,' I replied. Dylan seemed to effortlessly skip over the sand, as I laboured over every breath.

'I think we get another litre about three miles over that ridge,' Dylan chatted away.

I couldn't reply – partly because we were now going up an incline and partly because the news was too depressing to contemplate. I lurched awkwardly through a stretch of deep sand. Every time I took four steps forward it felt like I was sliding back three.

'Migs did well to pull it together last night, didn't he?' Dylan said, determined to continue his chatter as I wheezed alongside.

'Fantastic!' I managed.

I wasn't the only one to have struggled after the first day. It had been adrenaline-fuelled and many of the competitors had damaged themselves by running too hard and not taking on sufficient salt. Thanks to Cordelia's amazing nutrition notes, I was totally geared up on how much salt to take and how to manage my calorie intake, but many weren't. Migs, totally mismanaging his electrolyte balance in the heat and humidity, had spent his first night throwing up with horrendous headaches.

Thankfully, with a rousing Tent 98 effort, we sorted him out. It was a difficult task, but together we force-fed him the salt tablets and drinking water, restoring his electrolyte balance. A lesser man might have had his morale completely crushed by finding himself vomiting and nauseous at the end of the first day but Migs was a tough one, and wasn't going to give up so easily.

'Yes,' I managed, inwardly marvelling at how Migs had taken it easy through the start of the second day and now seemed to be stronger than ever, undoubtedly powering on somewhere ahead of us. 'He's got some stamina.'

'Do you know how many people dropped out after yesterday?' Dylan asked.

I looked at him, blinking away the sweat – he seemed totally oblivious to my near collapse. At last, we wrenched ourselves over the summit of the hill and, after a moment's pause, once I had regained my breath, I managed to answer.

'No,' was all that I said.

'Loads,' Dylan quickly replied, still itching to chat. He started to run again, and I laboured to follow. 'Imagine coming all this way and failing after the first couple of days – incredible! I heard a hundred people have dropped out. That's almost one in seven – all already failed!'

'I suppose, if you collapse, there's no coming back from it,' I said, feeling very close to doing exactly that.

'I dread to think how many of us have been dripped.'

The rules stated we were allowed one IV drip in cases of marked dehydration but if we needed to be dripped twice, we were removed from the race.

'Well, it's hard to keep hydrated in forty-six degree heat, running marathons over the desert and carrying a backpack,' I reasoned. I think I had a little more sympathy for our fellow lunatics' plight than Dylan.

'Meh!' Dylan protested. 'Only forty per cent of the race is sand like this, the rest is rocks and tracks – amazing how the desert landscape changes so much, isn't it?'

Dylan was right; the terrain did vary dramatically, ranging from endless stretches of undulating sand to massive flat plains littered with rocks the size of a man's head. Although twisting an ankle at the start would have caused massive problems, the real assassin, aside from poor water and salt management, were the fine grains of sand working their way into sweat-filled running socks and between toes. As feet pounded over rocky hard terrain, the fine sand particles lacerated and chewed up the feet as effectively as wrapping them in sandpaper. Most competitors had gaiters, which they looped around their running shoes before undertaking a sandy section of the course. Migs opted to change his socks at every checkpoint, whereas Dylan and I pressed on. I had brought a pair of gaiters but promptly snapped them as I put them on for the first time, whereas Dylan, for some reason, simply wasn't worried.

'There's the checkpoint!' Dylan suddenly chirped.

I looked up. To my utter relief, flags were waving on the horizon. We were halfway through the day – there were *only* another twelve miles to go. I blinked away a wave of fatigue and trotted on to get my stamp and receive my rationed litre of water.

'We're well within the time limit,' Dylan said, glancing at his watch. 'Not bad at all!'

As I opened my water and took an over-generous gulp, another familiar face walked over to join us. Omar squinted his one good eye and crouched down in front of me.

'I think today is a test,' he said.

'A test?' I enquired.

'Yes, logically, today is the today we will find hardest,' he continued. 'I think, if we get through today, tomorrow is no problem. Today our bodies realise we are in this for the long term, today we adapt to the desert or we suffer, our bodies will scream with pain.'

I didn't need to hear this. 'Very profound Omar,' I said. 'I think when we get through today, my body at least will scream with the pain tomorrow as well.'

'I thought Day Four was supposed to be the big one – the longest day – double marathon stage throughout the night,' Dylan piped up cheerfully.

'You're a ray of sunshine on a cloudy day, Dylan,' I said.

'Come on,' Omar grinned, standing up, 'we still have a long way to go, we'll cover it together.'

Galvanised into action, the three of us trotted off into the dunes.

I hadn't spoken for the best part of an hour by the time we approached the end of the stage. Having counted to eight thousand in my head to get me to the day's finish line, I hobbled into camp, only to see John by the medical tent. I didn't know I had any energy left in me, but I sprinted over.

An attendant looked up at me.

'We had to remove him,' the voice said. I could barely see his face for the way the sun was making me squint. 'He just collapsed on the course. He'll . . . .' The voice turned horribly serious for a second. 'He'll be okay,' he went on, 'but not for a little while.'

'His race is over?'

'Some people just won't make it to the finishing line. It's as simple as that.'

John's eyes were open, and he rolled them at me, defeated. I couldn't tell if that look was imploring me to go on and finish the race victorious, or to get out of this forsaken desert. Unable to look at him any further, I retired to our tent and collapsed myself.

Moments later, Omar and Dylan appeared, sinking into their mats.

'His size finished him,' Omar said as we lay in the tent, immobile and exhausted.

'How do you mean?' Dylan asked.

'He gets allocated the same water as you or me but he's the size of both of us put together – surely he needs more water?' Omar looked at me for scientific clarification.

I nodded sadly. It was the same with cows or horses, elephants and giraffes. At the end of the day, we were just animals like any other.

'Larger people have larger metabolic loads,' I mumbled as Migs came into the tent. 'They need more water.'

Migs stopped, looking at each of us in turn. 'I spoke to John,' he said. 'He's out for good. He's got kids back home, doesn't think he can risk pushing himself. He'd been vomiting uncontrollably when they found him. I think he was pretty brave calling it a day, I've no doubt he would have tried to drag himself onwards if he hadn't had a family to get back to.'

It was a sobering thought. I found myself suddenly thinking of being back home, with all my wild and wonderful friends, the new family I'd found since joining Mr Spotswode's practice. It got me thinking about what I had to get back to. Cordelia, Leuwen, family and friends. A pang of homesickness washed over me. I reached into my pack and pulled out a set of magnetic draughts that Cords had given me as a parting gift, clearly not quite grasping the fact that I had to carry my stuff during the race.

Rupert, who had also just arrived in the tent with Chris, looked at me incredulously.

'We're on weight limits for our packs and you've brought a magnetic board game?' he laughed.

'My girlfriend thought it would help me make friends,' I replied. I tried to imagine what Nick would say if he saw I had brought such a luxury item.

'Obviously has a good impression of your conversation skills, then,' Migs said, rolling over and setting up opposite me.

We'd hardly played half a game before a deep dreamless sleep descended.

'How does he do it? There are only a handful of women in this race, but somehow Chris knows all of them!' Lee gasped, hobbling beside me. His feet were totally raw; it looked as if someone had taken a cheese grater to the soles.

I paused to wipe a trail of vomit from my chin.

'He has the chat,' I managed to say, just before throwing up again.

I struggled to work out how Chris and Rupert, both really nice guys, had got themselves into this situation. They had calmly informed us all they were lawyers and that Rupert had

had a bad knee for the last six months and hadn't been able to train. They were a constant and unfailing source of humour and calm stoicism. They were also completely selfless, dishing out excess electrolyte tablets they just happened to have, and worked as a closely-knit team, conquering the race with what appeared to be nothing less than relative ease. If they hadn't struck me as such honest unassuming blokes, I might have thought they weren't telling us the whole story about themselves. Their skill in the desert was unparalleled among our little cabal. Lee and I were beginning to slough off large pieces of our feet, but Chris and Rupert didn't have a single blister, or a single hair out of place.

'Maybe, he's got a clean shirt tucked away somewhere that he puts on when he goes around the camp,' I said as we shuffled forwards. 'That would make him stand out.'

We had reached the halfway mark in the race, we were all disgusting, but I was certain that I ranked the filthiest competitor in the event.

I had to blame it all on the chicken.

The previous night my attempts to simmer up a boil in the bag chicken had backfired.

Too tired to boil it properly, I gulped it down cold and, scant hours later, I found myself crouched outside the tent, retching until it seemed as if my entire insides were forcing their way out. Naturally, this was very bad news.

Predictably, the diarrhoea was not far behind. I spent the next ten hours squatting over shallow depressions in the sand, wiping the cold sweat from my forehead, making silent entreaties to the gods of the desert that, if they could stop this, I myself would stop at nothing to irrigate their plains and turn them into a lush, fertile kingdom.

Sleep barely came to me that night and by the time my

fellows were slowly getting up, loosening stiff joints and muscles, and wondering what that unearthly smell was that seemed to be hanging about the camp, I knew that I was in for about the worst eighteen hours of my life. Today was the longest stage of the race – and the way I felt this morning, I would have struggled to get into the practice back home.

I set out to a barrage of cajolements and vaguely encouraging grins from my compatriots. Perhaps I was still delirious, for I kept thinking I could see Leuwen gambolling along beside me, or Cordelia waving from the next dune. Once, I was certain I could hear Sam whispering in my ear. 'This is another fine mess you've gotten us into,' he seemed to be saying.

For the first time ever, Sam was right.

Dylan stuck with me through the day. Keeping a safe distance – a cloud of stench drifted alongside me, my clothes stained with vomit and all the other results of my night's endeavours – he kept pace with me and kept me going. As we ran, my body seemed to drop into autopilot. I was a zombie, completing a zombie marathon across a zombie landscape. I couldn't eat anything, the heat was unrelenting and I struggled to keep even my rations of water down. When I could think at all, all that I could think of was the big danger of losing all my electrolytes as it was very hard to take salt tablets on an empty stomach.

'You'll end up dead in a ditch,' I heard Sam laughing. 'Carrion for the desert!'

'You'd like that, wouldn't you?'

'At least I'd get another holiday to Ibiza . . .'

'I'll haunt you, make sure you go back to Samos.'

A sudden voice reached out to me. 'Who are you mumbling at, Luke?'

I squinted up. Dylan was still running alongside me but

now he seemed to be wagging his tail, a horrible hybrid of Dylan and Leuwen.

'Dylan,' I said, 'I'm the happiest I've ever been in the world ever.'

'That's the delirium talking,' Dylan replied. 'Come on, mate, only fifteen miles left to go!'

By nightfall, I was really lagging, and even Dylan had pushed a little way ahead. I fancied I could see him keep looking back, as if to make sure that the desert hadn't totally swallowed me up. As I lurched awkwardly on, all I could think of was the endless mockery that Sam and Rob would dish out to me should I stop. But then, I'd already managed to keep on my feet far longer than I had thought possible. I began to wonder if it would really be so unforgivable to just lie down now and wait for the helicopters to come.

I thought of Samos, and I thought of India, and I thought of all the other thousand places in the world I one day wanted to go. I thought of Mr Spotswode and Giles and all the good they had done back home and how I, one day, wanted to do that good for animals everywhere. Somehow, it gave me new fire. The prospect of failing the charity drove me another five miles and then the fear of letting Cordelia down gave me a last surge of energy.

Somehow, long after everyone else, and only seconds before the stage of the race was formally closed, I stumbled into camp. I wanted to let out a wild, victorious howl but all that would come out was a simpering gurgle.

As I flopped down on the sand, watching the sun set over the Sahara, a figure shuffled over and crashed down beside me. It was Lee, the policeman, and he was also in a battered state. His feet were raw and he could hardly move through the sand.

'You made it,' I gasped.

'Only part of me,' Lee replied. He lifted up his feet, but they were torn to shreds by the relentless sand. 'I left the rest of them out in the desert.' If he had had the energy, he might have grinned.

'Just twelve miles left!' Dylan beamed at me through the first light.

I opened my parched lips a fraction. My legs felt like blocks of cement. I shook Lee until he woke up, and instantly he winced.

'Bugger off,' he managed.

'585 of the 731 competitors left!' Dylan said irrepressibly. 'You know, someone is in a coma, someone else has had a heart attack and I heard that one of the girls had a stroke! I need to check with Chris about her, but, you know, they've given out a record number of IV drips this year. Apparently the humidity has been right up!'

Casting an envious glance at Dylan, who seemed immune to any form of hardship, I looked down at my own swollen feet. I wondered if they would hold together long enough to carry me the final distance.

'The orchestra were amazing last night weren't they?'

I turned to see a rangy man I didn't recognise come and sit down near our tent. He seemed to be scanning the horizon expectantly.

'The orchestra?' I was nonplussed.

'The Paris Philharmonic!' the man exclaimed. 'Don't tell me you . . .'

I shrugged. 'I was tired,' I said.

Apparently, the Paris Philharmonic orchestra had joined us in the desert for our last night in the tents. The men around me said that the music had been so uplifting and the euphoric atmosphere in the camp rousing, but somehow I had missed the whole thing.

'You must have been half-dead!' Dylan cried.

'Three quarters,' I replied.

As we all stirred and readied ourselves, I realised that this was it. There was no way any of us were not going to make the last stage. Even if we had needed to drag ourselves by our teeth, we were going to get through.

I looked at the rangy man. 'How's your race going?'

The tiny backpack marked out the newcomer as a professional who was running in the race to win. I fancied I had seen him once or twice before, skipping over the dunes faster than I could sprint downhill on concrete.

'I'm only fourth,' he said, his eyes focused on the horizon. 'I'll need to go very fast today.'

'You do this every year?' I asked.

'I do them all over the world, but with this one, it is hard to beat the brothers,' he said quietly. I knew who he meant. The Ahansal brothers were famous; they were *Marathon des Sables* legends and always seemed to come first and second. 'Perhaps this year, it is my time . . .'

Bidding the stranger good luck, I saw Dylan raise his eyebrows.

'Different league to us, pal,' I said.

Dylan watched the runner disappear to get ready for the final leg.

'I guess that's the beauty of the race. No matter what your level, ultimately it's a challenge with yourself,' he said soberly.

I shook my head. There Dylan went with his philosophy again!

'I mean, if you're an elite ultra endurance athlete, it throws up different difficulties to the ones we have, who are just striving to complete the distance. You could say it's even harder for the people who can't run at the speed of light and end up spending double the amount of time in the baking sun. It's not like we have any extra water and at least the elites get out of the sun fairly sharpish! The elites are in it for the bucks, us amateurs are in it for the deeper reasons – the personal quest.'

I looked at Dylan in vague disbelief, but what the heck – two could play at this game. 'They say everyone gains something special from it,' I said.

Dylan looked at me, a big grin forming on his face.

'Except the guy in the tent next door who's had to have his toes amputated.'

I tried to join in the laughter, but I couldn't. I could hardly feel my own toes anymore and, having seen the state of Lee's, I didn't want to tempt fate. I'd taken a bunch of toes off a greyhound a few months ago, and I didn't fancy having the same thing done to me.

I started to jog on the spot, but only for a second; I didn't have the energy to spare.

'And on that note, with the very real risk of becoming part of your macabre list of statistics, let's get it done before I fall apart,' I said.

'See you on the other side!'

It was the shortest leg of the race, but I joined the throng of cripples at the back of the field and hobbled towards the finish line. I imagined Leuwen charging around in the sand, barking at me in excitement, all my friends and family waiting for me at the finishing line. I must have passed hours in that delirious daydream, for suddenly I found myself running hard on the home straight, passing an old man seemingly in his seventies and an obese Australian girl who heaved herself forward and gave me a big thumbs-up. Where paratroopers had failed, these two would be victorious. There was probably a lesson in that but I was too drained to see it.

A sense of euphoria filled me – whether it was a state of delirium induced by chronic dehydration or the feeling that I was almost at the end of one of the most physically demanding challenges of my life, I had no idea – but I knew that the charity was possible, that it was going to work. And, suddenly, I knew that I was going to win Cordelia's heart – this desert race was a small step to prove to her I was a winner. I imagined falling into her arms off the plane. She would look at me and tell me I was an idiot, but she'd be impressed nonetheless. Then, as if by magic, the practice mobile would ring, and we'd be jetting off to operate on some donkey who'd fallen off a tower block, or a dolphin who'd taken a wrong turn and ended up in a local lake.

The finishers' archway was only a hundred yards ahead. I slowed down, breathing it all in. Across the line, the others were already waiting: Dylan and Omar, Lee and the rest. I must have slowed down too much for, before I noticed what was going on, the seventy-year-old man and the obese Australian girl were ahead of me.

I didn't care. I just didn't care.

I considered the conversation Dylan and I had had that morning as I surged across the finish line. This whole race had indeed been a competition with myself. Looking up, I saw all seven of my friends lined up along the pathway, clapping and cheering my last steps.

It almost brought a tear to my eye. Despite their own weariness, they had all waited to make sure I made it to the end. They weren't quite the family and friends I had left in England but they would do for today, I thought to myself, they would do for today.

To Be a Pilgrim

'So you did it?' Sam's voice buzzed down the phone.

'Lost all my toenails but I'm officially back, £4k raised,' I replied proudly. 'This charity is going to happen, Sam.'

'And, dare I ask . . .'

I stayed silent.

'Cordelia!' he barked.

'All part of the plan, buddy,' I said. 'I can feel it.'

'In your water?'

I thought about not dignifying it with a response. 'Yes, Sam,' I said. 'I can feel Cords in my water.'

'Okay okay, tell me what it was like out there,' Sam said.

I stretched out on my sofa. Leuwen was still sniffing at my feet. He'd been fascinated by them ever since I came back. Some dogs can sniff out cancers, tumours, liver disease; mine could sniff out the fact that I had smelly feet.

'It was . . . *sandy*,' I replied.

'Profound. Well, all I can say is thank goodness I didn't come on holiday with you for that one. You total idiot!'

I was glad I had done it, but there was no way I was going back there again. I'd trudged back home with more difficulty than I'd had running across the desert. Everything seemed to weigh a thousand tonnes. Leuwen had greeted me at the door, where Rob had dropped him off, and had almost bowled me over when he threw himself forward.

'So,' Sam went on, 'how much more pleased was Leuwen to see you than Cordelia?'

'That's not a nice question,' I said evasively. 'But he wagged his tail a lot.'

'Did she wag anything?'

Leuwen licked at my feet. I ushered him away. It wasn't going to help.

'We had a great welcome back dinner – that's all I am saying.

It was good to hear his voice again – the real voice this time, not the ghostly one that had jibed and cajoled me through the desert.

'Look, I've got some good news. I've got myself a woman.'

I whooped down the phone. At the end of the sofa, Leuwen leapt back in surprise. With a dogged look, he hurtled to the window, convinced an intruder was on the way. I was going to have to give him some more training.

'No, she isn't blind, before you ask,' Sam said. 'She's a zoo vet – her name is Jane.' He seemed immensely proud.

'Does she do a lot of work with gorillas?' I asked.

'You are such a fool,' came the response.

'Seriously though, is she Jane and you Tarzan – how does it work?'

I'd been laughing a full minute before I realised the line had gone dead.

Heading off to work the next morning, I loaded Leuwen in the car and gingerly eased myself behind the wheel. My feet were still sore and they felt funny without any toenails, but with each day I was recovering and I felt fantastic as I headed for my first day back at work.

I decided to take the scenic route. I'd come here wet behind the ears, but now it really felt like home. Perhaps it had taken the desert to put that in perspective.

When I pulled into the practice car park, Rob was waiting. When Leuwen saw him, he rose on the back seat and pressed his face to the glass.

I rolled up alongside him and wound down the window.

'Morning, *Trustee*,' I beamed.

'Morning,' Rob replied. There was something sombre about his voice.

'I've already got your duties stacked up, mate,' I told him.

'Luke, well done on the race, never would have thought it . . .'

'Honestly, I've got a list a mile long . . .'

'Luke!' Rob's eyes made me lay off. In the back seat, Leuwen let out a little whine. Even he'd picked up on something.

'Don't tell me you're backing out?' I began, venturing a tentative laugh.

'Luke, we can't wait to hear all about the adventure, but I need to talk to you before you go in.'

I looked at Rob, perplexed. 'This is a bit clandestine isn't it? What's going on?'

Rob opened the passenger door of my car and got in. Leuwen's tail beat steadily on the back seat in greeting.

'You want me to drive? What have you done? I can't help you cover up a murder, Rob.'

'Luke, would you give me a break.'

I kicked the engine back into gear and idled the Car of Power back out of the car park. I didn't know why, or where I was driving but sometimes it's just best to drive. We mooched around the village, cutting a circuit of the local fields.

'Luke, there is no easy way to tell you this and I couldn't do it on the phone,' Rob began. 'It's Mr Spotswode.'

Instinctively, I hit the brakes. The car lurched to a stop in the middle of the road. Up above, the morning sun beat down. It really was a beautiful day.

'What is it, Rob?'

'You need to know that Mr Spotswode has been taken ill.' Rob paused. When Leuwen's head appeared between us, both of us began to tease his ears, as if it would make the news easier to bear. 'He's retiring from the practice at the end of the month.'

I stared at Rob, dumbfounded.

'Is this a wind-up?' I asked, deeply hoping that it was.

Rob shook his head sadly, still petting Leuwen.

'He's retired, Luke. The partnership's dissolving, and the practice is probably going to change hands. I don't know what else to tell you,' he said heavily.

The end of the month was only two weeks away. I slumped back in my seat. A motorcyclist overtook us on the blocked road, waving back in disgruntlement.

'When did this happen?'

'We were told last week, while you were gone. Mr Spotswode was taken ill about the same time you flew off to Morocco. It's a serious business.'

'What is it, Rob?'

I hardly wanted to know, but something compelled me to ask the question.

'I don't know exactly,' Rob said levelly. 'He isn't going to die or anything, but it's serious, Luke. He can't work here full-time anymore. You know how he is – he wouldn't be going if he didn't have to.'

'And no one thought to send me a message?' I demanded. Seconds later, I knew I was being petulant, and tried to rein it in. 'I was off gallivanting in the desert, and nobody . . .'

'We all agreed not to tell you in case it messed up your chances. It isn't public knowledge, Luke, not yet. Holly and I were only told at the end of last week that he wasn't coming back. No one outside the practice knows about this, before you start wondering.'

I sat there, speechless. So much had changed in such a short period of time. I pictured the entrance to the practice; I couldn't imagine walking in without Mr Spotswode there to greet me. I'd learnt more from Mr Spotswode and Giles than I ever had from endless seminars and lectures back at vet school.

'How are things round the practice?' I finally asked.

Rob shrugged evenly. 'Giles is managing things, but he's really gone into his shell. It's hit him harder than anyone. I think they'll probably sell off the farm business. The clients don't know what's going on, other than that Mr Spotswode is ill. They're bringing gifts left, right and centre. I don't know how they're going to take the news.'

'So he's definitely not coming back?' I said, grasping for that final straw.

'He retires on the 31st.'

I rubbed my face with my hands and looked at Rob.

'Blimey,' I managed.

'Blimey indeed,' Rob replied.

Mr Lock stood opposite me, his face etched with deep concern and a hand resting on the eight-month-old golden retriever between us.

'I just found Barney in the yard holding his leg up,' Mr

Lock began. 'No idea how he did it, must have been a blasted rabbit hole. Is it a nasty one, Luke?'

I looked down at Barney, who wagged his thick tail in greeting and held out his front leg for me to examine.

'It's nice for him to see a friend down here. He seems quite pleased to be at the surgery!' Mr Lock continued.

'He's probably hoping Leuwen will bound into the room so they can have a play,' I said fondly, stroking Barney.

'Where there's no sense there's no feeling – isn't that so, Barney!' I said, patting his head. 'Right, let's have a look at this leg shall we?' I said as my fingers gently began to trace towards the break.

There was no blood on the hair, but the lower part of the limb felt limp and, sure enough, halfway up the leg I could feel where the injury had taken place.

'Well, it hasn't gone through the skin,' I said, looking up at Mr Lock.'That's a good sign. It feels as if it could be quite straightforward, but we'll only know with an X-ray and once we get in there to repair it.'

'He definitely needs an anaesthetic then? You can't bandage it, let it heal the old fashioned way?' Mr Lock asked, wringing his hands together for the first time.

'He's a big dog,' I replied with a smile. 'A splint might work but it might not hold it straight enough and we'd end up with a deformed leg. The best way to get the two ends together again is to prevent the movement of the bones and that means we can't have them rotating or twisting round. I think he'll need a plate in his leg.'

'A plate! Hear that Barney, you're going to become bionic!' Mr Lock gave a forced laugh, but he was clearly worried about the whole procedure.

'This way we can not only check the break is as

straightforward as I think, we can also do a proper job, and get him a hundred per cent in about twelve weeks. We need him perfect so he can catch those rabbits and get his own back!'

'Leuwen is going to be upset – no one to charge round with for a while,' Mr Lock replied, trying to put on a brave smile.

'You've got him in here right away,' I said. 'I can X-ray him this morning and Giles is free, so we have the expert ortho-paedic surgeon on hand. I promise you, we'll get Barney fixed in no time, you don't have to worry.'

Mr Lock bent down and nuzzled his forehead into Barney's brow. Barney stuck out his tongue and gave his owner a big friendly lick.

'Well, I'll leave him with you then, Luke,' Mr Lock said, though he hadn't quite suppressed the trembling in his voice. 'Sorry to land you with an op on your first day back. You'll keep me posted?'

'Absolutely,' I replied, and as Mr Lock left the room, I gently carried Barney out the back and went to talk to Giles.

We got started straight away. Once Barney was prepped and we were ready to go, Giles gestured for me to pick up the drill and indicated where he wanted me to position it.

'Go steady with it,' he instructed. 'Once through the bone, you have to stop immediately or you'll damage the tissue underneath.'

It was the first major fracture repair I'd done, and I care-fully followed every direction Giles issued. Thinking Giles would want to do the surgery, and knowing Barney couldn't be in better hands, I'd assumed I would be sent out to the farms and it had been a real surprise when Giles had instructed Holly to clear my diary so I could join him in the operation.

The break itself wasn't too bad – an overriding transverse

fracture of the radius and ulna. Being fresh, it was easily reducible and the bones could be repositioned with little difficulty. The hard bit was ensuring that the plate we were fixing was fully supportive and would let the bone fuse again with minimal movement.

'That's good, now, let's get the screws in here,' Giles said, peering intently at the leg.

The plate fixed, I looked up at Giles.

'Steady hands, good job,' he nodded. 'The Sahara hasn't addled your brain. So you can now do luxated patellas, cruciates and plate a broken leg – your skills are building.'

'I think I need a bit more practice to say I can plate a broken leg,' I replied, 'but it was a brilliant experience. Thank you.'

Giles had seemed sad throughout the operation. He regarded me now, studiously, the same way he would look at a fractured bone or crushed paw.

'A lot has changed in two weeks, hasn't it?' he finally said.

I glanced across at Holly. She had been with us through the operation, but she now seemed immersed in monitoring the anaesthetic and had her stethoscope firmly in her ears.

I nodded. I didn't know what else to say. 'Giles,' I began.

'You'll have heard that the practice is going to be sold and Mr Spotswode is retiring,' he continued.

I focused on placing my skin sutures as Giles cleared his throat.

'Well, Luke, we have a buyer.'

I stopped. I realised that my hands were shaking, and I didn't want poor Barney to suffer that.

'A buyer?' I asked.

'It's a corporate company. A big chain.'

It was like a vile curse to Giles. He'd spent his life in this small independent practice, but he and Mr Spotswode had always been flying in the face of progress. It was the twenty-first century, after all, and corporate veterinary practices were marching across the country like an army in the days of old.

'They're not interested in the farm work, Luke. We need to sell it off before they consider buying us out. They'll then run it as a small animal practice, part of their chain.'

In silence, I tied off my last suture and looked up at Giles. I couldn't imagine Giles as a small animal vet in a corporate, run by non-vets who were often interested in the business for the money it would generate. I thought suddenly of the valuers falling on the farms during Foot and Mouth, like a plague of locusts.

'But Giles, you'll miss the farm work,' I said.

Giles nodded.

'More than you can imagine,' he replied. 'That's why . . .' He paused, struggling to find the right words. 'Luke, I'm leaving too.'

I sighed and laid down my instruments. Holly had shuffled out of the room now, and I felt more alone than I had in the desert.

'Are you sure?' I asked, though the look on his face told me that Giles had thought about this deeply. For him, there was no other option.

'I'll probably go to New Zealand to live with my brother, but I'm weighing up my options. I'll be tied in here for six months or so once the sale goes through, but after that I'll leave. I'm not cut out to be a small animal vet, Luke.'

'You could stay though, be independent again?'

Giles shook his head sadly. 'I'm forbidden to branch off and set up on my own around here for obvious reasons – it would scupper the whole deal for all the other partners.' He allowed himself a fleeting grin. 'But what an opportunity it would be! If I wasn't a partner and wanted to have a go at setting up a new practice, now would be the time to do it.'

Giles was eyeing me oddly. I found myself stroking Barney again, soothed by the rhythmic rising and falling of his chest.

'Once the farm side is shut down, I'm sure some local vets will have their eye on our farms and not be intending to pay us for an introduction. And there's all the equipment we have here, too. It's just going to go to waste . . .'

The silence lingered again. Perhaps I was delirious again, or perhaps just stupid.

'Look, Luke . . .'

Giles raised his bushy black eyebrows. I couldn't believe what I thought he was hinting at.

'We'll get a pittance for the farm side, Luke. Practices don't buy farms – they poach them off other practices. Farmers are their own men. I worked damn hard to build up our farm contingent, and it's all going to waste – unless someone makes the most of it. This opportunity is there on a plate – you know what I'm saying.'

'Giles, I can't possibly . . .'

Before I could continue, Giles raised a hand and hushed me.

'Think about it. We both know you aren't going to stay five minutes when the practice gets taken over. You're not a corporate vet, Luke. Hasn't this crusading off to Samos and India taught you that about yourself?'

My mind was reeling. Setting up the emergency service had been one thing – but I'd had the full support of the practice and Sheila to help me run it. Taking on a farm practice was a different matter entirely – it was big business, not just covering on-call.

Holly reappeared, sensed the silence in the room, and, after quickly checking the anaesthetic again, beat a retreat.

'It's just that this practice: you, Mr Spotswode, everyone here – you've given me so much. This is what I want to do for the rest of my life and that's down to you. I don't think I could work for a corporate, Giles, but setting up on my own – it never occurred . . .'

'Just like this conversation,' Giles said, giving me a wink and ungloving. 'Give it some thought, Luke. Life rolls on. Sometimes you don't get to pick the way it goes, but sometimes – just sometimes – it rolls your way.'

I looked up at Giles and nodded. As he turned to leave, I looked down again. The operation was over, Barney was fixed and a whole world of change loomed on the horizon.

As Barney was taken back to his kennel to recovery and Giles headed off to his office, I went through to prep to check on some blood results I had taken earlier, my mind reeling with everything we had just discussed.

'Somebody, anybody, I need a hand here!' Rob bellowed from the cattery.

I set down my papers and hurried through. Rob stood with his hands cupped around a small furry object, a look of mild panic on his face.

'What's going on?' I asked.

'I just picked him up to discharge him and the whole wound opened up. The little blighter's gone and chewed through his stitches. The clients are waiting and the more he wriggles, the worse it's going to get!' Rob paused to catch his breath. 'Bugger!' he cried. 'I didn't even do the surgery!'

I edged closer and peered between Rob's hands.

'It's a mouse!' I exclaimed.

'Well done Sherlock, your powers of deduction are second

to none!' Rob tried to calm the mouse down, but his attempts were futile. 'This is no ordinary mouse, Luke. This is Ernie, a mouse belonging to a six-year-old boy. He had a large growth removed from his side this morning.'

'The mouse, or the little boy?' I quipped.

'Shut up Luke, this is serious!'

The mouse squeaked in Rob's hands.

'Deadly serious,' I replied.

'Look, the little boy's been worried sick about this mouse. He's out there now, with his mum, to pick it up!'

I hurried to the door, craned around to look at the waiting room. Sure enough, a little boy was out there, eagerly waiting the return of his pet. He was in a wheelchair, his mother by his side.

'What are we going to do, Luke? I can't give him back like this!'

That much was evident. I could see half the mouse's abdominal muscles through Rob's wriggling fingers.

'Two anaesthetics in a few hours aren't going to be good for this little fella,' Rob went on, 'and I can't put him down or it'll completely open up – and then he's done for!'

'What do you want me to do?' I grinned, peering at the little face poking out between Rob's fingers.

'I'm working on that one,' Rob said, his face racked with indecision. 'You could go take a long walk off a short pier, for a start!'

I paused. Something hit me, like a bolt from the blue.

'Why on earth did you put a mouse in the cattery?' I asked.

Rob pulled an exasperated expression. 'Well, Barney was making a racket this morning and it was so quiet in here, I thought, all things considered, the mouse would have a better time of it.'

'As long as you don't let it go and it scurries into the wrong cage by mistake!' I said, stifling a smile.

'Being eaten by a cat is the least of its worries,' Rob replied.

'Do you want me to go and tell the kid there's a problem?' I said.

Rob's eyes widened. 'NO!' he barked.

'That was a "no thank you", was it?'

'Sorry,' Rob said. 'I promised the boy that Ernie would be okay. We have to sort it, now.'

I pondered for a moment.

'Can we glue it?' I said.

'I don't know. Do you reckon it will hold?'

'The skin is pretty thin,' I reasoned, 'but at least the mouse won't chew through the glue – we also won't need to anaesthetise it. I mean, the wound is fresh, it has to be our best option – but I've never used glue on a mouse before.'

'First time for everything!' Rob said, a glimmer of hope flashing across his face. 'Come on Luke, chop to it!'

I dashed out of the cattery, grabbed the tissue glue from the fridge and raced back.

'Do you want to hold it steady and I'll glue?' I said, unscrewing the top off the bottle.

'Right, be careful, we need to make sure the skin doesn't overlap,' Rob said. 'It's a nice mouse, it shouldn't bite.'

'Shouldn't bite? You sound like half the clients!'

Little Ernie looked up at me, his impossibly sweet face twitching in the bright light. I looked at the gaping wound on its side; the poor creature had completely unzipped itself.

Gently inverting the bottle, I placed three drops on the skin and quickly held them together.

'What a good mouse! He isn't moving at all, I've got the edges together, I think it's working!' I flashed Rob a big grin.

At first, Rob grinned back but then as he looked down, his face took on a horrified expression.

'What?' I asked, still smiling. 'You look like . . .'

'You're not wearing gloves!' Rob suddenly blurted.

'No, it's fine, I've also just come from surgery, I'm clean.'

'No, you idiot!' Rod said, a hint of panic creeping into his voice. 'It's tissue glue! The last time I looked, your fingers were designated as tissue, unless you've got plastic skin!' Rob stopped. 'I think we've just jumped from the frying pan into the fire.'

As realisation dawned on me, I tried to flex my fingers apart.

Ernie gave a little squeak. Not one of my fingers could move. I looked Rob in the eye. There was panic between us now.

'I'm stuck to Ernie,' I said, trying and failing to remain calm. 'What on earth do we do now?'

'I have no idea,' Rob replied.

The mouse gave another little squeak and I placed my other hand underneath it.

'Stop moving your hand,' Rob said irritably. 'It's frightened.'

'Not a massive surprise considering how things have turned out,' I retorted. 'You've shut it in a cattery for the day and now the poor creature is stuck to my fingers! Why didn't you remind me to wear gloves?'

'Remind you? I'm trying to hold the mouse together, you were supposed to be helping me fix it – you're a vet, remember!'

'Look, you told me to run and get the tissue glue – wasn't it an emergency?' I snapped back.

Suddenly, the door to the cattery flew open. Holly stood there, screwed her eyes up, and paused.

'Oh . . . sorry,' she began, turning as if to leave.

'Holly!' I shouted. 'We're in trouble! Big, big trouble.'

'I didn't realise you were having a secret meeting,' she continued, still oblivious to our predicament. 'But the noise is carrying and the clients can . . .'

'Holly, we're not having a secret meeting, we're trying to help this . . .'

I didn't get a chance to finish. Too late, Holly had seen the mouse and let out a loud squeal. Quickly, she clapped her hand over her mouth.

'Holly, pull yourself together,' Rob said, more and more frustrated with every moment that passed.

Holly slumped against the wall, her body shaking with laughter as she pointed at Ernie, her eyes widening into saucers. She tried to speak but no words came out of her mouth.

'Brilliant, let the comedy continue,' Rob breathed, his face flushed. 'Look, you stay here, I have to go and tell the client we'll be with them shortly – they've been waiting for fifteen minutes, they'll be getting worried.'

'Don't you go anywhere, we need to get this poor mouse off my finger!' I cried.

As Rob walked out the door, I turned to look at Holly.

'How do you dissolve tissue glue, Holly?' I asked.

'Why is there a mouse in the cattery, anyway?' Holly managed, gulping for air.

'Holly, seriously, that's the least of Ernie's concerns! You have to help me figure out how to free him, he's totally stuck.'

I looked down at the little ball of fur. He regarded me quite calmly. Thankfully, Ernie didn't seem at all distressed. Ever since I'd kept him still, he hadn't squeaked once. In fact, he seemed very relaxed as he looked around the room, one side of his body completely adhered to my finger and thumb.

Holly walked over and gave him a little stroke.

'It's a very calm mouse, isn't it?' she said.

'Calm for the moment, but I can't imagine he's having the best day of his life,' I replied.

'If anything happens to him, at least he'll be in easy reach for mouse to mouse resuscitation,' Holly giggled.

'Honestly Holly, it's not funny,' I replied, unable to raise even a half-smile. 'Next you'll be telling me to oil him if he squeaks!'

Holly set herself off again and I raised my eyes to the ceiling. 'Holly, please calm down, we need to think.'

'You mean, you want me to be quiet as a . . . mouse,' Holly gasped.

I sat down on the floor, lowering Ernie to my lap as I did so.

'This is one hell of a prosthetic. I don't know how we're going to sort this, it's a nightmare,' I said, testing the full extent to which Ernie was stuck. 'I've managed to stick his whole side to me, I can't pull him off!' I groaned. 'I'll tear him in half!'

'I'll go and ask for some advice,' Holly said, bolting for the door before another wave of laughter paralysed her.

What felt like hours but can only have been a few minutes later, the door opened again and Rob strode in.

'Haven't you got it off yet?' he asked.

'No, I haven't got it off yet. I've only got one free hand – what do you expect me to do? Cut my fingers off?' I retorted.

Rob sat down beside me and placed his head in his hands.

'I told the client that Ernie was still a bit sleepy. They've gone to the shop next door for twenty minutes.'

'Twenty minutes and counting. That was at least fifteen minutes ago!'

'This boy is going to be mortified if we can't get Ernie off your fingers,' he said.

'Holly went to ask around if anyone knew of something that might be able to dissolve the glue,' I replied.

We sat there in muted silence, both of us lost in our own thoughts.

'Big changes ahead then,' Rob said quietly.

'Giles seems to think I should set up on my own and take the farm clients for starters,' I blurted.

Rob reared back. In my hands, Ernie followed him with his gaze.

'Really?' he asked.

'He said they have to sell the farm side of the business, he can't take it on because he's legally obligated to the sale of the practice as a whole. He's in a state, Rob. He's put all that hard work into building the farm practice and now, all of it's going to fall by the wayside.'

'Won't the partnership lose money if that happens?' Rob asked.

'Giles didn't seem to be too worried about that. The whole conversation just caught me by surprise, mate. What do you think?'

'I think you look damn stupid with a mouse stuck to your finger.'

I shot him a look. 'About the practice,' I said.

'I think it's nuts,' Rob said. 'But it is a rare opportunity, Luke. You'd have a farm practice in the blink of an eye. The farmers like you, you'd do a good job, but . . .'

'But what?'

Before Rob could reply, Ernie squeaked sadly. He was getting bored with being stuck in a rut as well.

'But why stop there?' Rob went on. 'Why not make it mixed, really take it on?'

I sat in silence. 'What about you, Ernie? What do you think?'

'He thinks he wants to get off your finger!' Rob sighed. 'Where's Holly?'

He stood, as if to go after her, but I called him back. We had more to discuss. In a weird way, I felt hostage – a captive in a cattery, with a mouse stuck to my fingers with glue.

'How about you – are you interested?' I asked, my mind racing at the possibilities. Perhaps this didn't have to be sad. Perhaps there really could be something good coming from Mr Spotswode's retirement. If Rob and I joined forces, we'd have an incredible start.

Rob was at the door. He angled his head out. From the look on his face, I could tell that Ernie's owners were back.

'It's too late, Luke,' he said quietly. 'I haven't told anyone yet but I've just been accepted for a residency in ophthalmology at Bristol vet school. I'm going to specialise.'

I looked down at Ernie. For some reason, his eyes widened. Even Ernie was shocked at this news.

'I wasn't going to tell you right away, not with all the practice upheaval. You know, it's difficult enough.' He paused. 'We've all got to get out, Luke, make our own way . . .'

I fell silent again. Rob slumped against one of the cattery cages.

'Look,' he said, 'I'm going to stay in the area. I'll be able to help you out with cover – I want to keep my hand in anyway.' He paused. 'You've got to do this, Luke, with or without anybody else. Heck, you don't need us anymore. You're running the emergency service, you've got this charity idea bubbling along, you've just run across the whole Sahara desert! You know you can do this.'

'Me and Ernie,' I said, lifting aloft the little mouse doomed to be my life long companion.

'It's an amazing chance – open a practice, keep the spirit of

333

what's it all about alive. Who wants to be a corporate nine-to-five small animal vet focused on vaccine sales? Where's the challenge in that – no on-call, having a social life – I mean, it almost becomes a normal job! Neither of us could handle that!'

I laughed and then lifted Ernie to my eyeline. 'What happens if he dies?' I wondered. 'Stuck to me forever, and then just dying . . .'

Rob shook his head. 'The mark-ups, the targets, the commercial thrust of business making animals into pound notes – Mr Spotswode must be sick to his core about what's going to happen!' he continued. If we hadn't been constrained by the cattery, he would have been staring wistfully into the middle distance.

I wondered what Mr Spotswode was thinking now. Suddenly, it hit me how much I was going to miss him. The practice felt different already, knowing he was going to leave us.

'It'll take months to sort out if I go for this,' I said. 'I need to check my contract.'

'If anyone is going to manage it, my money is on you,' Rob said.

I swelled with pride. Despite my having just stuck a mouse to my finger, my friend and colleague still believed in me. That was real friendship right there.

Suddenly, Holly burst back into the cattery, breathless.

'Sorry it took me so long,' she said. 'I've asked everyone and I think we have a plan.'

'Where is it then?' I replied looking at Holly's empty hands.

'You need to come to the prep room, I've got the solution in the tub table,' Holly said earnestly, casting a furtive glance at Ernie, her face starting to crease up again.

'Go out there?' I balked. 'With a mouse stuck to my finger?'

'Stranger things have happened . . .' Holly began.

'What?' I demanded. 'What stranger things?'

'Well, Giles offering you the farm practice for a start!'

I looked at her.

'I wasn't *so* engrossed in that anaesthetic that I went deaf, Luke.'

I sighed and gently stood up.

'You'll have to shield me,' I said to Rob.

'Shield you?'

'In case anyone sees!'

'You want a bodyguard now, Mr High-and-Mighty?'

'Damn right I do!'

With Rob closely flanking me, we walked out into the prep area. Holly had seemingly told the entire practice what was going on, for everyone was gathered there, a guard-of-honour to welcome back their Sahara-conquering hero and his sidekick, Ernie the mouse. Even the receptionists had left their posts to come and witness poor Ernie's predicament.

'I don't believe this,' Rob muttered. 'You are never going to live this one down.'

'Still our exotics specialist then, Luke?' one of the receptionists asked, beaming.

I felt my face going red as people clustered around to look.

'Give Ernie some space,' I said, pushing my way over to the tub table. 'Holly, let's get this done.'

When there was no response, I looked back to see Holly clutching the sides of the tub table, struggling to stay upright. Tears leaked down her face.

'It's not funny,' Rob said in his most sanctimonious tone. 'We have to get poor Ernie off Luke's fingers – there is a little boy, a little mouse and great big lump of a vet who are depending on it!'

Holly, having collected herself, nodded her agreement.

Dipping a small amount of cotton wool into the solution, Rob gently wiped around the edges of the miserable mouse.

'It's not working,' Rob said exasperated. 'He's really stuck fast.'

'He really is going to be there forever,' I moaned.

'Cords is not going to be impressed. Next time you're out to dinner, you'll have to order for three!'

Before I could bite Rob's head off, the door to the prep area opened again and Giles walked purposefully towards me.

Looking down, he tutted quietly.

'I'm sorry,' I whispered. 'It's just that, well, the wound had broken down and we thought tissue glue was a good solution . . .'

Giles didn't say a word. In silence, he reached out and grasped Ernie firmly.

With a swift motion, he yanked Ernie free. The poor mouse gave an almighty squeak as I gave a shout of surprise. His might have been in victory, but mine was in sheer embarrassment.

Holding the hapless Ernie out for Rob to take, Giles looked at me and slowly shook his head. 'Like a plaster, Luke. Rip them off like you would a plaster!' He grinned. 'So much still to learn. Stick to cows for now – that's my advice.'

Giving me a subtle wink, he promptly turned, exiting to a round of applause from the staff.

Ernie gave another little squeak in agreement and sat looking around, resting on the palm of Rob's hand.

'Well, the good news is that the wound looks great and the skin is fine,' Rob said.

'And the bad news is that Ernie is now entirely bald down one side and Luke has hairy fingers!' Holly exclaimed.

Hanging my head, I gave Ernie a gentle stroke goodbye and disappeared off to the office, hairy fingers and all.

It was a pleasant, balmy evening, and while the locals were out walking in the fields and lounging in their gardens, there was peace and quiet at the pub. Sheila, Rob, Holly, Cordelia and I sat round a table in the beer garden. I cupped my hand around my pint, but couldn't feel the coldness in my palm. Mouse fur, it turns out, is the perfect insulator.

'Here's to the best laid plans of mice and men!' quipped Rob.

Mr Spotswode had come into the practice earlier that day to congratulate me on the marathon and invited me into his office for a chat. It had been a huge relief to see that he was not totally out of action.

'So what did he say?' Sheila asked.

I took a long pull on my pint and the others crowded round to listen.

'He just wanted to say well done on the Marathon. And, well, we had a bit of a heart-to-heart about things,' I replied, desperately trying not to be embarrassed.

'Quite the special one, then!' Rob said with a smile. 'Private chat with Giles and private chat with Mr Spotswode.'

'Not that private with Giles,' Holly piped up. 'I heard every word!'

'The invisibility cloak of a veterinary nurse,' Sheila interjected.

'So what did Mr Spotswode actually say?' Rob asked, 'Or was it a private, *private* chat?'

'Private, *private*,' I said.

'Quite right too,' Sheila chipped in.

'But I've made a decision,' I said. 'I'm going to start my own practice.'

There was a momentary silence around the table. All of them knew that it was on the cards. I'd been thinking about it since Giles planted the seed but this was the first time I had said it out loud.

'The journey of a vet,' Rob said. 'You spend years qualifying, then more years actually learning the job, and finally you get to do what you truly love. It's a bit like an epic pilgrimage.'

'What are you going to call it? Are you going to need a head nurse?' Holly quickly asked.

'One question at a time!' I spluttered. Some of my beer had gone down the wrong way, and I hurried to wipe the dribble off my chin before Cords saw.

'Be careful what you wish for Holly, or you'll be drawn into his net as well,' Sheila said, laughing, and giving Cordelia a conspiratorial wink.

'You need a name first of all, that's really important,' Cordelia said.

Mulling it over whilst taking a large swig of beer, I thought about what Rob had said.

'Pilgrims,' I said with a smile. 'I'm going to call it Pilgrims Vet Practice . . .'

'Now *that* has a ring to it! Let's drink to that,' Rob said, raising his glass.

Cords and I were the last to leave the pub that night. As we wandered out into the darkness, I saw a familiar shape at the end of the yard. Leuwen bowled his way between me and Cordelia.

'Don't you leave him tied up?' she asked.

'He knows his way around,' I grinned, calling him to heel.

We wandered along the moonlit lane, as Leuwen bounded ahead. There were a lot of things changing in our lives, but there was one thing I never wanted to change. She had been there, waving me over every sand dune in the desert. She had been there while I brawled in the car park to protect the honour of her car from a madman's urine. She had been in every one of Rob and Sam's jokes for the past six months and more.

'Setting up the charity, setting up a practice – you've got an exciting time ahead,' said Cordelia, her arm linked through mine.

We stopped where two roads met. One branched back towards Mr Spotswode's practice, soon to be no more. The other wound into darkness, to my home and an uncertain future.

'It's going to be fun, big decisions to be made,' I said softly, looking into her eyes.

'What do you mean, big decisions? Not for me, I'm staying put!'

Further down the lane, Leuwen barked. I didn't call for him. A rabbit darted from a hedgerow and away.

'Well, have a think about that,' I said. I reached into my back pocket and produced an envelope. When I pressed it into Cords' hands, she looked uncertain. Not breathing a word, she opened the envelope. Her eyes widened and she looked up at me in the silvery light.

'Two tickets to India!' she exclaimed, flinging her arms around my neck.

'I'd love it if you'd join me for a little trip,' I said, smiling through her hair. 'There's something I've got to ask you . . .'

ACKNOWLEDGEMENTS

Writing this book has been great fun – sections have been written in between consults, other bits in the few minutes before morning surgery, other bits last thing at night! It would have been impossible without the support of Cords, my family, friends and work colleagues who all gave me the space to ensure I got it written on time. Rob Dinsdale, my agent, who guided me through the process and patiently read the drafts as they came through, encouraging me along the way, as well as Heather and Elly at HHB. Lisa and the team at Two Roads for having the faith in taking on an unpublished author, giving me a chance and being so supportive.

The biggest acknowledgement has to be to those individuals who helped and inspired me to become a vet and do what I love doing. My career was moulded by the characters of the book – some have been subtly changed and others merged together, but they know who they are and I am indebted to every single one of them. Particular mention should be made of Mr Spotswood, Giles, Rob and Sam, who had the patience to mould me at the very beginning.

Finally, my Mum – who, aside from unfailing parental support and encouragement throughout every single step of my life, gave me an omnibus edition of the James Herriot collection in 1990 and inscribed in the front of it: 'In twenty years time, maybe you'll have stories to write a bit like these!' Well, here you go Mum, let me know what you think . . .

© Luke Gamble

LUKE GAMBLE graduated from Bristol University in 1999 as a vet and spent a year as Clinical Scholar in large animal medicine and surgery at Cambridge University. Although primarily a mixed practice vet and based in his New Forest surgery, Pilgrims Veterinary Practice, his extracurricular work with the Worldwide Veterinary Service charity (which he founded in 2003) takes him much further afield and was the subject of two TV series on Sky 1. He also runs an emergency service for animals in Dorset and a pet travel company.

Luke is a black belt in karate, has run 152 miles across the Sahara to raise money for his charity (and to impress his wife) and in 2010 was awarded the J A Wight (James Herriot) Award by the British Small Animal Veterinary Association for outstanding contributions to the welfare of companion animals. Luke is married and lives in the New Forest with his two children, a Ridgeback and a bossy rescue cat called Charlie.

www.wvs.org.uk

**TWO
ROADS**

stories ... voices ... places ... lives

Two Roads is the home of fabulous storytelling and
reader enjoyment. We publish stories from the heart, told
in strong voices about lives lived. Two Roads books come
from everywhere and take you into other worlds.

We hope you enjoyed *The Vet: my wild and wonderful friends*.
If you'd like to know more about this book or any other title on
our list, please go to www.tworoadsbooks.com or scan this code
with your smartphone to go straight to our site:

For news on forthcoming Two Roads titles,
please sign up for our newsletter

We'd love to hear from you

enquiries@tworoadsbooks.com   Twitter (@tworoadsbooks)

facebook.com/TwoRoadsBooks